To my students—past, present, and future

Contents

Figures

Plates

Plate 1   Harris Berger. Courtesy of Harris Berger.

Plate 2   Alan Merriam. Courtesy of Indiana University Archives.

Plate 3   Mantle Hood. Courtesy of Society for Ethnomusicology.

Plate 4   Anthony Seeger. Courtesy of Society for Ethnomusicology.

Plate 5   Virginia Danielson. Courtesy of Virginia Danielson.

Plate 6   Ingrid Monson. Courtesy of Society for Ethnomusicology.

Plate 7   Benjamin Brinner playing gender to accompany a Javanese
shadow play performance by Midiyanto, Cowell Theater, San
Francisco. Courtesy of Rebecca Bodenheimer.

Plate 8   Peter Manuel. Courtesy of Peter Manuel.

Plate 9   Kay Kaufman Shelemay. Courtesy of Kay Kaufman Shelemay.

Plate 10   Ruth M. Stone. Courtesy of Ruth M. Stone.

Plate 11   Feme Neni-Kole. Photo by Verlon L. Stone.

Plate 12   George Herzog. Courtesy of Archives of Traditional Music.

Plate 13   Hugo Zemp shooting his film *The Song of Harmonics*, 1990.
Courtesy of Hugo Zemp.

Plate 14   Adrienne Kaeppler. Courtesy of Adrienne Kaeppler.

Plate 15   Bruno Nettl. Courtesy of Bruno Nettl.

Plate 16   Regula Qureshi. Courtesy of Regula Qureshi.

Plate 17   Moses and John Woni viewing a video playback of their
performance. Photo by Verlon L. Stone.

Plate 18   Jane Sugarman. Courtesy of Jane Sugarman.

Plate 19   Margarita Mazo. Courtesy of Margarita Mazo.

Plate 20   Cornelia Fales. Photo by K. A. MacDonald.

Plate 21   Ellen Koskoff. Courtesy of Ellen Koskoff.

Plate 22   Martin Stokes. Courtesy of Martin Stokes.

Plate 23   Daniel B. Reed. Courtesy of Daniel B. Reed.

Plate 24   Daniel Avorgbedor. Courtesy of Daniel Avorgbedor.

Plate 25   Mellonee V. Burnim. Courtesy of Mellonee V. Burnim.

Preface

Ethnomusicology has been variously defined as the study of any and all of the music of the world, the study of music as culture, or the study of music as human experience. Each of these definitions moves into different dimensions of inquiry, but all of the definitions expand the study of music.

Ethnomusicology is a field of inquiry that is half a century old, and many ethnomusicologists espouse the centrality of theory to this enterprise. Theory, whether appearing explicitly or implicitly, is an important mark of a distinguished ethnomusicologist. Whether an ethnomusicologist is studying the inner workings of a string quartet playing Mozart or the playing of the horse-head fiddle in the popular music of Mongolia, theory has its place and significance. Nevertheless, there are generally limited discussions of theory in either general books devoted to ethnomusicology or in specific ethnographies of musical practice.

This book addresses ethnomusicological theory directly and explicitly, exploring some of the underpinnings of various approaches and analyzing differences and commonalities in these orientations. The study also explores how ethnomusicologists have used these theories in their ethnographic research, exploring the particular circumstances of the theoretical application in ethnomusicology.

Theories for Ethnomusicology

The work of many ethnomusicologists today shows affinities for certain theorists or concepts that theorists in the social sciences and humanities have offered. Particularly at the beginning of ethnographic accounts, ethnomusicologists cite theoretical ideas that they associate with their work. Some ethnomusicologists go further to then interweave the concepts with the data as they develop their manuscript. Other ethnomusicologists sprinkle theoretical terms—*deconstructionism, gaze, role of ideology*—in their analysis without attributing in detail the sources for these ideas. A very few ethnomusicologists engage in detailed theoretical discussion, developing their own theoretical angle, critiquing theories of other researchers, and talking about where their work fits into the conversation. These latter ethnomusicologists are definitely in the minority, though, and theoretical discussions are more typically brief and cursory in most ethnomusicological accounts.

Although theory is regarded as necessary for ethnomusicology, detailed theoretical development may be lacking. This situation should not be surprising, considering that few courses are devoted to theory in ethnomusicology within the curricula of ethnomusicology programs. Theory is often integrated into classes focusing on other topics, such as fieldwork, and theory is seldom a featured topic. Alternatively, students generally learn about theory in seminars that are located in neighboring disciplines like anthropology, linguistics, musicology, or folklore.

The history of the field serves to illuminate the present situation. On one hand, the anthropological influences on the discipline have helped emphasize the importance of theory and its place in ethnomusicological studies. Certain musicological influences, on the other hand, have contributed to the emphasis on studying music from the perspective of a phenomenon that exists most importantly as an aesthetic object and creative process.

Thus, although most ethnomusicologists would acknowledge the importance of theory, I would posit, that based on published material in the field, a small number would also argue for an extended explication of theory. Those scholars of the social science orientation have stressed the importance of theory in orienting projects from the beginning. Other scholars from a more musicological background have argued for avoiding theory and going to the field with a blank slate, awaiting the inspiration of the music to be studied for a theoretical conclusion. The compromise that has been tacitly reached with regard to theory appears to be that though theory is invariably mentioned and pointed out in ethnomusicological work, few studies detail the role and involvement of theory in an explicit and extended way. Perhaps what fuels this tacit compromise is the ambivalence about starting research with an orienting framework. As Harris Berger (1991a) poses the question, "Can theory explain the phenomena of expressive culture, or does each individual item . . . transcend generalizing frameworks?" (31).

In many cases, ethnomusicologists have drawn from a variety of theories or approaches, and the boundaries between them are treated as porous and permeable. To try and pigeonhole various ethnomusicologists as espousing this or that

Plate 1 Harris Berger. Courtesy of Harris Berger.

particular theory would be to ignore the reality of practice within the field. Many scholars mix and match theories with considerable ease, and this book explores both how those various theories have been used in conjunction with one another and on what bases these combinations may or may not be compatible.

The practice of present-day ethnomusicologists to draw on multiple approaches is not unlike that of Charles Seeger (1886–1979) Seeger (1977) embraced at least three different approaches to his work. He relied on the work of Henri Bergson, for his interest in intuition and mystical faith as a basis for studying music; on Bertrand Russell, for his way of combining mystical faith with logic; and on Ralph Barton Perry, who supplied the rationale he later employed to explain the relation between music and language as well as an overarching framework for combining his interdisciplinary interests (Greer 1998:21–22).

At certain points in the history of ethnomusicology, a particular theory has lit up the landscape and been embraced as the nearly perfect explanation for musical phenomena. The appearance of paradigmatic structuralism, best known through the work of anthropologist Claude Lévi-Strauss, appeared to offer such a solution in the early 1970s. The meeting of the Society for Ethnomusicology in 1972 included a number of papers that demonstrated that palpable excitement. Yet by the latter part of the decade, a diminishing number of references to structuralism could be found in the current work of ethnomusicologists, and other theories were now favored in conference papers and ethnographic studies.

The theories in the social and humanistic sciences, when compared with one another, may at first seem to bear no resemblances. I would point, however, to Wayne D. Bowman's (1998) comment in his book *Philosophical Perspectives on Music:* "[A]midst the striking diversity, there do exist discernible patterns, convergences of perspective, recurrent disputes and problems."

My mentors, Alan P. Merriam and Charles Boilés, instilled a keen interest in and concern for theory in me during my days as a student. This was reflected in my dissertation, which included an extended discussion of theoretical assumptions that framed my study of Kpelle cuing in performance (Stone 1979:1–65).

When I began teaching at Indiana University more than twenty-five years ago, I inherited what may be the most consistently taught graduate course in ethnomusicological theory, "Paradigms in Ethnomusicology." This class was patterned on one by the same name that Boilés had taught in the Department of Folklore and Ethnomusicology at Indiana University some years earlier. In that class, he examined linguistic approaches to ethnomusicology. I expanded the course to include a broad range of theoretical approaches, and over the years I have continued to add to the range of theories addressed with the goal of exploring common themes among the various approaches. Several years ago, the Ethnomusicology Institute, in recognition of the importance of theory to the training for students, added another course in theory—an advanced theory course—which, in addition to the "Paradigms in Ethnomusicology" course, is required of all doctoral students who specialize in ethnomusicology at Indiana University.

Many of the ideas offered in this book were first discussed in the "Paradigms in Ethnomusicology" class. Ideas on theory also emerged in lectures to students at other universities, including those from the University of California, Santa Barbara; University of California, Los Angeles; University of Ghana; University of Malawi; New York University; University of Michigan; and the University of Zimbabwe. Through their probing questions and keen observations, the students and other audience members provided the basis for changes and amplifications. The chapter on history, for example, was added to the manuscript at the suggestion of students after I had written an initial draft and let them read and critique it. Thus this book should be read as a summary of numerous dialogues that have ensued over some twenty-five years of lively exchange.

This work presents my views on the advantages as well as limitations of these theoretical approaches in ethnomusicology. Such explorations show that no theory encompasses all issues of inquiry. Ethnomusicologists have judged some theories better than others for their work at certain points in history, and not all ethnomusicologists would agree on what the best theories might be. But these orientations are, at best, partial in their explanatory power.

Theories often incorporate aspects from earlier approaches and thus build from earlier work. Thus they may share some aspects of earlier theories in orientation. In this way, theories overlap and interrelate in ways that complicate the best attempts to build tight categories.

My goal here is to show that, whether acknowledged or not, theory underlies ethnomusicological inquiry and even implicit theories have a bearing on the analyses that result from our fieldwork. The trick is not to obscure the study of music making with clumsy or inappropriate frameworks. Theory should ultimately make ideas transparent and strengthen the quality of the intellectual conversation.

This book explores the underlying ideas within the humanities and social sciences to which ethnomusicologists have referred. The basic assumptions of these theories are explained and compared in order to understand relationships. Examples are offered of how ethnomusicology as a field of inquiry has used and adapted these theories.

Each chapter centers on a distinct theory or cluster of theories that have been or are presently important to the studies produced by ethnomusicologists. In most cases the treatment includes the following:

1. Definition of the theory
2. Basic assumptions of the orientation
3. Examples of the theory in ethnomusicology
4. Critical examination of theory for ethnomusicology

A final chapter draws some general conclusions about the status of these theories, showing how they converge at some points and diverge at other points.

A number of people have assisted me in the work on this book, and I would like to thank them for their efforts. Each class of "Paradigms in Ethnomusicology" students, beginning in 1980, has contributed to making this book what it has become. Furthermore, a number of students worked more intensely on the project by serving as assistants or conducting specialized searches. To Susan Oehler, Paul Schauert, Charles Seymour, and Jessica Anderson Turner, a special thanks. To Kimberly Marshall, who conducted a detailed review of the manuscript, a special word of appreciation. To Anthony Guest-Scott who prepared the illustrations, my appreciation for your skill and care. To Keith A. MacDonald, who helped with photo research, I'm grateful for your help and instruction. To Harris Berger, who has continued to stimulate my thinking about theory long after he took the class, I'm grateful for our discussions. To my colleagues Daniel Reed, Sue Tuohy, Portia Maultsby, Mellonee Burnim, Charles Sykes, Dick Bauman, Nina Fales, Marina Roseman, Greg Schrempp, and David Shorter, who have been part of important intellectual exchanges, your ideas have sustained me. To my daughter, Angela Keema and son-in-law Keith, you have made my life a joy. Finally, to Verlon, my husband, you've been my anchor. I would like to thank the following reviewers Ellen Koskoff (Eastman School of Music), Gregory F. Barz (Vanderbilt University), and Stephen Blum (Cuny Graduate Center).

In the end, I take responsibility for the ideas offered here. The interpretations are mine and reflect my own particular point of view about theory as it is practiced in the field of ethnomusicology.

Ruth M. Stone
Bloomington, Indiana

References

Berger, Harris M. 1999a. "Theory as Practice: Some Dialectics of Generality and Specificity in Folklore Scholarship." *Journal of Folklore Research* 36(1): 31–49.

Bowman, Wayne D. 1998. *Philosophical Perspectives on Music.* Oxford and New York: Oxford University Press.

Greer, Taylor Aitken. 1998. *A Question of Balance.* Berkeley: University of California Press.

Seeger, Charles. 1977. *Studies in Musicology 1935–1975.* Berkeley and Los Angeles: University of California Press.

Stone, Ruth M. 1979. "Communication and Interaction Processes in Music Events among the Kpelle of Liberia." PhD diss., Indiana University.

Inquiry in Ethnomusicology

Ethnomusicologists carry out research about music performance, about music experience, and about music performers using concepts that are drawn from inquiry in the social and natural sciences as well as the related areas of music and the humanities. A number of concepts anchor the language that surrounds "theory" as well as other aspects of research in ethnomusicology. These ideas are essential to the extended discussion of theory in ethnomusicology.

Paradigm

One starting point in the conceptual apparatus of theories is the idea of paradigm. **Paradigm** means "pattern, exemplar, example" (Oxford English Dictionary 1986). The concept became a very popular in academic circles with the publication of Thomas Kuhn's book, *The Structure of Scientific Revolutions* (1962). Kuhn defined paradigm as the shared understandings and agreements that form the lens used by scientists to proceed in conducting "normal science" (1962:10). When a revolution in scientific research occurred, he maintained, a particular paradigm changed, giving way to a new procedure for conducting research.

Paradigms or exemplars include sets of assumptions that are not necessarily obvious but describe those things that make up the world and are models for how we can inquire about them. "Acquisition of a paradigm and of the more esoteric type of research it permits is a sign of maturity in the development of any given scientific field" (1962:11). Because they are often implicit, they are out-of-awareness and not altogether obvious.

Kuhn outlined a set of chronological phases for paradigms: (1) a pre-paradigm stage, (2) crystallization of a dominant paradigm with the beginning of a normal science, and (3) scientific revolutions. Scientific revolutions are marked by those

---

Paradigm

- Model or example
- Shared understandings about research procedures

---

moments when there is a shift; a new paradigm takes over and becomes the dominant exemplar.

Although Kuhn's ideas have had a long-lasting influence in scholarship, they have also been subject to critique on a number of fronts. Some scholars have felt that Kuhn's conception of paradigms made these models incompatible, one with another, in a way that was not necessarily typical of the interpenetration of research ideas with one another. Other researchers observed that Kuhn saw the scientific community as separate from society in general. But Paul Hoyningen-Heune (1993) maintains that many scholars misread Kuhn's early formulation as well as ignored his later formulations, which led to some of the misunderstandings.

We might consider what paradigm characterizes ethnomusicology today. Alan Merriam proposed in the 1960s a three-part "model" that addressed (1) music sound, (2) behavior in relation to that sound, and (3) conceptualization about music (1964:32–33). That exemplar has been widely quoted and cited over the years. Yet Merriam staunchly maintained, in class lectures and conversation, that ethnomusicology as a whole possesses no single paradigm.

Mantle Hood, Merriam's contemporary, maintained that ethnomusicology is "a field that has almost as many approaches and objectives as there are practitioners" (1971:1). Merriam did not see the situation as quite that diffuse and posited that there were, more or less, two approaches to ethnomusicology—what he liked to call the "two horns of the dilemma"—one that derived from the anthropological perspective and another that was inspired by the musicological viewpoint.

Plate 2 Alan Merriam. Courtesy Indiana University Archives.

Plate 3 Mantle Hood. Courtesy SEM.

More than twenty years after Merriam's influential publication of *The Anthropology of Music,* Timothy Rice, in his article "Toward the Remodeling of Ethnomusicology" (1987), referred to Merriam's work as "[p]robably the best example of an effective model in the recent history of ethnomusicology." Anthony Seeger, in responding to Rice's call for remodeling ethnomusicology, questioned the need for consensus in the field. He noted, "It is possible to think of models as dialectical, of a field as a ferment, and of debate as a method for advancing ideas." Seeger went on to advocate for "different approaches." He said, "I have always envisioned the Society for Ethnomusicology as a place where people who are studying music from very different perspectives can report on their work as well as listen to or read each other's reports." Referring back to his ancestor, he commented, "Instead of everyone going the same route, [Charles] Seeger suggests a field in which we all travel in different directions, reporting back to each other on what we have seen, heard, or discovered on our travels. Rather than providing a single point of departure, the field and the Society for Ethnomusicology provide a place to report on our arrivals" (Anthony Seeger 1987a).

Richard Middleton, reflecting a perspective from British musical studies, envisioned a field called "cultural musicology," as he wrote in 2003. Recognizing a number of trajectories of scholarship, he said, "Nonetheless, different approaches are interacting, and with increasing intensity, such that it is clear that a **new paradigm** may well be on the horizon" (2003:1). For Middleton, culture forms the common denominator in ethnomusicological studies that derive from a variety of disciplines.

Plate 4 Anthony Seeger. Courtesy SEM.

Ethnography as a Shared Aspect

Although there might not be complete agreement on a single paradigm, ethnomusicologists can establish certain points of convergence among competing paradigms. The single most important shared aspect among the paradigms of ethnomusicologists at present is **ethnography** as a way of carrying out research. Ethnography typically involves face-to-face observation of and participation in performance. It "embraces the descriptive details" (OED 1986) of how people create, perform, and critique music in societies around the world, including our own. Essential to ethnography as conducted by ethnomusicologists is fieldwork carried out on location among the people who perform—wherever on the globe they may live, including local communities in close proximity to the everyday world of ethnomusicologists. As Deborah Wong observes,

> Ethnographic work means having direct, sustained contact with people and their activities—it means talking with them and spending time at it. . . . At some point, you transform the accumulation of particularities (personal

---

Ethnography

- Research emphasizing face-to-face interaction
- Research rich in descriptive details

histories, opinions, alliances etc.) into another medium—a book, a film—in which you probably try to make some larger points about broader matters implicitly or explicitly suggested by the particularities. (2004:8–9)

Thus most ethnomusicologists share ethnography as a means of carrying out research. Although there may be overlapping ethnomusicological paradigms, ethnography does form an area of at least partially shared understandings. Researchers from a variety of persuasions value the fieldwork experience for the gathering of data in ethnomusicology.

Fieldwork employs close and sustained interaction—often face-to-face—with the people whose music is the focus of study. Fieldwork implies immersion into the everyday life, musical performances, and other aspects of the society in which they live. Following the immersion experience, a fieldworker produces written accounts—field notes—of the experience, which then serve as data for later analyses. Sometimes that same fieldworker also becomes adept at performing the music he or she has been studying and then reproduces it in performance and teaching settings.

Fieldwork may involve living in a far removed geographical setting or working in a nearby location that, nevertheless, provides a view different from the everyday world of the ethnomusicologist. As a research practice, fieldwork sets the ethnomusicologist apart from most other music researchers, although it is partially shared with folklorists, anthropologists, oral historians, and sociologists.

In most ethnomusicology programs, students conduct fieldwork as part of their course of study. Ph.D. candidates are typically expected to conduct 8 to 12 months of sustained fieldwork in preparation for writing their dissertation. In this way, fieldwork is an important component of the dissertation process.

The field where research is conducted may constitute more than one geographical location. Because people live in dispersed communities around the world, the field for some researchers has become multiple geographic locations. Kay Kaufman Shelemay, in studying Syrian Jews who have settled in New York, conducted fieldwork not only in Brooklyn but also in Mexico City and in Jerusalem, to understand the music of the people who had originated in Aleppo, Syria (Shelemay 1998).

Although fieldwork unites segments of ethnomusicologists, there are points of divergence in the paradigms. This divergence owes much to the musicological training and orientation of some ethnomusicologists, and social scientific training and orientation of other ethnomusicologists. Further, ethnomusicology may be lodged within a department or school of music or, less commonly, in a department

Fieldwork

- Participant observation research
- Immersion in everyday life and performance

of anthropology, folklore, or linguistics. Such associations may influence the research practices of ethnomusicologists in these various areas.

In my own case, for example, being a part of a folklore department for all of my career has no doubt influenced my interest in and analysis of texts and in particular an epic text—the Woi epic—even though I looked at it in the larger context of a musical performance (Stone 1988).

Partially Shared Ideas

Ethnomusicology is a social enterprise in which data are shared and ideas are exchanged. These ideas are exchanged in professional meetings where papers are delivered and comments made about the ideas offered. They are shared in public discussions on the Internet or in print or electronic publications. These ideas, although they are exchanged, are only partially shared. Knowledge in ethnomusicology depends on experience. That is, anything that we know in ethnomusicology, if it is to be meaningful, must be brought into relation with experience or background knowledge. Just how this happens depends on our particular orientation.

I recall a trip that my colleague Portia Maultsby and I took to Zimbabwe in the mid-1980s. As we watched a performance of musicians in Murewa, a town a few miles from the capitol of Harare, we each posed different interpretations. Portia typically saw parallels to African American practices. I related what I heard to West African sounds with which I was familiar. And we grew to realize how our interpretations of Zimbabwean music were influenced by our past experiences, each past deriving from a different configuration of personal biography.

Theory

There are other concepts in the field of ethnomusicology that ground analysis and deserve elucidation. **Theory** is one overarching such concept. Few researchers would agree on a definition of theory, but many more agree on what theory *does*. "Theories, then, are more than merely abbreviated summaries of data, since they not only tell us *what* happens but *why* it happens as it does. Any worthwhile theory should thus perform the double function of explaining facts already known as well as opening up new vistas which can lead us to new *facts*" (Kaplan and Manners 1972:11). Theories suggest explanations not only for the phenomena that invoked them in the first place but for other phenomena as well.

Theory

- Explains why something occurs
- Creates new horizons of knowledge

Theory that is closely tied to specific data is grounded theory—where the specific connections between theory and data can be documented. Though the sociologists who developed grounded theory included detailed method for employing it, ethnomusicologists generally use it in a more generic sense (Glaser and Strauss 1967; Strauss and Corbin 1990).

Theory vs. Descriptive Statement

To contextualize theory further, let us compare it to the **descriptive statement**. A descriptive statement refers to "events occurring in a specific space-time context" (Kaplan and Manners 1972:13). Theoretical generalization, in contrast, refers to highly abstract relationships under which descriptive statements can be submitted as special instances.

Over the course of nearly a year of research in Liberia, West Africa, I had come to realize that those cues to end dances were associated with instances of entertainment music. In ritual contexts, these cues were absent or obscured. A theory served to explain a great number of cases and situations—not only those I had observed but those that I had not yet seen and heard.

From my own research on performance among the people of Gbeyilataa, I could derive the following *descriptive statement*:

Descriptive Statement Example

As the women from Gbeyilataa watched the videotape of their performance, Lopuu commented that Keema has "cut the edge" when she turned and brought her arm in an art to her waist.

With a number of related descriptive statements and some interpretation on my part, I then developed the following theory to explain the earlier event.

Theory Example

Cutting-the-edge dance cues are characteristic of music that is considered entertainment in nature and quite absent in ritual events.

When students in music departments or schools take courses in music theory, they are studying the logic of sounds relating to other sounds, particularly harmonic progressions. In ethnomusicology, we consider the sort of theory with which we are contending to be much more general and abstract than the logic of chord progression. A theory in ethnomusicology might be one such as Alan Lomax's theory offered in *Folk Song Style and Culture*.

Descriptive statement
• Describes events in a specific space and time

Theory Example

Song performance can characterize a culture in terms of basic structural elements such as complexity and subsistence level, political structure, complementarity and sexual mores. (1968:98)

Range of Theory

Theories show enormous range in level of generality. The level of generality involves the radius of the explanatory shell or the extensiveness of the sorts of events to be considered such as might be distinguished in the range between macrotheory versus microtheory. If we take

- Theory 1: Instruments in Gbeyilataa village in Liberia are classified by the local musicians as either struck or blown.

This could be considered a theory with limited generality and limited abstractness. But, if we take

- Theory 2: Instruments across the world are classified by ethnomusicologists as aerophones, membranophones, idiophones, or chordophones.

Then we have a theory of extended generality but not extended abstractness. In the third instance, consider

- Theory 3: Specific instruments across the world are associated with specific colors, times of the day, and moods.

This theory could be considered to exhibit extended generality as well as extended abstractness, for the instruments are associated with symbolic ideas that extend beyond sorting and grouping.

Finally, some theories have much more explanatory muscle than others and are evaluated according to the number or types of cases they can explain. Some theories may be considered more powerful than others, and that judgment will be the basis for choosing one theory over another.

Types of Theory

Ethnomusicologists refer not only to theories that derive from Western academic scholarship, and by extension Western philosophy, but from the various cultures where research is conducted. Because these indigenous theories are often implicitly rather than explicitly stated, they are not always easily discerned.

Nevertheless, I would argue that much in ethnomusicological thought derives from abstractions and theories held by musicians and peoples from the cultures we study. As Shelemay notes in the introduction to her study of Syrian *pizmonim,*

> Over time, it became clear that insider perspectives not only had determined the central unit of study, but had opened pathways for its interpretation as well. (1998:2)

In another case Wong points out,

> Theory is made by people thinking through the valences of their moment. Regarding theory as part of cultures makes visible the conditions of its construction—i.e., the fact that theory, like any part of culture will be inflected with the power play of race, ethnicity, gender, sexual orientation, class, etc. (2004:317)

In the end, theory making is not a privilege of the elite but a process in which we all engage, and awareness of diverse theories created by the musicians we study comes with careful listening and observing.

Theoretical Orientation

As ethnomusicologists prepare and plan a research project, **theoretical orientation** might best describe the frame of reference they use. This orientation draws from theoretical issues and contains some assumptions or things that researchers hold to be true as they begin to work.

Some ethnomusicologists staunchly maintain that they want to enter the field with a blank slate. They do not want to go in with an orientation. Such an approach, no doubt, harkens to the ideas that have been held about music as an object that does not rely on any external element but stands as an independent entity and should be understood as such. Music, they contend, exists separately from context.

I maintain that meaning in music is socially created just as culture is socially created. Whether we acknowledge our theoretical orientation or not,

---

Theoretical orientation

- Creates a frame of reference
- Draws from theoretical issues
- Contains assumptions

we most surely possess one. We are experiencing the musical tradition we encounter and processing it against the backdrop of our previous experience. We have an implicit theoretical orientation whether or not we make it explicit.

How might one state a theoretical orientation? Virginia Danielson encapsulates her theoretical orientation for *The Voice of Egypt* as follows:

> This book addresses the issue of agency in society, particularly the role of the exceptional individual in expressive culture. Theoretically it rests on the rather large literature that has become known as practice theory as well as the literature associated with cultural studies. I am particularly indebted to the work of Raymond Williams, whose *Culture and Society* accounts successfully in broad social terms for a good number of English literary "stars." (1997: ix)

Danielson succinctly locates her work in practice theory and cultural studies, identifying Raymond Williams as a scholar on whom she relies in accounting for the behavior of an exceptional individual.

Veit Erlmann positions *Nightsong,* his work on migrant work song in South Africa, by saying this:

> In the account that follows, I have adopted a writing strategy that, like the title of the book, highlights rather than obliterates the foreignness and shifts that

Plate 5 Virginia Danielson. Courtesy of Virginia Danielson.

marks ethnographic translation. . . . I attempt to position my account of *isic-athamiya* within contemporary efforts to insert agency and performativity into anthropology. (1996a:xiii)

He identifies with theories of agency and performance in setting up his account.

A third theoretical orientation is offered in Ingrid Monson's *Saying Something* where she addresses jazz improvisation.

> My commitment to the value of vernacular or insider knowledge places me at odds with a considerable body of work in cultural studies, and my serious engagement with poststructuralist thinking places me similarly at odds with established eth- notheoretical thinking in ethnomusicology. Consequently, a secondary theme of this book is the reconciliation of ethnomusicology's traditional preoccupations with post structuralism. (1996:7)

Monson, in stating her theoretical position, suggests that she is challenging another theoretical orientation—that of the poststructuralist thinking.

All these theoretical orientations then suggest ways of selecting, conceptu- alizing, and ordering frameworks in preparation for research processes. These orientations ultimately help to generate theories through the course of research as data are obtained and interpreted.

Plate 6 Ingrid Monson. Courtesy SEM.

Method

Once a theoretical orientation or general framework is identified, we can then identify **method** for carrying out the research. Method is "the process by which [an ethnomusicologist] generates an abstract view of the situation. In this way [method] comprises *how* the [ethnomusicologist] decides *what* social phenomena are relevant to his descriptive project at hand and how he deals with these in developing his account or theory" (Phillipson 1972:79). In other words, method is how we get at our research. In contrast, **methodology** is "the study—description, the explanation, and the justification—of methods" (Kaplan 1964:19).

Method in Ethnomusicology

One method many ethnomusicologists use is **participant-observation**. This method provides for varying degrees of involvement with a culture, depending on the techniques employed and that place the researcher more or less at the participant end of the spectrum or more or less at the observer end of the spectrum. Ingrid Monson describes the observation end of the spectrum and many things one can learn about a culture:

> I attended many performances, observed the multiplicity of business and social activities taking place inside New York's jazz venues, and became something of a regular at several clubs. I imagine my presence may have drawn the notice of some: a normally unaccompanied women, usually seated at the bar

Method

- General way an ethnomusicologist conducts research

Methodology

- Explanation and justification of methods

Participant-observation

- Approach to research involving varying degrees of observation and participation in a cultural setting.

(where no minimum was charged), who talked to musicians during the intermissions. (1996:16)

Participant-observation at the participant end of the spectrum may involve a general immersion in daily life of a society. As Jane Sugarman recounts,

> We spent most of our time participating in farming activities with our host family: stringing tobacco, chopping wood, threshing wheat, irrigating fields, picking vegetables, herding oxen, baking bread. (1997:8)

Such activities led to a deepening understanding of issues and values that are critical to the creation of the music. John Blacking, many years earlier, also reported on the participant end of the spectrum when he detailed his research among the Venda of southern Africa:

> I learnt the songs both from adults and from children. On some occasions I made deliberate mistakes, and was therefore especially interested if I was not corrected. (1995a [1967]:33)

Archival work may be another method that ethnomusicologists incorporate into their research. Archival materials cover many media, from recordings to field notes of other researchers, newspaper articles, correspondence, artifacts, photographs, and various kinds of documentation for the recordings. All of these objects contribute to our understanding of historical events.

> Historical collections made by listeners give indications of what was important to them, what not, and sometimes why. Historical resources permit comparison of events as they occurred with later reflections on the same events (Danielson 1997:7).

Archival knowledge forms part of the discourse that is important to ethnomusicologists and is a method shared with other disciplines such as history, musicology, and others. In all of the archival work, the researcher is interpreting data collected by others, often at a time some distance in the past. (These data also help respond to Rice's call for reinserting the historical dimension into ethnomusicology [1987:480].)

Archival work

- Research of materials housed in archives
- Study of recordings, fieldnotes, newspapers, letters, photographs, artifacts

Techniques in Ethnomusicology

Techniques are "specific procedures used in a given science or in particular contexts of inquiry in that science" (Kaplan 1964:19). A number of techniques that ethnomusicologists employ include sound and video recording, still photography, transcription of music or speech, and the writing of fieldnotes. Ethnographic interviews—playback interviews, life history interviews, and questions from an interview schedule—all constitute yet another series of techniques.

Ethnomusicologists frequently mention their techniques as they introduce their books. For example, Shelemay notes, "The team effort results in a large collection of **field recordings** and **interviews** deposited in the Sephardic Archives" (Shelemay 1998:2; emphasis added). Or Sugarman comments on techniques used in Eastern Europe:

> I . . . turned increasingly to **playback interviews** structured around **audio or video recordings** (see Stone and Stone 1981). Here the advantages of video were immediately apparent. Not only was it easier to identify all participants in a singing occasion, but the songs could be correlated more precisely to other activities taking place. (1997:21; emphasis added)

Regula Qureshi comments on her techniques used in Asia:

> The music of Qawwali reflects its ethnographic setting. An extensive oral repertoire (**recorded** 433 performances of 261 songs with 179 tunes) is performed and transmitted by hundreds of Qawwals at different local Sufi centres (I **recorded** 83 groups at fifteen centres). (1995 [1986]:14; emphasis added)

In each case, the ethnomusicologist begins with either audio or video recordings and then structures interviews of various kinds adjacent to or with those recordings.

Assumptions

Assumptions, held by any ethnomusicologist venturing to the field to do research, are taken-for-granted knowledge. These are concepts, theories, or ideas that at any particular *moment* are beyond question. They are accepted

---

Techniques

- Specific procedures an ethnomusicologist uses to conduct research
- Field recording, transcription, and interview

Assumptions

- Concepts or theories that are held to be true and beyond question at a given moment
- Taken-for-granted knowledge

as given "until further notice" (Schutz and Luckmann 1973:4). Yet in the process of any project, these assumptions yet may become the basis for inquiry.

Benjamin Brinner tells us in his introduction to a study of the Javanese gamelan about his assumption:

> The Chomskyian concept of linguistic competence and its offshoots should not be taken **apriori** as the standard for the more inclusive concept of musical competence proposed here. I prefer to start with the **assumption** that these competences are essentially different, allowing the phenomenon of musical competence to be judged on its own merits while leaving open the possibility, indeed, the desirability of comparing it with linguistic competence at a later date. (1995:2–3; emphasis added)

In my own work about music event among the Kpelle of Liberia (1982: 7–10), I outlined eleven assumptions I was making in conducting the study, beginning with, "Music is communication," and including "Meaning in music is created by participants in the course of social interaction." I continued with, "The social relationship among event participants is based upon the simultaneous experiencing of the performance in multiple dimensions of time," and ended with, "The ethnomusicologist makes inferences about music event interaction by engaging in interactional behavior."

Plate 7 Benjamin Brinner playing gender to accompany a Javanese shadow play performance by Midiyanto, Cowell Theater, San Francisco. Courtesy of Rebecca Bodenheimer.

Jocelyne Guilbault, in her study of *zouk* in the West Indies, offers an assumption to situate her work within the field:

> The premise on which this study is based **assumes**, as Peter Manuel has observed, that music functions not merely as a passive reflection of broader sociocultural phenomena, but also as an active contributor to the processes of cultural change. (1993:xvii; emphasis added)

These statements of assumptions then cordon off those things, which scholars take to be true and are not questioned as ethnomusicologists embark on their research. It is important to identify assumptions so it is clear from the start what areas are not open to question—at least at the outset. Now there are of course many cases where evidence may change those assumptions at a later point in time.

Over the years of reading proposals submitted for research, I have noticed that some scholars begin by describing certain assumptions about a body of music to be studied. Very quickly as the research questions are presented, it becomes evident that some concept stated as an assumption is also being posed as a research question. Although one may end up, in fact, questioning one of the assumptions because of unexpected data, one needs to be clear from the start where the investigator is placing and situating the work, and what aspects are initially **not** open to questioning.

Plate 8 Peter Manuel. Courtesy of Peter Manuel.

Hypothesis vs. Research Question

The **hypothesis** is part of the research package that science employs and is sometimes mentioned in ethnomusicology. In science, the hypothesis helps focus the research process and identifies the locus for experimentation. Typically, the hypothesis is stated in a "If . . . then" statement. The experiment or observation that follows proceeds to test that specific hypothesis.

Ethnomusicologists, for the most part, are conducting research that is focused on a much more preliminary stage of investigation. They frequently find themselves among the first scholars to investigate a musical topic in a particular location. They often do not already know enough about the music they study to frame an appropriate hypothesis. Furthermore, their interests are generally much broader than can be appropriately encompassed in a specific hypothesis or a related set of hypotheses. There are also a great number of variables, and there may be difficulty in isolating one or two hypotheses at that stage in the research.

Research Questions

Rather than hypotheses, several broad questions typically frame and guide ethnomusicologists as they conduct research. These **research questions** are encompassing in nature, and, like the theoretical orientation, are quite general and abstract. For example, these were Danielson's questions for the study of the Egyptian singer Umm Kulthūm:

> Why was *this* individual, among many other entertainers, so important? . . . What were the material circumstances of a commercial singer's life? How did she make her way? In what respects was Umm Kulthūm's career typical? How was she affected by the operations of institutions such as record companies and theaters? What was her effect on musical life and in what ways were her actions informed or constrained by precedents? Where were her performances situated in the larger processes of life? (1997:2–3)

Hypothesis

- Identifies the locus for experimentation
- Typically stated in an "if . . . then" statement

Research question

- Broad question that frames the research
- Typically general and abstract

These questions imply a study that begins with the performance of the singer but moves to explain larger social processes that interrelate with that performance.

Sugarman framed her study of singing at Prespa Albanian weddings with these questions: "How is it that these families have developed such a strong sense of place? What is it about weddings that make them so central to the life of the community? And why is it so important that everyone sing at such a celebration?" (1997:7). Like Danielson, Sugarman firmly embeds her study in the larger social setting. Her guiding research questions help her determine what data to collect as she proceeds with fieldwork. And both scholars are asking why music seems so vital to the conduct of the larger social life.

The research questions that Brinner poses focus on the actual performance of the music and the relationship to competence. He begins his study of Javanese gamelan by asking, "How do they do what they do?" and follows with, "How do musicians make music together?" (1995:1). Despite different research questions, an assumption of a social basis for performance seems shared by all of the scholars—Sugarman, Brinner, and Danielson.

Guiding research questions derive both from what is already known about a specific musical issue and from the theoretical orientation that the researcher uses. Research questions give strong clues about what data will be vital to the ethnomusicologist.

Study Object

The most explicit statement about the focus of a research project is identification of the **study object**. Theoretical orientations and research questions may provide a few hints, but they may not directly address the unit of analysis. Certain of these units or study objects may be associated with a specific approach. Among early comparative musicologists, for example, the "song" was the unit of analysis. Study of these recorded or experienced objects yielded scales or pitch inventories, which could then be compared. Later, structural-functional scholars, influenced by anthropology, took the community as the study object. For many years, these ethnomusicologists studied all music making within a geographically bounded unit such as a village. A *song* versus a *community* forms quite disparate study objects that each yield much different results.

Today we have yet other study objects that serve to center our studies. My own research among the Kpelle for example, has taken the **music event** as a point of focus. In doing so, I have argued that the event is a unit of analysis with saliency for the Kpelle people. The event is bounded and set apart from

---

Study object

- Unit of research
- Units include song, individual, event, repertory, community, genre

everyday life and is where sound and behavior are united in musical interaction. Often Kpelle musicians say, "Kwa loi belei su" ("We are entering the inside of the performance"). The Kpelle mark the boundaries as they speak of the "inside" of the performance (Stone 1982:2).

Monson identifies her study object as **jazz improvisation**, centered on interaction in this multiple sense. Stressed here are the "reciprocal and multi-layered relationships among sound, social settings, and cultural politics that affect the meaning of jazz improvisation in twentieth-century American cultural life" (1996:2). Thus although she begins with a musical process, Monson also links this process to much broader issues of race and culture. She also indirectly comments on the structural-functional definition of community when she says, "By stressing the activity of music making as something that creates community, I am purposefully moving away from the idea of community that is defined exclusively by a particular geographic location or a particular social category, such as race, class, or gender" (1996:13).

Shelemay chooses a **repertory of songs**, *pizmonim*, as her study object and she tells us she intends to "document and interpret the *pizmonim* tradition for the recent century" (1998:1). She even comments on the choice of study object: "In contrast to most ethnomusicological projects, where the unit of study slowly emerges during the course of ethnographic research, the central focus here was identified before the process of fieldwork began in consultation with members of the Syrian Jewish community in Brooklyn" (1998:1).

Timothy Rice presents his study object:

> I've made two **individuals**—Kostadin Varimezov (a historically important instrumentalist) and his wife Todora Varimezova (a knowledgeable singer)—the center of the study. By following the history of their interaction with the world into

Plate 9 Kay Kaufman Shelemay. Courtesy of Kay Kaufman Shelemay.

which they were thrown, I hope to show (1) how they have defined themselves in interaction with that changing world; (2) the dramatic changes in that world over the seventy years or so of their lives; and (3) what aspects of that world—of that culture—are opened to our understanding by musical sounds, performances, and contexts acting as symbols. (1994:8)

We are presented by these ethnomusicologists, then, with a variety of study objects:

1. Song (comparative musicologists)
2. Event (Stone)
3. Musical process—jazz improvisation (Monson)
4. Repertory of songs (Shelemay)
5. Individuals (Rice, Danielson)
6. Community (Merriam, Blacking, Monson)
7. Genre of musical performance (Sugarman)

For the present discussion, what are interesting are the implications of these choices for theory in ethnomusicology. Using a song as a starting point for a study is very different from using a community as a starting point. If individual songs form the focus, then elements of these songs become the most likely areas of examination. In contrast, if community is the object of study, then the research will embrace a whole range of performances and inevitably treat the

Plate 10 Ruth M. Stone. Courtesy of Ruth M. Stone.

details of individual songs differently. Furthermore, where Blacking (1995a [1967]) and Merriam (1964) took the community as a starting point, studying musical performance within a bounded geographical area, Monson (1996) took a virtual community of musicians and followed them into a variety of settings. In the latter case, they were a community bounded by interests not geography. Like Monson, in my own doctoral research (Stone 1982), I studied musical groups from neighboring villages and traveled wherever they went to perform, again transcending the idea of studying music within an isolated geographic area.

Each choice of study object has a theoretical basis. In Merriam's case, drawing from a structural-functional theoretical framework, he was interested in the interrelationship of the music system with other parts of the cultural system. In my own case, drawing on symbolic interaction and phenomenology, I was most interested in events, and those events took place in a variety of neighboring geographical settings. I wanted to understand processes of interaction within that united behavior and sound. Merriam depended on a defined geographical area; in my own case I depended on the events that transcended village boundaries. Neither approach was right or wrong. Rather, each approach revealed different kinds of insights.

Although the different study objects that ethnomusicologists select relate to different theoretical orientations, they also connect to a variety of method and techniques. A paradigmatic structuralist would be far less interested in the details of a feedback interview, for example, than a phenomenologist might be. Thus, in this work, we associate certain techniques much more closely with certain theoretical approaches than with others.

We also need to check how certain techniques and methods align with the overall theoretical orientation to ascertain their compatibility. For example, a phenomenologist is unlikely to begin research with a schedule of fixed questions. Rather he or she would conduct broad observational research initially to investigate what questions may be important to the musicians themselves before developing a list of questions.

Alignment of theory with method and technique is critical to the process of inquiry. There needs to be integration in terms of assumptions being made about the research process, and how these parts fit with one another. It is not good enough to have a theory in mind as we conduct research. The theory needs be compatible and integrate appropriately with the rest of the inquiry process.

Certain theoretical orientations have developed one or another parts of the inquiry process to a different extent. Some approaches are more elaborated in terms of theory, others more developed in terms of method or technique.

Ethnomusicologists are actively publishing exciting new work about music of the world's peoples, and they seek to understand the basis of the inquiry. What approaches are being used? How do they compare to one another? What are the differences and the points of unity? How have approaches to this field changed from the early days of the discipline? How are the parts of the inquiry interrelated in each approach?

We can examine each approach as distinct and separate, but ethnomusicologists often draw from several approaches simultaneously. Our look at specific studies will reveal something of how scholars actually conduct their studies and combine what will be described here as distinct theoretical orientations.

References

Blacking, John. 1995a [1967]. *Venda Children's Songs: A Study in Ethnomusicological Analysis.* Chicago: University of Chicago Press.

Brinner, Benjamin. 1995. *Knowing Music, Making Music: Javanese Gamelan and the Theory of Musical Competence and Interaction.* Chicago: University of Chicago Press.

Danielson, Virginia. 1997. *The Voice of Egypt.* Chicago: University of Chicago Press.

Erlmann, Veit. 1996a. N*ightsong.* Chicago: University of Chicago Press.

Glaser, Barney G., and Anselm Strauss. 1967. *The Discovery of Grounded Theory: Strategies for Qualitative Research.* Chicago: Aldine.

Guilbault, Jocelyne, with Gage Averill, Edouard Benoit, and Gregory Rabess. 1993. *Zouk: World Music in the West Indies.* Chicago: University of Chicago Press.

Hood, Mantle. 1971. *The Ethnomusicologist.* New York: McGraw-Hill.

Hoyningen-Huene, Paul. 1993. *Reconstructing Scientific Revolutions: Thomas S. Kuhn's Philosophy of Science.* Translated by Alexander J. Levine. Foreword by Thomas S. Kuhn. Chicago: University of Chicago Press.

Kaplan, Abraham. 1964. *The Conduct of Inquiry: Methodology for Behavioral Science.* San Francisco: Chandler.

Kaplan, David, and Robert A. Manners. 1972. *Culture Theory.* Englewood Cliffs, N.J.: Prentice-Hall.

Kuhn, Thomas S. 1962. *The Structure of Scientific Revolutions.* 2nd ed. Chicago: University of Chicago Press.

Lomax, Alan. 1968. *Folksong Style and Culture.* Washington, D. C.: American Association for the Advancement of Science.

Merriam, Alan P. 1964. *The Anthropology of Music.* Evanston: Northwestern University Press.

Middleton, Richard. 2003. "Music Studies and the Idea of Culture." In *The Cultural Study of Music,* eds. Martin Clayton, Trevor Herbert, and Richard Middleton. New York and London: Routledge, 1–15.

Monson, Ingrid. 1996. *Saying Something: Jazz Improvisation and Interaction.* Chicago: University of Chicago Press.

Oxford English Dictionary, The Compact Edition. 1986. 2 vols. Oxford: Oxford University Press.

Phillipson, Michael. 1972. "Theory, Methodology and Conceptualization." In *New Directions in Sociological Theory,* ed. Paul Filmer et. al. Cambridge: MA: MIT Press, 77–118.

Qureshi, Regula Burkhart. 1995 [1986]. *Sufi Music of India and Pakistan: Sound, Context and Meaning in Qawwali.* Chicago: University of Chicago Press.

Rice, Timothy. 1987. "Toward the Remodeling of Ethnomusicology." *Ethnomusicology* 31(3): 469–88.

———. 1994. *May It Fill Your Soul: Experiencing Bulgarian Music.* Chicago: University of Chicago Press.

Schutz, Alfred, and Thomas Luckmann. 1973. *The Structures of the Life-World.* Chicago: Northwestern University Press.

Seeger. Anthony. 1987a. "Do We Need to Remodel Ethnomusicology?" *Ethnomusicology* 31(3):491–95.

Shelemay, Kay Kaufman. 1998. *Let Jasmine Rain Down: Song and Remembrance among Syrian Jews.* Chicago: University of Chicago Press.

Stone, Ruth M. 1982. *Let the Inside Be Sweet: The Interpretation of Music Event among the Kpelle of Liberia.* Bloomington: Indiana University Press.

———. 1988. *Dried Millet Breaking: Time, Words, and Song in the Woi Epic of the Kpelle.* Bloomington: Indiana University Press.

Strauss, Anselm L., and Juliet M. Corbin. 1990. *Basics of Qualitative Research: Grounded Theory Procedures and Techniques.* Newbury Park, Calif.: Sage.

Sugarman, Jane C. 1997. *Engendering Song: Singing and Subjectivity at Prespa Albanian Weddings.* Chicago: University of Chicago Press.

Wong, Deborah. 2004. *Speak It Louder: Asian Americans Making Music.* New York: Routledge.

Chapter 2

Cultural Evolutionism and Diffusionism in Comparative Musicology

Ethnomusicology, as a field of study, developed in the post–World War II environment of the 1950s. Much early work in ethnomusicology owed a great deal to the earlier field known as **comparative musicology**, or *vergleichende musik-wissenschaft*, defined by Guido Adler as "the comparison of the musical works—especially the folk songs—of the various peoples of the earth for ethnographical purposes, and the classification of them according to their various forms" (Adler 1885:14).

> By 1961 the use of "comparative musicology" as a label had disappeared except in historic references; while it appeared later (Kolinski 1967), it was no longer applied to the field in general but rather, to a portion of it. (Merriam 1977:192)

The "Berlin School of Comparative Musicology" began with the research work of Carl Stumpf, a psychologist and philosopher, and his assistant Erich M. von Hornbostel, a twenty-four-year old student with training in philosophy and chemistry. In a multidisciplinary constellation—that also included Otto Abraham, Fritz Bose, Marius Schneider, Mieczyslaw Kolinski, and George Herzog—Stumpf worked to build a collection of recordings in the Psychological Institute of Berlin University for research purposes, which later became the Berlin Phonogramm-Archiv.

Comparative musicology

- Comparison of various musical works of various peoples of the earth
- Nineteenth-century field of study that was prominent in Europe, particularly Germany

---

Cultural Evolutionism: Assumptions

Two theoretical orientations, which derived from anthropology, dominated European comparative musicology. The first was **cultural evolutionism**, which held that all cultures are on an evolving track, some having reached a more developed state than others at any one time. This approach helped establish a clear differentiation between "civilized" and "primitive" cultures (Sanderson 2002). Several assumptions grounded cultural evolutionism:

1. **Cultures evolve from simple to complex, and as they do so they move from primitive to civilized.**

   Cultures and societies are always progressing. The direction of that change moves always toward the more complex.

2. **Music evolves from simple to complex within societies as they progress.**

   Comparative musicologists pointed to attributes that distinguished pentatonic from heptatonic scales. Pentatonic, also called "gapped scales," were not as fully evolved as the heptatonic scales they maintained. And the reasoning was that as these cultures developed more fully, the "gaps" would be filled and the scales would eventually become heptatonic or possess seven tones within the octave rather than just five tones.

3. **Societies are built of fairly coherent and functional systems that interrelate to one another.**

   The evolutionists viewed societies as much more tightly integrated than most diffusionists did on the whole. Nevertheless, there was a general idea among comparative musicologists that societies possessed a degree of coherence.

4. **Certain musical practices may occur in multiple societies because of shared human psychological structures as those groups of people evolve through a particular level.**

   In cultural evolutionism, musical practices are bound to spring up in multiple locations, depending on where a particular people are on the evolutionary spiral. These multiple sources are a form of polygenesis. It is quite normal to expect similar inventions in multiple locations.

Cultural evolutionism

- The theory that all cultures are evolving to ever-higher states and some cultures have reached a more developed state than others
- Supports the idea of polygenesis

By invoking evolutionism, cultures could be differentiated according to their place in the evolutionary scale. Inevitably, Western music represented the most evolved state, and other cultures were by this scheme of reckoning less developed.

Comparative Musicology: Cultural Evolutionism

Evolutionary theory pervaded Stumpf's work. In his article on the Ballakula Indians, he "suggested that a tonal system with stable steps required an intellectual development . . . whose consecutive stages and inner properties no one has yet demonstrated for us in a psychologically credible way" (Stumpf 1886a:426), a task to which he later devoted himself in his book on the "origins of music" (Stumpf 1911). With historical records unavailable for the "early stages," the "line of development" sketched by Stumpf quite naturally employed both ethnographic parallels and a psychological hypothesis (Schneider 1991:299).

Along with grand schemes of evolution, there have been more detailed studies of the evolutionary aspects of a single genre of music. Percival Kirby, for example, proposed a developmental sequence for the musical bow of southern Africa. In that scheme he suggested that the musical bow, first of all, came from the hunting bow when the arrow was fired (Kirby 1934:193). The second stage developed from the hunter tapping the string with an arrow. The third stage resulted when a number of bows were placed together on the ground and tapped by a single person (Merriam 1967b:94). All of this theory building derived primarily from inference rather than detailed ethnographic investigation.

One might decide that the culture of people who use a simple hunting bow as a musical bow must be more ancient than that of people who have multi-string instruments. But making such a claim might not be borne out by the facts. Alan Merriam noted, "The possibility of using evolutionary schemes in reconstructing culture history is not particularly bright" (1967b:95).

Critique

1. **Grand theories of social change were constructed that were not anchored in ethnographic details.**

   It is difficult to refute or support many of the claims of cultural evolutionists because their theories were not grounded in facts but rather in conjecture.

2. **All other cultures, according to this orientation, were judged to be less culturally evolved than Western cultures.**

   There was a hegemonic tilt to the orientation that served to elevate Western cultures above other cultures and societies. This aspect of the theory must immediately cause us to wonder about the soundness of the structure.

Cultural Evolutionism: Contribution

1. **The cultural evolutionism orientation attempted to account for historical patterns.**

   There was some merit in attempting take into account changes over time in broad regions of the world. The idea was bold and certainly ambitious.

2. **The cultural evolutionism orientation attempted to compare vast expanses of culture one to another.**

   The intention could be seen as interesting and not without merit, although in its execution it could not be judged successful by most any measure.

Diffusionism

The second orientation, **diffusionism**, also came from anthropology and described the spread of cultural practices, including music performance, from one location to another often over long distances and the passage of time. One of the key American scholars associated with diffusionism was Franz Boas (1858–1942), who was born in Europe but spent a major part of his career in the United States. He showed a keen interest in culture traits and how they diffuse over time from one place to another. His version of diffusionism was anchored in particular facts and relied on movement of a much smaller scale than many of the European scholars.

Diffusionism in the discipline of folklore was embodied in the historic-geographic method and constituted the study of folktales and their spread from one place to another over time. Research allowed one to reconstruct the point of origin of cultural practices and artifacts.

Diffusionism: Assumptions

1. **Cultural traits diffuse or move from one place to another over time.**

   We can find a cultural object such as the hooked drumstick in India as well as in West Africa. Using diffusionism as an explanatory theory, we might proceed to reconstruct the route by which the stick moved from one location to another.

Diffusionism

- The theory that cultural traits move over time and space out from the point of origin
- Supports the idea of monogenesis

2. **There is a single point of invention and over time the trait moves outward from that original location.**

Unlike cultural evolutionism, diffusionism does not allow for multiple sites of independent invention. There is a single point of invention or monogenesis. Common elements are assumed to have moved from one point to another, and research constitutes creating the path of movement from the place of origin to another location. Over time culture clusters or cultural circles (*Kulturkreislehre*) develop, where related traits occur.

3. **Societies are built of many traits that exhibit various origins and histories.**

This situation may result in somewhat incoherent wholes because of the varying origins of different parts of the culture. The result is a patchwork quilt arrangement of varying components.

Comparative Musicology: Diffusionism

Musical diffusionism was an area of considerable research for comparative musicologists, and they studied the movement of instruments as well as musical pitch inventories or scales among other traits.

Diffusionism Example: Drum Bracing Technique: Indonesia and Africa

Musical instruments were part of the evidence that Leo Frobenius, for example, pointed to in theorizing about diffusion between Indonesia and Africa when he pointed out that "the Indonesian method of bracing drums reappears on the West African coast" (Frobenius 1898:640–41).

Diffusionism Example: Cycle of Blown Fifths: Oceania, Latin America, Southeast Asia, Africa

Part of the evidence Erich M. von Hornbostel used in developing his theory of scales was that "a large number of exotic scales found in use among peoples widely separated both historically and geographically, as well as ethnologically, may be derived *in some regular manner* from that cycle of blown fifth" (Kunst 1948:5). Hornbostel and other scholars found evidence in the tunings of panpipes from Oceania to Latin America and xylophones from Southeast Asia and Central Africa. As Jaap Kunst concluded, drawing on diffusionism without directly saying so, "There are various indications pointing to the probability that the cultural influence manifested in the tunings here referred to originally emanated from China" (Kunst 1948:5). Thus he maintained that China was the point of origin, and that with the cycle of blown fifths the way of organizing the pitches spread out from China to Southeast Asia, Oceania, Latin America, and Africa—a very great distance indeed. Kunst was simultaneously pointing to cultural evolutionism when he maintained, "Now it is a matter of general agreement among musicologists that scales with definitely fixed, as it were 'objectivated' intervals *must* be products of a high cultural level" (Kunst 1948:5).

Diffusionism Example: Xylophone Tuning: Africa and Asia

The comparative musicologists looked to comparison of pitch inventories to explore connections between Southeast Asia and Africa. Hornbostel began with a study of the pitches from two African xylophones (Bavenda and Mandingo) and four Burmese xylophones. In the end, the pitches, expressed in vibrations per second, were amazingly similar for Africa and Asia (Hornbostel 1911:601–15).

Nearly fifty years later, Arthur M. Jones, missionary and devoted amateur comparative musicologist, researched material from similar regions, employing a broader set of musical characteristics. He found that the Chopi, Malinke, and Bakuba in Africa used a nearly identical beginning absolute pitch, just as Cambodian and Javanese musicians did on their xylophones. He discovered the octave was divided into equal steps of nearly identical size. The variations were always less than half a step (Jones 1960:36–47).

This claim has not been widely discussed in ethnomusicology. Rather, ethnomusicologists have turned to issues of different sorts and much more limited in scope. Nevertheless, because we do have evidence of Africans traveling to Arabia and Indonesia as part of the Arab slave trade, the spread of African musical traits is not altogether surprising (Jeffreys 1961:16).

Diffusionism Example: World Instrument Classification

Curt Sachs (1929) in his book on musical instruments, *Geist und Werden der Musik Instrumente,* defined a theory for musical instruments around the world in which he designated twenty-three strata, drawing on distribution patterns. These strata or circles could be labeled from oldest to most recent just as the layers in an archeological excavation could be labeled. The most widely distributed strata were the oldest.

Hornbostel looked at instruments worldwide and compared his own strata with those designated by Sachs. He found much agreement, although there were differences on particular points. In the end, Hornbostel arrived at twelve groups for Africa (note VI and VIa). The groups were designated as follows:

I. *Earliest Cultures.*
  1. Universal.
     Strung rattles.
     Bull-roarer.
     Bone-flute.
     Scraped idiophones.
  2. Universal—sporadic in Africa.
     End-blown conch trumpet.
  3. Sporadic everywhere it occurs.
     Percussion-rod.

    II. *"Ancient Sudan."*
       1. Extensive but not universal.
          Gourd rattle? Cylindrical drum.
          Mouth bow.

    III. *"West African."*
       1. West and Central Africa, South and East Asia—South America.
          Slit-drum, globular-flute.
          Log-xylophone, nose flute.

    IV. *"Mid-Erythraen"*
       1. E. Africa, S. and E. Asia—South America.
          Pan-Pipes, stamping-tube, central-hole flute, (gourd drum), single-skin
             hourglass-drum.

    V. *"Pan Erythraean, Early"*
       1. Indonesia—Africa.
          Gourd-xylophone, iron bell, cup-shaped drum.

    VI. *"Pan-Erythraean, Late"*
       1. India—Africa.
          Bow with gourd resonator, harp-zither with notched bridge.

    VIa. *"Hova."*
       1. Indonesia—Madagascar
          Flat-bar zither, tube-zither.

    VII. *Ancient Southwest Asia—Ancient Egypt.*
       1. Proto-Hamitic? Animal horn.
       2. Pre-Islamic. Bow-harp.
       3. Post Islamic. Double clarinet,
          Tanged lute.

    VIII. *Buddhism.*
       1. Buddhist Asia, sporadically in NW Africa.
          Double-skin hourglass shaped drum.

    IX. *Pre-Christian, West Asiatic.*
       1. Arabia, E. Asia, Sudan.
          Bowl-lyre.

    X. *Post-Christian, Pre-Islamic.*
       1. W. Asia—Indonesia, W. Africa.
          Hooked drumstick.

    XI. *Islam.*
       1. NE Africa, W. Asia—Indonesia.
          Tanged fiddle with lateral pegs.
          Kettle drum. (Hornbostel 1933:299–301)

Later, Sachs reduced his twenty-three strata and Hornbostel's twelve groups to three. In doing so, he specified the following assumptions that both he and Hornbostel employed:

    1. An object or idea found in scattered regions of a certain district is older than
       an object found everywhere in the same area.

2. Objects preserved only in remote valleys and islands are older than those used in open plains.

3. The more widely an object is spread over the world, the more "primitive" it is. (Sachs 1940:62–64)

In Sachs's and Hornbostel's work, a massive amount of evidence was brought together and, as Merriam points out, the "logic is carefully buttressed by fact" (Merriam 1964:100). The problem came in determining whether the diffusionary process occurred as they inferred it had or whether it happened in some other way. More recent work in diffusion has focused on more restricted areas in which there is some evidence for historical unity. In other words, in the last thirty years, scholars, conducting studies of diffusion, have confined themselves to problems of much smaller scope for which verification of facts is more possible.

Diffusionism: Critique

1. **Although diffusionism presents an order of events and relative time sense, it does not indicate a precise or chronological sense of time.**

   The concern with history is not anchored in calendrical dates or absolute time. Rather it is more a placing of one aspect before or after another.

2. **It is difficult to predict how a trait will be accepted by a group of people.**

   Neighbors may not take a trait, whereas people living a long distance away will quite readily adopt it.

Diffusionism: Contribution

1. **Diffusionism attempted to explain culture change over time and space.**

   By comparing traits, diffusionism sought to account for variation as well as stability of traits, whether they occurred in music or folktales or religion.

2. **Diffusionism attempted to identify similarities across cultures, even those that were widely separated.**

   In this way, the orientation looked for connections from one group of people another. Certain peoples, separated by great distance, possess traits that on the surface at least appear to be similar and, therefore, merit study.

The Implications of Cultural Evolutionism and Diffusionism

These two orientations coexisted in the comparative musicologists' world and were alternately, and sometimes simultaneously, invoked at various moments. Diffusionism and evolutionism used different explanatory routes to understand musical phenomena in the nineteenth century. But in the end, they helped differentiate so-called high cultures from the so-called primitive cultures. They created a hierarchy of societies and, by extension, musics. These two theories, then, served and supported the thrust of colonialism as the Western powers ruled over their outposts all over the world. These intellectual formulations echoed the superiority of the West and classified the music of other parts of the world in relation to the West.

Comparing Evolutionism and Diffusionism

Figure 1 compares the major approaches of comparative musicology, cultural evolutionism and diffusionism. Although it is fairly easy to recognize the flaws with these approaches, and the resultant tendency to classify the music of places like Africa as oldest and therefore simplest, these theories have an amazing tenacity not only in ethnomusicology but in popular culture as well. The media and movie industries of the West perpetuate the views put forth as a result of these theories with a force and power that is hard to refute through scholarly articles in academic journals.

When I was director of the Archives of Traditional Music, we were contacted by Disney Studios for examples of African music to be used in a soundtrack for a film. We selected several samples from recordings made in Africa and sent them to the Disney staff to see if they would like to use the full selection of any of the samples. A short time later, they responded that what we had sent did not sound enough like Africa for their purposes. We interpreted that to mean the samples were not stereotypical enough of what they considered to be African and did not fit the Hollywood notion of African music. Thus the notion that African music was repetitive, simple, and predominantly drumming was what they, no doubt, expected.

Even within ethnomusicology, these diffusionism and cultural evolutionism theories were explicitly employed up to the middle of the twentieth century. Andre Schaeffner, for example, corroborated Sachs's twenty-three strata of musical instruments among the Dogon of Mali, West Africa, in a study published as late as 1956 (Schaeffner 1956:29–30).

The comparative musicologists shared some assumptions about "folk" or "primitive" music. They pointed to the "absence of relatively developed and autonomous 'systems' and 'languages'" (Blum 1991:13). Béla Bartók referred to

	Evolutionism	Diffusionism
Origin of Trait	Multiple	Single
Accounts for time	Yes	Yes
Oldest = Simplest	Yes	Yes

Figure 1 Evolutionism vs. Diffusionism

"styles" which made possible "spontaneous gratification of the musical instinct or impulse" among Hungarian peasants (Bartók 1933:268; see also Suchoff 1997). Hornbostel described a "low level of musical culture" (1928:38) that precluded an organized set of musical tools. The roots of such assumptions went back to the late eighteenth century when Jean-Jacques Rousseau had noted two types of musical systems. One was characterized by "artifice and theory" and the other by "nature and practice." Thus one could analyze the former with rules, whereas the latter were "melodic inflections, each of them necessarily apprehended and reproduced as a whole" (Blum 1991:13).

Contemporary Indigenous Examples of Cultural Evolutionism

Diola of West Africa

Some ideas contained in these theories can be found in more recent studies that do not make specific reference to them. Judith T. Irvine and J. David Sapir connect musical structure to social structure among the Diola of West Africa. One of the things they observe is the greater diversification of music roles over time. Virtuoso performers would not have fit the older Kujamaat Diola way of life (1976:79). The roles have become more elaborate, more developed over time. In other words, the roles have evolved. These empirical observations do not necessarily support or refute these earlier theories of evolutionism and diffusionism but rather show that patterns or theories can be used to explain phenomena of a limited time and space. Furthermore, the progress from simple to more complex is a pattern that may be observed without the other baggage of the evolutionary theory. And the empirical discovery of such patterns does not mean that one has made inaccurate observations or that such situations need entail all that was part of evolutionism.

Kpelle of West Africa

Another contemporary case of a musical event becoming more elaborate over time involves my own fieldwork. Musicians living in the Kpelle area in Liberia explained to me in the middle of 1970s how they frequently borrowed a song from another village. That song entered their repertoire as a kind of empty shell. Then they began, over time, to embellish it and develop it.

During 1975–76, I observed how the song "Koli-gong-song," imported from a neighboring village by the Gbeyilataa ensemble, was developed. First, the group added a dance pattern to accompany the singing of the song. Then they found some ritual objects, gnarled pieces of wood that they said represented the accoutrements of the chief of the witches. These objects were then put in the center of the performance arena, and sometimes dancers picked up the pieces and danced with them. As the musicians described the changes, they emphasized the ever-elaborating aspect of their evolving performance.

Although the Kpelle musicians with whom I worked would not invoke evolutionism, they made clear that over time they had added to the original song in inventive ways—elaborating and enhancing this borrowed song. The Kpelle performers of Gbeyilataa were evolving a performance in a way that they valued and deemed aesthetically pleasing without invoking the theory of cultural evolution and all of the accompanying assumptions.

The two examples from communities in West Africa are much more circumscribed and local than the theories of cultural evolutionism utilized by comparative musicology. They show that we do indeed find cases of evolutionism that can be supported by the ethnographic fact of music performances and music roles becoming more complex over time.

The Legacy of Comparative Musicology

Comparative musicology grew as a small but enthusiastic group of researchers from across the scientific spectrum realized the possibilities for using music in studying the growth and spread of one aspect of culture. The multidisciplinary roots of ethnomusicology were clearly evident in this period, and the complex intertwining of science and humanities in the study of music began to appear.

Comparative musicology lived precariously at the edge of the academy. Although, for a brief period, it was recognized in Berlin as a subject to be taught, its tenure was somewhat brief in the early 1900s, and the famous Berlin Phonogram Archive was moved from the Psychological Institute to the Ethnographic Museum. The Second World War and all the ravages that accompanied it in Hitler's Germany did not help comparative musicology become an established and entrenched university discipline. The picture is fascinating as we compare it with the present-day interest in ethnomusicology even as the field still searches for disciplinary independence in the academy.

The dominant theories of the comparative musicology of 1900 to 1935—diffusionism and evolutionism—continue to have enormous influence on thinking about music. These theories offered a very hierarchical conception of cultures in which comparison of Western music to music of the "Other" inevitably revealed forms that were less developed, less sophisticated, and less complex in the world of the "Other." Although we can readily see the problems, their effects permeate much thinking within the academy and among the larger public today. We will also see how aspects of evolutionism and diffusionism have links to more contemporary theories, and how the legacy of these ideas is embedded at certain points with current paradigms.

The early 1900s in Europe were both exciting times of discovery as Europeans explored the world and the rich music found there. These were also the times when scholars attempted to systematize and master this music of the other. The colonial impulses from this period continue to reverberate today in various theoretical formulations. In diffusionism, one found a mirror of the colonial powers where the center represented the purest form of a trait, which then spread to the periphery. The colonial powers on a larger scale were the center of force that spread to the edges.

Comparative musicologists thought globally and looked for universals. They were ambitious and comprehensive. To their detriment, they did not examine certain details of performance in ways that later scholars would deem essential. But no one could accuse them of thinking small.

In many ways, the framework they offered was exciting, boldly sketched, and a fine legacy. In other ways, the theories that dominated the period continue to haunt the work we do today. Thus a minimal understanding of the stage as they set it is critical to examining in some detail theory in ethnomusicology today.

References

Adler, Guido. 1885. "Umfang, Methode und Zeil der Musikwissenschaft." *Vierteljahrsschrift für Musikwissenschaft* 1:5–20.

Bartók, Béla. 1933. "Hungarian Peasant Music." *Musical Quarterly* 19:267–89.

Blum, Stephen. 1991. "European Musical Terminology and the Music of Africa." In *Comparative Musicology and Anthropology of Music,* eds. Bruno Nettl and Philip V. Bohlman. Chicago: University of Chicago Press, 3–36.

Frobenius, Leo. 1898. "The Origin of African Civilizations." *Annual Report of the Board of Regents of the Smithsonian Institution* I: 640–41.

Hornbostel, Erich M. von. 1911. "Über ein akustiches Kriterium für Kulturzusammenhänge." *Zeitschrift für Ethnologie* 43:601–15.

——. 1928. "African Negro Music." *Africa* 1:30–62.

——. 1933. "The Ethnology of African Sound-Instruments," *Africa* 6:277–311.

Irvine, Judith T., and J. David Sapir. 1976. "Musical Style and Social Change among the Kujamaat Diola." *Ethnomusicology* 20:67–86.

Jeffreys, M. D. W. 1961. "Negro Influences on Indonesia." *African Music* 2:16.

Jones, Arthur Morris. 1960. "Indonesia and Africa: The Xylophone as a Culture Indicator." *African Music* 2:36–47.

Kirby, Percival R. 1934. *The Musical Instruments of the Native Races of South Africa.* Oxford: Oxford University Press.

Kolinski, Mieczslaw. 1967. "Recent Trends in Ethnomusicology." *Ethnomusicology* 11:1–24.

Kunst, Jaap. 1948. "Around von Hornbostel's Theory of the Cycle of Blown Fifths." *Medeling* 76:3–35. Amsterdam: Publication of the Royal Institute for the Indies.

Merriam, Alan P. 1964. *The Anthropology of Music.* Evanston: Northwestern University Press.

——. 1967b. "The Use of Music as a Technique of Reconstructing Culture History in Africa." In *Reconstructing African Culture History,* eds. Creighton Gavel and Norman R. Bennett. Boston: Boston University Press, 85–114.

——. 1977. "Definitions of 'Comparative Musicology' and 'Ethnomusicology': An Historical-Theoretical Perspective." *Ethnomusicology* 21(2):189–204.

Sachs, Curt. 1929. *Geist und Werden der Musikinstrumente.* Berlin: D. Reimer.

——. 1940. *History of Musical Instruments: The Rise of Music in the Ancient World East and West.* New York: Norton.

Sanderson, Stephen K. 2002. *Social Evolutionism: A Critical History.* Oxford: Blackwell.

Schaeffner, André. 1956. "Ethnologie musicale ou musicologie comparée." In *Les Colloques de Wégimont,* ed. Paul Collaer. Brussels: Elsevier, pp. 29–30.

Schneider, Albrecht. 1991. "Psychological Theory and Comparative Musicology." In *Comparative Musicology and Anthropology of Music*, eds. Bruno Nettl and Philip V. Bohlman. Chicago: University of Chicago Press, 293–317.

Stumpf, Carl. 1886a. "Lieder der Bellakula-Indianer." *Vierteljahrsschrift für Musikwissenschaft* 2:405–26.

——. 1911. *Die Anfänge der Musik.* Leipzig: J. A. Barth.

Suchoff, Benjamin, ed. 1997. *Béla Bartók Studies in Ethnomusicology.* Lincoln and London: University of Nebraska Press.

Chapter 3

Structural-Functional Approaches

As we begins to look at the first theoretical area that ethnomusicologists employed in the post–World War II era, a word about the makeup of theories in ethnomusicology is appropriate. A student in one a Paradigms in Ethnomusicology class remarked one day, "There are few orientations that are 'pure' in ethnomusicology." Indeed, aspects of what are described as a theory in ethnomusicology are often employed in conjunction with other theories.

Ethnomusicologists are not alone is combining approaches at a time when the scientific community has become enamored with theories from a wide range of disciplines. Even the structure of musical forms has provided inspiration for scientific thinking in other disciplines. With the blurred, messy intermingling of theories across disciplines in mind, we turn then to an approach with a rather awkward but quite aptly descriptive label.

Structural functionalism arose as a theoretical orientation of British social anthropologists, seeking to challenge cultural evolutionism and diffusionism. Anthropologists sought ways of addressing the shortcomings of the nineteenth-century theories (Turner and Maryanski 1979: 29–31). They turned to structural functionalism as a remedy to the problems they detected in the theories on which the comparative musicologists had relied.

The seeds for this approach that proved most salient for scholarship in the 1950s and 160s came from such scholars as Constantin Brăiloiu. In an article that first appeared in Paris in 1931, this Romanian musicologist recognized the importance of music as it relates to social life when he said,

> The analysis of musical forms, though still necessary, would become secondary and would retain only the importance of one means among others. In this case, organic processes, such as the alteration of an Archaic repertory by an urban or

---

Structural functionalism

- Studies social phenomena in terms of consequences for broader society
- Focuses on various systems (political, kinship) that interrelate to one another

suburban infiltration . . . would be more interesting . . . to the man of science, than the sporadic preservation of ancient specimens. (1984:60)

As early as the 1930s, comparative musicologists saw the value of connecting music to the broader social life for the purposes of analysis. To set the scene, in its broadest sense,

> [F]unctional analysis examines social phenomena in terms of their consequences for the broader society. . . . In many ways functionalism emerged as the science of the "body social," for it was felt that if insight into the parts of the human body could be achieved by determining how they affected bodily states, the same would be possible for society. (Turner and Maryanski 1979:xi–xii)

Assumptions

The fundamental premises of structural functionalism are based on Emile Durkheim's idea of *social* solidarity. What makes individuals work together in groups?

As Alfred R. Radcliffe-Brown, the main theoretician asserted, *function* is one important part of this orientation. Things—institutions, rituals, customs— function to keep the individuals acting as a groups. This is why for Radcliffe-Brown *function* is related to social structure. Furthermore, Radcliffe-Brown distinguished *structural functions* from *biopsychological* needs as outlined by Bronislaw Malinowski (1944).

Malinowski, in contrast, focused on the collective satisfaction of biological needs as justification for social solidarity. People could better satisfy their biological needs—food or shelter, for example—in groups; that is why individuals work together. Malinowski held that to describe *how* a lung worked, we would be describing the *form* of the process. But a description of *why* the lung is operating in a certain manner is a concern for **function** (Moore 1997:133).

For Radcliffe-Brown, function was the contribution an institution makes to the maintenance of social structure that serves to reinforce social solidarity. Structural functionalism rests on a number of assumptions:

1. **Social systems maintain themselves in certain kinds of societies for significant intervals of time in a steady state, during which time a high degree of social solidarity characterizes the relationship among its members.**

   From 1930 to 1955, the overwhelming number of structural-functional studies was based on fieldwork in African societies located in countries

---

Function

- Contribution an institution makes to the maintenance of social structure

under colonial, especially British, control. The research conducted in these societies focused on looking at the integrated systems that constituted these societies. The results of these studies had the effect of confirming the rightness of maintaining indirect British rule.

2. **Structural-functional studies focus on groups, especially those organized along territorial, kinship, and political lines and the interrelationship among different systems within a group.**

For this reason, community studies characterized structural-functional inquiry, and the main question was how a bounded society was put together. Alan Merriam's training had been in this approach, and he explained, in classes I took with him, how when he went to the Basongye area in Zaïre, he began by surveying the village where he settled, trying to discern the organization of various groups within the town. His intent, following structural functionalism was to discern the interrelated systems that kept the Basongye people together as a distinct culture.

This approach was in contrast to the strategy I was proposing for my own work some years later. I intended to locate two musical groups and follow them on their performance circuits, moving to the wider context later.

3. **Little useful historical information can be obtained from most "primitive" peoples because of their lack of written records.**

This assumption resulted in a distinct separation, until the 1950s, of synchronic structural-functional studies from diachronic inquiry in anthropology and, by extension, ethnomusicology. That is, structural functional studies focused on the **ethnographic present** in contrast to diachronic inquiry where the emphasis would be on inquiry about history or human interaction over time. This single assumption affected the study of ethnomusicology for many years. Early ethnomusicologists focused on studies of the contemporary practice, assuming that little of historical value could be learned from societies without history.

4. **The structure of a sociocultural system can be compared to a living organism.**

There is a vital interrelation between the parts of a structure of a society. The metaphor of a living organism provided a useful model for a sociocultural system in the structural-functional paradigm. The origin of the doctrine of **holism,** defining anthropology as unique because of its focus on *all* aspects of society—political, religious, and kinship—can be found in this approach. This assumption also helps create the focus of music studies—the system is the point of emphasis, not the individual musician.

Ethnographic present

- A romanticized timelessness attributed to many cultures before Westernization

Sociocultural system
• Entity of interrelated parts and the relationships created between the parts

Holism
• Approach that examines something in its entirety • Approach in anthropology that focuses on all aspects of society

5. **A sociocultural system involves a complex of interdependencies between parts and processes.**

   As Talcott Parsons advocated, a system is a concept around which all sophisticated theory in generalizing disciplines must be organized. And his work moved across the boundaries of a number of disciplines to explore how behavior relates to organization (Turner and Maryanski 1979:83). The religious system is related to the music system, for example. These parts of the system are bound together through processes such as rituals, where religion and music intertwine and serve to reinforce and bind together these parts.

6. **There is interdependency between a cultural complex and its surrounding environment.**

   The structural functionalists do maintain an interest in where the cultural system with which they are concerned fits into the larger context. They are focused on reified and definitively bounded cultural complexes that, nevertheless, relate to one another and to the surroundings, including the physical environment.

7. **The ultimate concern is to account for the internal functioning of cultural systems.**

   This assumption involves a concern with the functions of cultural practices as they maintain, perpetuate, and integrate the culture. These functions provide the mechanism for cultural systems to operate and to reproduce themselves. They are the things that keep individuals bound together in groups.

Structural Functionalism: Critique

1. **Is a culture really a complex of interrelated systems?**

   As with any approach to studying human behavior, there have been criticisms of the structural-functional approach. Perhaps most serious has been the identification of a methodological weakness in assuming the reality of such systems. How do we know these integrated systems have an empirical basis? How do we test to see if this is how society is put together? That is, what can we do to be sure they exist? Because it is difficult to conduct the research to test these systems, which are already assumed to exist, the effect is that of a tautology. We become enmeshed in a circular argument and have no clear and easy proof.

2. **Structural functionalism favors equilibrium and does not account well for change.**

   A second criticism that has been leveled is that structural-functional research is biased toward equilibrium. Structural functionalism assumes that cultures are well-functioning units that have propelled the culture as a fixed and unchanging entity through time. It also assumes that all conflicts eventually serve to reinstate equilibrium in the society. The structural-functional approach, therefore, favors situations that are static and is somewhat ill suited to situations of change.

3. **Functions are uniform within the entire system.**

   A third criticism, voiced by sociologist Robert K. Merton, is that standardized social items are assumed to be functional for the entire social or cultural system or all individuals within the society. Whether these items uniformly fulfill functions should be questioned, not assumed, he maintains (1996:72–73).

   Scholars such as Edmund Leach (1965) examined dysfunction and the pressures that can be brought for change in a system. As a result, he modified the structural-functional approach to make the model more dynamic and allow for disruptions to the equilibrium.

4. **Structural functionalism lacks explanatory power.**

   A fourth, and fairly damaging, criticism is that functionalism lacks explanatory power and does not go beyond the facts that it intends to explain. One has a musical system that one assumes is bound to other parts of the social cultural complex system. Yet there is difficulty knowing if that is, in fact, the case. A good theory should help us move beyond the facts as we observe them, and this is not easy with structural functionalism.

Structural Functionalism: Contribution

Despite the criticisms leveled at structural functionalism, certain positive attributes need to be pointed out.

1. **Structural functionalism provides an integrative approach to the study of human interaction, bringing together several aspects of culture.**

   Structural functionalism aims to generalize and find laws for the interworking of the parts of society. In doing so, it presents an umbrella or holistic approach to the study of human societies.

2. **Methodologically, structural functionalists have achieved a great deal through extensive ethnography.**

From the method aspect, structural functionalists' work led to considerable achievements. One of the advantages of trying to discover all of the interrelated aspects of a society has been that, of necessity, one spends a great deal of time in that society learning about it. Method, in this case, involved rigorous fieldwork as the researcher sought to find interconnections that tied the parts of the system together. Structural functionalists like Malinowski and Radcliffe-Brown contributed to the participant-observation method of fieldwork.

Structural Functionalism in Ethnomusicology

Although anthropologists, including Radcliffe-Brown, mentioned the music system as part of the larger sociocultural complex, it was really Merriam who, in his book the *Anthropology of Music* (1964), described in some detail what was implied by the structural-functional approach in ethnomusicology. In his chapter "Uses and Functions," he noted,

> Descriptive facts, while in themselves of importance, make their most significant contribution when they are applied to broader problems of understanding the phenomenon which has been described. We wish to know not only what a thing is, but, more significantly what it does for people and how it does it. (1964:209)

In other words, Merriam saw functionalism as moving beyond the *what* and extending to the *how*. Merriam defined *function* as the "understanding of what music does for human beings as evaluated by an outside observer" (1964:209). He proceeded to list some possible functions of music in a society:

- Aesthetic enjoyment
- Communication, particularly of emotion
- Symbolic representation
- Physical response
- Enforcement of conformity to social norms
- Validation of social organizations
- Contribution to the continuity and stability of culture
- Contribution to the integration of society

Each of these functions reinforced the image of structural functionalism as it was employed in anthropology. These functions were generally oriented toward maintenance and stability of the sociocultural system.

Radcliffe-Brown (1933) himself, although not an ethnomusicologist, discussed the extreme sense of unity and harmony produced by dance for the Andamanese islanders, which he identified as an integrative function. Richard

Waterman summarized the contribution of music to the continuity and stability of Yirkalla culture in Australia in pointing out that as an enculturative mechanism, music reaches into almost every aspect of life. Waterman says,

> Throughout his life, the Aboriginal is surrounded by musical events that instruct him about his natural environment and its utilization by men, that teach him his world view and shape his system of values, and that reinforce his understanding of aboriginal concepts of status and of his own role. (1956:41)

Kwabena Nketia (1958) pointed out that music functions as tribal solidarity for Yoruba musicians in Accra. Alan Lomax went even further to assert that music is the summary of the sociocultural system, the index of other systems. "Song presents an immediate image of a cultural pattern" (1968:6).

John Blacking pointed to children's songs among the Venda people of southern Africa that he noted, for anyone who wanted to be socially accepted, functioned as a mechanism of social acceptance. He said, "Knowledge of the children's songs is a social asset, and in some cases a social necessity for any child who wishes to be an accepted member of his own age group" (1995a [1967]:31). He went on to show that for young Venda boys, songs function to "crystallize and confirm certain norms of behavior—that it is disgraceful to neglect one's herding duties, to play with girls, or to stay with one's mother after a certain age" (1995a [1967]:32). As evidence of its effect, John Blacking suggested, "some or all of the *processes* used by a society in the organization of its human relations are used to organize available music sounds" (1969:53).

Although structural-functional ideas are most prominent in ethnomusicological literature of the 1950s and 1960s, the effects of the approach continue even today as scholars adopt other orientations. I think of Christopher Waterman's work on Yoruba popular music, *Jùjú,* in which he says,

> My aim is to illustrate how one aspect of Yoruba culture—that is music—has both reflected and played a role in shaping patterns of social identity. I also attempt to show how large-scale economic and political structures articulate with and broadly condition the localized microprocesses of musical performance. (1990:3)

Here the approach Christopher Waterman is using in the 1990s still assumes music as a part of a larger sociocultural system and his interest is in studying the articulation among music and social identity, political systems, and economic structures. The idea of cultures made up of interrelated systems continues to persist long after narrow structural-functional studies have given way to other approaches.

I have cited studies where the structural-functional approach is invoked, but we cannot look to an extensive and exhaustive musical ethnography where this orientation is deeply explored. Although Merriam provided a prescriptive statement for using structural functionalism, he did not himself ever publish a detailed ethnography of the Basongye in Zaïre among whom he carried out considerable research. Nor was his study of Flathead Indian music in North America such a work that it could be cited as a model of structural functionalism (1967a).

Structural Functionalism in Ethnomusicology: Critique

The problems with using structural functionalism in ethnomusicology parallel those in anthropology:

1. **Music is presented as part of a system in equilibrium.**

   In the first place, structural functionalism presents us with an equilibrium model that makes the explanation of change difficult, if not impossible. Such a model hardly explains some of the rapid changes many ethnomusicologists are observing in their field sites around the world. For example, how does the widespread practice of African American hip-hop in Malawi destabilize the existing music in the face of globalization? Such developments challenge the structural-functional model in its classic conception.

2. **The holistic approach to music makes the detailed research of any one aspect of music difficult.**

   We have here a holistic approach that makes it difficult to research any one aspect in detail. The realities of this second critique became evident to me one day as I spoke to Merriam about his research. When he went to Lupupangye in Zaïre, he began his study not with a look at the music but with a census of the village, then a kinship study. He felt compelled to examine the various systems, at least superficially, to better understand how they articulated with the music system. Only then did he feel free to begin studying the music. The requirements of knowing something of the other systems constituted a heavy obligation. As we talked, I argued for beginning at music and moving outward from there, and in the mid-1970s Merriam accepted that as a reasonable premise. He acknowledged that the study of the system could result in a deemphasis on details that might be important to an ethnomusicologist.

3. **There is difficulty in establishing just what a musical system is and the nature of its boundaries.**

   A third critique of structural functionalism is the problem of establishing the reality as well as the boundaries of a musical system. To what extent **is** this a system, and from whose perspective is it a system? Hip-hop might arguably serve to reinforce social solidarity among African American youth in the United States. But what function does it serve for the grandmothers who are part of African American society but hate the hip-hop music?

4. **Different music within any complex cultural system may be differentially susceptible to change.**

   A fourth critique is that different types of music within the system may be more or less susceptible to change. Yet structural functionalism does not provide for these differences that might show up in a field setting. For example, among the Kpelle of Liberia, ritual music is intended to continue unaltered while entertainment music ideally changes rapidly.

Structural Functionalism in Ethnomusicology: Contribution

All of these criticisms do not obviate the fact that structural functionalism has made some distinctive contributions to our study of music around the world.

1. **Structural functionalism allows an ethnomusicologist to study music in a manner that integrates it with the sociocultural complex surrounding it.**

   This approach provides a model where music is integrally seen as part of the larger culture. Thus the study of other parts of the society has relevance for an ethnomusicologist employing this orientation.

2. **Structural functionalism attempts to explain the role of music in bringing people together and integrating a community.**

   Music serves to promote stability and cohesiveness within the larger system. The establishment of this point is a critical one. For although it may seem common sense to think of music as part of a larger system, this thinking is quite counter to another view that has been dominant. This other view holds that music is a system unto itself and not meshed with everyday life. Music is special and unusual—standing out from all else. Many students in music schools have been taught this latter view and would find the structural-functional view quite antithetical to the accepted view that is so taken for granted by many ethnomusicologists.

Related Approaches: Music System as an Organism

The idea that music is one system within a society where there are multiple systems that interact and interrelate needs to be examined next to the theoretical orientation in Western art music analysis where music itself is seen as an autonomous, living organism. Victor Zuckerkandl, as one of the most enthusiastic proponents of music as organism, provided a model whereby music could be understood as something special and independent. The system aspect developed, in this instance, as the interrelationship of parts within the music system itself. And many scholars of Western art music have relied, at least implicitly, on Zuckerdandl's model. Thus Zuckerkandl would argue that aspects of consonance and dissonance derive from the acoustical properties of sound (1956:364), not from a socially derived concept.

Interestingly, the notion of a system with interrelated parts exists both in the anthropologically influenced structural functionalism and in the musicologically based music as organism. The first is much more comprehensive and extensive in its scope, conceiving of the whole as an entire culture made up of interrelated beliefs and practices, including music. The second is much more specific and deliberately excludes a broader societal influence, focusing only on music within a society. Nevertheless, both use the model of an organic whole made up of functioning systems that are essentially integrative and equilibrium oriented.

Structural-Functional Analysis of Two Kpelle Music Cases in Liberia

Solidarity Function

Observing the details of how a theoretical orientation is employed is important to developing a more in-depth understanding of any theoretical approach. In the following section, I take some of my own ethnographic data and apply a structural-functional explanation. In doing so, I'm in no way advocating for such an approach, nor was that my theoretical explanation for my work. Nevertheless, it's a useful exercise to both clarify points of a theory and to show what the effects of such a theory may be. I should note that in subsequent chapters, I sometimes use my own data and at other times employ the data of other scholars in providing the examples at the end of each chapter.

Among the Kpelle of Central Liberia, music serves to reinforce the authority and solidarity of the Poro and Sande societies, of which all adults are expected to be members. These interlinked fraternal societies are a critical component of the larger Kpelle society, and music plays a vital role in sustaining the institutions.

The Poro or Sande society dominates the land for a designated period of time. The Sande, to which women belong, controls the land for three years at a time, and the Poro controls the land for a subsequent four years. During that time, the spirits of these various societies manifest themselves by musical sounds. The "voices" are created by blowing into globular pottery flutes. In this area of West Africa, visual masks are not used, and musical sound is the emblem of the spirits. Vocal disguise and guttural or high-pitched sounds indicate the movement of the spirit in the village on any particular evening.

As young people are secluded in the forest during their period of education into the Poro or Sande, they spend time learning to dance and sing. Musical performance is considered part of normal adult behavior, and as they learn to become adults, they practice performance as part of that maturation. Particularly talented young people receive special instruction and may go on to apprentice themselves to master performers. Certain instruments are associated with performance. In the Sande, for example, a struck tortoise shell slit drum is well known.

As the Poro or Sande session concludes, and the young people are presented as new adults with new names and new personas, a celebration draws the village and neighboring peoples together to celebrate the event. In the case of a Sande graduation, the young girls enter the edge of the village and remain secluded for three days in a hut guarded by the Sande elders. Faces are painted with white chalk for they are in a transitional state, no longer belonging to the old life but not yet fully adult either. As the ceremony proceeds, they receive new clothes, new names, and are eventually brought into the village proper. There they proceed to display their music and dance skills for the assembled crowd. Whatever discord may exist among people at that time is put aside as the crowd exults in the return of these young girls who have emerged as young adults and survived the rigors of the Sande training.

The young girls dance in precise, carefully executed steps as they present themselves with passive facial expressions to the crowd. The dance is a visual and symbolic representation of their newly expressed adulthood. The movement and the underlying drum and gourd rattle music reinforce the Sande society and its place within Kpelle society. For the Sande, and its counterpart the Poro, society represents the ultimate authority that binds the Kpelle people together into a larger cohesive group. On this special day, marked with feasting and drinking, the power of the Sande is vividly expressed through ceremony and music. Music reinforces and supports these institutions and the larger Kpelle society.

Music as Release Function

In another Kpelle situation, music can function as a release valve for protest. Performance may serve to restore people to a state of equilibrium. Criticism of people in authority should not be voiced aloud in speech but may be sung in veiled and allusive song texts.

During the period leading to the Liberian civil war that broke out in 1988, the Kpelle people became increasingly distressed by the repressive acts of the military leader, Samuel K. Doe. At the funeral of a former cabinet member, James Gbarbea, who happened to be Kpelle, the Kpelle choir from St. Peter's Lutheran church seized the opportunity not only to honor the deceased but to express deeply felt grievances about the present political climate.

Feme Neni-Kole was a singer in the Sande society and often invited to sing at funerals in her home village. In one of her song texts on the occasion of the Gbarbea funeral, Feme sang of people who bear false witness in the present regime.

> Ah, Jesus is the *zoo* [ritual priest].
> Only the Holy Spirit is a *zoo*.
> The tutelary sprits we catch, we hide them.

Plate 11 Feme Neni-Kole. Photo by Verlon L. Stone.

> Only Jesus is the *zoo* . . .
> Bearing false witness will not appear in heaven, we all know the inside.
> The big, big human sacrifices we make . . .
> Bad witchcraft doesn't happen in heaven . . .

With Feme's knowledge of the "inside," she could bring to the "outside" or to public scrutiny the deeds of the Samuel Doe government. She pointed out in her song lyrics that the public knows about the atrocities and that they will be found out. The guilty people will be punished in time. She sang boldly of people who had been killed for political purposes and called them "human sacrifices." In this song, as she could not do in speech, she accused the Doe government of a litany of atrocities. As Feme led the singing, her hands danced in gesture and she turned, first to one side and then to the other, to underscore her words as she would have done in a Sande song. The Christian song was directly shaped by core Kpelle ritual structures. Yet she could use it to protest an atrocity in a very carefully defined way that would not destroy or threaten Kpelle society ultimately.

In a powerful grafting of images, Feme compared first Jesus and then the Holy Spirit to a *zoo* (ritual priest). The Christian cosmology was set next to the Kpelle cosmology and an equivalency created.

Thus music becomes a powerful medium to express protest of atrocities in a manner that provides escape from the grievances people feel without leading to a rupture that might be brought on by ordinary speech. The choir's pointed comments on the present regime provided an emotional outlet for the mourners who were brought together on this occasion, not just for an individual, but for the larger community.

The Place of Structural Functionalism in the Theoretical Repertoire

When ethnomusicological scholars began conducting intensive fieldwork in the early 1950s, structural functionalism constituted the so-called anthropological approach to research. Although we can't point to a large body of studies that developed as models of this approach, the fundamental notion of a system with integrated parts has survived and been important in succeeding theoretical models—a point that is explored later.

Structural functionalism was born in the climate of British colonial rule, and its intellectual history must take account of that background. The model that stressed stability and continuity rather than radical change served the political ends of control of the larger empire. Ethnographic studies served to lock cultures in the fixed ethnographic present.

The assertion that music is interrelated to other social systems was an important one. It radically departed from the widely held view that music was separate and distinct from the fabric of life. Thus began ethnomusicology's long exploration of connections between the different music and social systems. As ethnomusicology embraced this interconnection between music and other aspects of life, it took the rather radical step of acknowledging the connection to, rather than separation from, social life. Music was not just so many sounds but was now anchored to politics, kinship, religion, and economics.

The legacy of structural functionalism, then, is a significant one. For ethnomusicology became enmeshed in a systems approach that stressed the social context of music sound and no longer focused on just classifying sound and understanding the sonic dimensions.

The embrace of a "systems" approach by ethnomusicology, such as was offered through structural functionalism, greatly expanded the scope of ethnomusicology's study. For no longer was it enough to think of scales, rhythms, and consonance. Now nearly all dimensions of a society had some impact on musical life and needed to be examined.

Not all ethnomusicologists, of course, embraced or endorsed this view. But the impact was considerable. Although influences to use structural functionalism came from a number of quarters, the publication of Merriam's *The Anthropology of Music* in 1964 focused the structural functionalism theoretical orientation in ethnomusicology. In that work we find a succinct summary of how the approach is relevant to the study of music.

Structural functionalism has left an important stamp on our discipline, and its effects are widely felt at the beginning of the new millennium, although we cannot point to many scholars for whom it is a dominant orientation today.

References

Blacking, John. 1969. "The Value of Music in Human Experience." *Yearbook of the International Folk Music Council* 1:33–71.

———. 1995a [1967]. *Venda Children's Songs: A Study in Ethnomusicological Analysis.* Chicago: University of Chicago Press.

Brăiloiu, Constantin. 1984. *Problems of Ethnomusicology.* Translated by A. L. Lloyd. Cambridge: Cambridge University Press.

Leach, Edmund R. 1965. *Political Systems of Burma: A Study of Kadin Social Structure.* Boston: Beacon Press.

Lomax, Alan. 1968. *Folksong Style and Culture.* Washington, D.C.: American Association for the Advancement of Science.

Malinowski, Bronislaw. 1944. *A Scientific Theory of Culture.* Chapel Hill: University of North Carolina Press.

Merriam, Alan P. 1964. *The Anthropology of Music.* Evanston: Northwestern University Press.

———. 1967a. *Ethnomusicology of the Flathead Indians.* Chicago: Aldine.

Merton, Robert K. 1996. Ed. Piotr Sztompka. *On Social Structure and Science.* Chicago: University of Chicago Press.

Moore, Jerry D. 1997. *Visions of Culture: An Introduction to Anthropological Theories and Theorists.* Walnut Creek, Calif.: Altamira.

Nketia, J. H. Kwabena. 1958. "Yoruba Musicians in Accra." *Odu* 6:35–44.

Radcliffe-Brown, Alfred Reginald. 1933. *The Andaman Islanders.* Cambridge: Cambridge University Press.

Turner, Jonathan H., and Alexandra Maryanski. 1979. *Functionalism.* Menlo Park, Calif.: Benjamin Cummings.

Waterman, Christopher. 1990. *Jùjú: A Social History and Ethnography of an African Popular Music.* Chicago: University of Chicago Press.

Zuckerkandl, Victor. 1956. *Sound and Symbol: Music and the External World.* London: Routledge and Kegan Paul.

Chapter 4

Linguistic Approaches

Linguistic orientations to the study of music as human communication have been of considerable interest to ethnomusicology as well as other music disciplines. The close relationship between music and language has long been recognized. George Herzog's (1934, 1945) early investigation of drum language in Liberia on the west coast of Africa and his own training in linguistics, as well as musicology and anthropology, set up a model of interdisciplinary study and investigation that others in the field followed. Béla Bartók and Albert Lord's study (1951) of Serbo-Croatian folk song also devoted considerable attention to the linguistic elements.

Linguistic models have been viewed by a number of scholars as particularly appropriate to adopt for the investigations of ethnomusicology. A review article

Plate 12 George Herzog. Courtesy of Archives of Traditional Music.

on English language literature by Steven Feld and Aaron Fox (1994:25–33) points to what they term a "musico-linguistic" anthropology. They categorize the various approaches as (1) music and language, (2) music as language, (3) music in language and language in music, and (4) language about music among other topics. They note, "Music's poetic de-referentializing of language heightens the symbolic efficacy of is affective discourse, making it a sensitive gauge of both traditional and emergent forms of sociability and identity, and a key resource in both the constructions and the critical inversion of social order" (1994:43).

This chapter considers several linguistic approaches and their possible explanatory power for musical performance. Three in particular that we examine are ethnoscience, transformation-generative models, and semiotics.

Ethnoscience

William Sturtevant defined **ethnoscience,** also known as ethno classification, as "the system of knowledge and cognition typical of a given culture" (1968:475). Ethnoscience has also been called the "new ethnography," despite the fact that such a label implies a pejorative connotation for other kinds of ethnography.

Sturtevant explained that "a culture itself amounts to the sum of a given society's folk classifications, all of that society's ethnoscience, its particular way of classifying its material and social universe" (1968:475). The approach of ethnoscience was not new, for Malinowski had said, "the final goal of which the ethnographer should never lose sight . . . is briefly to grasp the native's point of view, his relation to life, to *realize* his vision of the world" (1922:25). He detailed his experience in the Trobriand Islands as he tried to capture that point of view in *Argonauts of the Western Pacific* (1922) and *Coral Gardens and Their Magic* 1965 [1935].

Ward Goodenough's explicit definition of culture as a whole was new and emphasized the knowledge that one possesses and the competence associated with it. He said, "A society's culture consists of whatever it is one has to know or believe in order to operate in a manner acceptable to its members" (1957:xx). This formed the basis of the work by ethnoscientists.

Considerable interest was generated by ethnoscience as scholars in the social sciences explored the use of this new approach in the 1960s and 1970s. Ethnoscientists assumed that humans make sense of the broad range of experience around them by understanding the world through a learned classification of experience. Some referred to it as a "method" for they felt it was better developed

---

Ethnoscience

- System of knowledge of a given culture
- Local classifications of a society

as a procedure of inquiry than as an explanatory model. Nevertheless, we can consider some of the assumptions made by practitioners of ethnoscience.

Assumptions

1. **Ethnoscience researchers are interested in the basic domains of culture and how the society defines those domains.**

   The focus here is on the mind and domains or basic areas of meaning but with sensitivity to particular contexts. That is, structures of the mind influence how the world is perceived and how sense is made of the world. Nevertheless, the interest is in the expression of those categories in local and specific settings because ethnoscientists assume that the classification system we use to make sense of the world is a learned one.

2. **Ethnoscience researchers rely primarily on language or linguistic data.**

   Language is important to ethnoscience because it is through language that cultural classification is transmitted. Although many other approaches also use linguistic data, the reliance in the case of ethnoscience on linguistic data is particularly prominent.

3. **The interest in context is primarily based on ideal behavior and shared knowledge.**

   Given that a common language holds the key to a culturally specific way of making sense of the world, researchers here are centered on a customary repertory and a knowledge that is homogeneous within the group under study. Ethnoscientists focus on culture understood as shared and somewhat fixed. Given these assumptions, the idiosyncratic variations of particular individuals are not of interest.

4. **Ethnoscience seeks to reduce knowledge to basic structures but not to assume cross-cultural similarity.**

   In this assumption, ethnoscientists, like the structuralists discussed later, are looking for the basic building blocks of human knowledge. But they are more limited than structuralists in their claims for similarity of mind structures. They are rather interested in ways particular cultures make sense of their world. Ethnoscientists emphasize the possibility of variation across societies and do not make sweeping claims across a vast expanse of human societies.

5. **Key concepts are the contrast set, paradigm, and domain.**

   This **contrast set** bears similarities to the concept of "oppositions," which is important to structuralists. A contrast set might be the pair of terms such as

---

Contrast set

- Two terms that are mutually exclusive but occur in an environment together

black/white. The contrast set is important to ethnoscientists because people organize their world by drawing oppositions. The two terms in a contrast set are considered mutually exclusive, but they occur in an environment together. A **domain** is the total range of meanings for the segregates or contrast sets. A **paradigm** is a set of segregates or contrast sets that can be partitioned by features of meaning. When one carries out **componential analysis,** one is studying a paradigm. (It is important to note the quite different meaning for paradigm here than the one presented earlier.)

6. **Researchers try to determine the most economical componential analysis that will define or generate their paradigmatic relationship.**

   The concern here is with predictability, economy, and inclusiveness. Ethnoscientists emphasize the need to be explicit about discovery procedures to improve replicability. All of these procedures have been applied to the study of kinship, color, body parts, and ethnozoology in the social sciences.

Critique

A number of critiques have been made of ethnoscience.

1. **Ethnoscience relies on structures of the mind that are difficult to investigate.**

   That is, ethnoscience assumes all people perceive the world in the same way. The disadvantages of the approach lie in the reliance on unarguable structures of the mind that all people are assumed to share. It is these structures that generate ethnographic facts according to ethnoscientists.

2. **Ethnoscience does not emphasize variations among people's knowledge.**

   Ethnoscience is not interested in the varieties of various people's knowledge. Rather, the approach assumes a shared knowledge among a particular group of people.

Domain

- Total range of meanings for contrast sets

Paradigm

- Group of contrast sets that can be partitioned by meaning features

Componential analysis

- Study of a paradigm or group of contrast sets

Contribution

Despite the criticisms leveled at ethnoscience, a number of contributions can be noted.

1. **Ethnoscience is a method that assists in discerning vocabulary in certain cognitive domains or areas of culture.**

   The use of ethnoscience in ethnomusicology is clearly important for eliciting vocabulary about music performance and music theory. The approach has helped dispel the sometimes voiced idea that non-Western people, for the most part, cannot talk about music or other aspects of their culture, nor do they possess a technical vocabulary to do so. Ethnoscience is directly concerned with indigenous vocabulary.

2. **Ethnoscience helps elicit indigenous knowledge.**

   Because of its focus on language, ethnomusicologists can employ the ethnoscientific method systematically to investigate areas of music theory in a particular society.

Ethnoscience in Ethnosmusicology

In his doctoral dissertation, Charles Adams (1974) carried out an ethnoscientific study of the genre or domain *lipapali*, loosely translated as "games," among the Basotho people in southern Africa. He discovered music to be a part of this domain, and his study helps us understand where music fits within a Basotho system of categorization. In the course of his investigation, he noted that the people he interviewed showed wide variation in their interpretation and evaluation of games, depending on individual experience. In the end, he concluded that this variation precluded, to some extent, a homogeneous game ideology. This homogeneous ideology was, of course, the goal of ethnoscience (see Assumption 3 earlier).

An even more fascinating discovery by Charles Adams was the concept that the Basotho expressed about "instrumental chaining." In instrumental chaining they designated the acoustical links between sound activator and producer. The greater the number of links, the more complex was the relationship. In such a system of thought, a musical bow whose string was being hit would be a fairly complex instrument with the stick as activator and the mouth cupped around the string modifying the sound as it resonated in the cavity.

Adams's study showed the complexity of mapping a domain that is central to the understanding of music performance. His work provided us with an important case study of ethnoscience for ethnomusicology.

A number of other ethnomusicologists have made excursions into ethnoscience or some variation of ethnoscience. Richard Haefer and Donald Bahr (1978) explored Native American music concepts. Carol Robertson (1979) studied the category of *tayil* among the Mapuche of Argentina. Hugo Zemp (1978,

Plate 13 Hugo Zemp shooting his film *The Song of Harmonics,* 1990. Courtesy of Hugo Zemp.

1979) conducted extensive investigation into categories of music theory among the 'Aré 'Aré of the Pacific region. Steven Feld (1981, 1982, 1984, 1988, 1991) elicited knowledge about musical practices and their linkage to the local ecology and social life among the Kaluli in New Guinea.

Adrienne Kaeppler, ethnomusicologist and dance ethnologist, said, "Ethnoscientific analysis as used in anthropology seeks to analyze culture (or parts of it) in such a way that the resulting description would be comparable to a grammar which enables an investigator to learn to speak a language" (1972:173). In her work, Kaeppler searched for dance analogies to phonemes—the smallest unit—and morphemes—the smallest grammatical unit—isolating terms for specific movements and then for combinations of those movements.

Charles Keil's (1979) study of Tiv classification of terms associated with music performance in Nigeria owes much to ethnoscience, although he does not use that label. He devotes considerable effort to eliciting indigenous concepts for making music and the meanings of the words associated with the concepts. In a later project, Keil explored music in daily life, demonstrating a wide range of vocabulary employed by people in describing everyday music experiences (Crafts, Cavicchi, and Keil 1993).

Plate 14 Adrienne Kaeppler. Courtesy of Adrienne Kaeppler.

Ethnoscience: Example from the Kpelle of Liberia

In my own research of music among the Kpelle people of Liberia, I used ethno-science methods to understand the categorization of musical instruments. At the end of a year's research, I wrote the names of all of the Kpelle instruments that had been mentioned by musicians and consultants on slips of paper. I asked Kpelle people who read Kpelle to sort and group the pieces of paper as they deemed best. I then wrote down the groupings and asked the individuals about their rationale for making the different choices. "From one of the very simplest of these sorting procedures, I could see a fundamental difference between assumptions of Western ethnomusicologists and most Kpelle persons in the underlying classificatory scheme for musical instruments" (Stone 1982:55–57) (See Figure 2).

Whereas the Western ethnomusicologist focuses predominantly on the material that is activated to cause sound, the Kpelle musicians and laypeople alike emphasize initially on *how* the human produces that sound. The Western ethnomusicologist thus ends up with *four* categories of instruments and the Kpelle, *two* categories. For the Kpelle instruments are either struck—(*ngale*

Instrument	Ethnomusicological Classification	Kpelle Classification
Kêe – gourd rattle	Idiophone	Ngale - struck
Fêli – goblet drum	Membranophone	Ngale - struck
Konîng – frame zither	Chordophone	Ngale - struck
Túru – transverse horn	Aerophone	Fêe - blown
Boo - flute	Aerophone	Fêe - blown

Figure 2 Kpelle Classification of Instruments.

means "to break")—or blown—(*fêe*). Subsequent research has shown that the Kpelle categories are shared by some of the other peoples in West Africa (Dan/Gio, for example).

Conclusion

Ethnoscience rests in the assumption that all people in a particular society share a common cultural way of making sense of the world. That may or may not be the case because variations in knowledge across a culture certainly occur. There is also the assumption that situations where elicitation takes place are similar to interaction. Yet we know that there are clearly differences between the ideal and the everyday interaction setting.

The height of interest in ethnoscientific ideas in ethnomusicology may have come during the 1980 annual meeting of the Society for Ethnomusicology where numerous panels and papers focused on the topic of "ethnotheory." Since that time, ethnoscience has continued to have an influence in the thinking and research of ethnomusicologists, although the methods of the 1970s have been somewhat modified. Ethnomusicologists continue to maintain an interest in local classification, but they do not, for the most part, create hierarchical models such as branching tree diagrams using those classifications such as those used by some ethnoscientists.

Transformational-Generative Models

Transformational-generative models in linguistics are associated with Noam Chomsky and are among the various kinds of structuralist grammars that were created by linguists and others. Hundreds of people flocked to Oxford University in the 1950s to hear this remarkable scholar (Lyons 1970). Even the press took note of Chomsky, who stated his ideas most forcefully in *Syntactic Structures*, published in 1957.

History

Structuralism in linguistics flowered with the work of Chomsky and his students and followers. But his work was based on the earlier research of Ferdinand de Saussure (1966 [1916]) and a group of Russian formalists, including Vladimir Propp (1958, 1984) and Petr Bogatyrev (1971). With these linguists, interest shifted from study of the history of individual words over time to a "structural system of relationships among words as they are used at a given point in time, or synchronically" (Tyson 1999:201).

Saussure differentiated between the underlying structure on which the language is built (*langue)* and the speaking of the language (*parole*). For these linguists the structure (*langue*) is the proper study object (Saussure 1966 [1916]). What is critical in this underlying structure are the differences we perceive between the different components. These differences are most readily identified in terms of opposites, referred to by structuralists as *binary oppositions*. We think of black/white, up/down, raw/cooked, red/green as examples of these binary oppositions.

An important idea for linguists who espoused structuralism was that words are linguistic signs consisting of signifier and signified. The signifier is a sound-image and the signified is the concept to which the signifier refers. A sound must therefore be linked to a concept. What sound is used to refer to a car, for example, is an arbitrary choice. In that vein, "we don't discover the world; we 'create' it according to innate structures with the human mind" (Tyson 1999:202).

The terms *transformational* and *generative* are to be understood here as grammars that show the changes that occur from the base structures to surface structures. A grammar is a set of rules. *Generative* implies that from these rules new combinations can be generated. *Transformational* means that changes occur so a **transformational-generative grammar** is a model that can generate all the possible statements from a certain set of base rules. In other words, these models are attempts to show the structure of a whole class of examples.

Assumptions

Let's begin by examining some of Chomsky's assumptions in constructing transformational and generative grammars.

Transformational-generative grammar

- Type of structuralist grammar associated with Noam Chomsky
- A set of rules
- Rules allow new combinations to be generated
- Changes occur as a result of the rules being applied

1. **Children are born with knowledge of the highly restrictive principles of universal grammar and the predisposition to make use of them in analyzing the utterances that they hear.**

   In assuming that people are born with structures and the predisposition to use these structures, Chomsky was even more explicit than Claude Lévi-Strauss—whose work is discussed Chapter 5—about what mind structures people shared. Such an assumption drew on Immanuel Kant and his ideas of unity of the mind (1955 [1952]).

2. **Creativity must be accounted for—that is, the capacity of all native speakers to produce and understand an infinitely large number of sentences.**

   Chomsky noticed how even small children could utter sentences, many of which they had never heard spoken before. He concluded that they were using a set of rules to predict utterances, which would make sense.

3. **A linguist cannot take the corpus of utterances at its face value. He must idealize the raw data and eliminate from the corpus all those utterances, which the competent native speaker would recognize as ungrammatical.**

   Structural linguists are interested in ideal rather than performed utterances, many of which would be considered ungrammatical by the rules of the language.

4. **A linguistic theory should not be identified with a manual of useful procedures.**

   In other words, a theory should serve to move beyond the data in providing an explanation and not simply be a how to set of directions. For example, Chomsky was not interested in teaching people how to speak correctly.

5. **Linguistic theory should provide criteria for choosing between alternative grammars.**

   As Chomsky saw it, some grammars provide more powerful explanations for utterances than others, and precision is needed to decide which grammar is superior.

Assumptions in Ethnomusicology

Transformational-generative models in ethnomusicology have been borrowed from linguistics, which make the following assumptions:

1. **A finite set of rules is capable of generating an infinite number of utterances or groupings.**

   Thus the ethnomusicologist can take a corpus of musical sound and create rules for generating not only that corpus but also other possible examples that conform to the rules.

2. **Deep structure is linked to surface structure by (a) developing rules for generating the deep structure, and (b) developing transformation rules for producing the surface structure.**

   These rules show the logic by which one level of the grammar is related to another level of meaning.

3. **The linguist is concerned with a person's competence or implicit knowledge and performance or behavior.**

   For the ethnomusicologist, the concern is with the implicit knowledge that one who knows the music possesses and can demonstrate to the ethnomusicologist.

Critique

1. **The basis of this kind of linguistic structuralism is the unarguable assumption of the unity of the mind.**

   One real disadvantage of this approach was that it was based on the premise of similar cognitive structures. This assumption could not be proved or disproved and was, therefore, unarguable.

2. **The focus is on the ideal over the enacted.**

   Scholars using these approaches assumed that the unity of mind allowed the researcher to take the ideal rather than concerning himself or herself with the messy details of the performance.

Other critiques that have been leveled at the use of transformational-generative grammars.

1. **Music performance as studied by ethnomusicologists generates a wealth of detail to be analyzed.**

   The disadvantage of these models is that in using these procedures, we discover the myriad details to be accounted for and find ourselves inundated by rules as we try to account for the details of a complex musical performance.

2. **Transformational-generative grammars of music performance could involve many rewrite rules to explain fully all of the dimensions of performance.**

   For anyone who has attempted to write a transformational-generative grammar, it becomes clear very soon how complicated musical performance is and how many rules must be written to describe the performance comprehensively.

3. **These transformational-generative grammars are based on the shared mind structures that pay little attention to issues of variation from one performer to another.**

   Because these models are built on assumptions about shared mind structures, they are not generally context sensitive. That is, they do not concern themselves with multiple interpretations of different individuals.

Critique of Transformational-Generative Models

The most comprehensive critique of these linguistic models came from Steven Feld (1974) who argued in "Linguistic Models in Ethnomusicology" against simply adopting a set of discovery procedures. Rather, he called for looking toward linguistics for ethnomusicological explanation as, for example, what people must know to understand, perform, and create acceptable music in a particular culture. The need for a comprehensive approach in regard to linguistic approaches was echoed by John Blacking who argued that,

> When the grammar of music coincides with the grammar of a particular person's body, cognitive resonance can be felt and apprehended partly because of learned social experience. But when the grammar of music coincides with the "musical" biogrammar of the human body, in the most general sense, cognitive resonance can be felt and apprehended regardless of social experiences. (1995b:240)

Contribution

1. **Grammars such as the transformational-generative brought logical clarity.**

   Noam Chomsky brought mathematical rigor and precision, which formalized the properties of alternative systems of grammatical description. This rigor was impressive for the clear way arguments could be made about the complexity of language.

2. **The transformational-generative grammar could subsume a great quantity of data for analysis.**

   One of the strengths of the approach was to analyze a great quantity of data succinctly. The rules could encompass and account for a great quantity of data.

There are a number of distinct contributions of transformational-generative grammars in the field of ethnomusicology.

1. **Transformational-generative grammars in ethnomusicology provide an elegant and economical way of representing sound.**

   The advantage of such models is that they bring formalism to analysis and provide for some orderly ways to examine the structure of musical performance.

2. **Analysis of pitches allows for easy segmentation and manipulation of sound.**

   Musical transcription that uses staff notation breaks sound into discrete pitches and note heads. These pitches and their groupings are quite amenable to segmentation and rule writing that is part of constructing a transformational-generative model.

Structuralism in Ethnomusicology

In the field of ethnomusicology, the flowering of interest in structuralism cul-minated in the early 1970s. A number of scholars who were familiar with this linguistic approach began to apply structuralism to the study of music, partic-ularly music sound.

We need to clarify here that structuralism, where a researcher is interested in relationships of a whole class of objects, is somewhat different from an inter-est in structure as in the form of an individual piece of music. Accordingly, the terms are used quite differently in theoretical discussions.

Ethnomusicologists found structuralism quite attractive. The formalism, embodying clear rules of procedure, had long been a goal of music theory. Thus discovery procedures used in language were adopted in analyzing music sound, sometimes without a careful explanation of the theory and assumptions underlying that procedure.

Examples in Ethnomusicology

Charles Boilés (1967) carried out one of the earliest attempts to create a transfor-mational-generative grammar. In his study of Tepehua ritual in Mexico, he cre-ated a complex grammar whereby specific musical intervals, such as a falling minor third, were tied to specific ritual gestures, such as a bowing motion. Later, Michael Asch (1972) created a set of prose rules for the sound organization of Slavey drum dances in Canada. Thus musical sequences acquired specific lexical meanings. In a related way, Fred Lerdahl (1983) worked with generative models in music theory.

Another kind of transformational analysis is J. David Sapir's (1969) gram-mar of Diola-Fogny funeral songs in West Africa. He employs transformational rules along with indigenous song structure terminology. Vida Chenoweth and Darlene Bee (1971) provide three models for visualizing musical syntax in music from New Guinea. They restate their analysis in generative rules with the goal of allowing ethnomusicologists to predict all the melodies possible within the system and to enable outsiders to compose within the system.

David Hughes (1988), building on earlier work of Alton Becker and Judith Becker (1979, 1983), developed a transformational grammar of *Gendhing Lampah* in Javanese music. His goal was to analyze the melodic features of the genre "with maximum completeness and elegance (in the mathematical and logical sense), *not* to test particular linguistic constructs" (1988:23). He con-cluded that each of the three subgenres that he was analyzing consists of "a sin-gle *gatra*-contour (or its inversion) at a deep level" (59). Thus he was moving between surface level—or the level of the performance—and the deep level, from which the surface level was generated.

Fremont Besmer (1974) took an entire year-cycle musical event in northern Nigeria and wrote a transformational-generative grammar. His study object was a much more inclusive one than other grammars and much broader in scope than most other studies of this type in ethnomusicology.

(pitch transposed ½ step down)

Figure 3 Cuing Sequence: Kpelle, Stuart's Rubber Farm, Bong County, Liberia

Ethnomusicology Example: Kpelle from Liberia

As a graduate student I carried out several analyses of music, drawing on the procedures of transformational-generative models. In the first, I attempted to write a grammar for the cuing system of a musical group used to let one another know that the event was about to pause. I wanted to know what the rules for this cuing were.

I first selected the data for analysis. These data were a twelve-minute slice of an event performed on July 24, 1970, on Stuart's Rubber Farm near Totota, Liberia, in Bong County, situated about 90 miles from the capital city. Within this twelve-minute segment of audio-recorded tape, I found eight "pause segments" or sequences of performance that resulted in a pause (Figure 3).

In constructing a transformational-generative grammar, my first step was to take all eight of these pause segments and to see what they had in common and how I could define segments within these events. (Remember that by the assumptions of this approach I did not need to be unduly concerned about how the Kpelle musicians themselves would segment these sequences.) In the end, I devised a first rule, also called "rewrite rule," which I presented as shown in Figure 4.

This is called a rewrite rule because what is to the left of the arrow, "cuing sequence," is equivalent to what is to the right of the arrow. In other words, cuing sequence can be rewritten as penultimate phrase leading to the ultimate phrase and then a complete pause in the cuing event. Cuing sequence can also be written with another scenario where the penultimate phrase is left out, to be replaced by the ultimate phrase and then a partial continuation. Within the brackets of the written rule, one or the other action must be included, although within the brackets there may be alternatives.

Within the performance, what I called the penultimate phrase was the female soloist singing this phrase: "I say *Posia* (master of ceremonies), blow the whistle." The female singer simply inserted this phrase within her melody so smoothly that it sounded like a part of the regular flow unless one listened carefully to the text. Now she was signaling the master of ceremonies to blow his whistle and thus reinforce her signal for a pause. The ultimate phrase consisted of the chorus singing a concluding phrase on the syllable ee–oo or some variation thereof, and the soloist coinciding with them on their phrase with a minor alteration. It may or may not include the master of ceremony blowing his whistle as well.

In the next rewrite rule (Figure 5) I labeled cuing specification. In other words, cues could be rewritten as always cue B, that is, the choral concluding

Figure 4 Rewrite Rule 1: Cuing Sequence

2.1 Cues → B (A + C)

Figure 5 Rewrite Rule 2.1: Cuing Sequence

phrase, with the optional inclusion of A, soloist singing "Posia . . . " and then the obligatory whistle blowing, or cue C, when A occurs. In all eight sequences I recorded, the choral ending always occurred. These choral endings could be enhanced by the penultimate soloist phrase and the whistle that followed. But these phrases were not always included. Now from rewrite Rule 1 we know that when the chorus and soloist sing, they sing the concluding phrase "oi–yo" or a variation thereof (B). The performance does not come to a clean stop. There's a partial continuation. I wrote another rule (Figure 6) to explain the number of cues in any pause. There can be one or three cues in any of these pauses; that is, the combination that always occurs in the universe of the sample of cutoffs that I recorded.

I wrote the third rule to explain just what was contained in the penultimate phase (Figure 7), which I had identified previously in Rule 1. That is, there is a female soloist who is singing the phrase "I say, Posia, blow the whistle."

The fourth rule defines the ultimate phrase, which always includes the chorus and soloist and may or may not include the master of ceremonies. Thus C is placed in parentheses, indicating it is optional and not necessary for inclusion (Figure 8).

The next two rules define what happens after the penultimate phrase and the ultimate phrase conclude (Figure 9). There is either a complete pause or a partial continuation. In the case of a complete pause, the audience commences talking after the music ceases. When there is a partial continuation, it is the drum and the chorus that may keep going.

One of the common things that many transformational-generative grammars in ethnomusicology do is to go into some detail on the matters of rhythm

2.2 Degrees of Cuing

[+ Cuing] ⟶ [1 Cue]

[3 Cues]

Figure 6 Rewrite Rule 2.2: Cuing Sequence

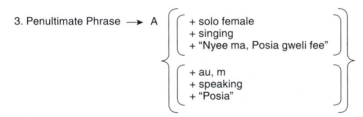

3. Penultimate Phrase ⟶ A
{
[+ solo female
+ singing
+ "Nyee ma, Posia gweli fee"]

[+ au, m
+ speaking
+ "Posia"]
}

Figure 7 Rewrite Rule 3: Cuing Sequence

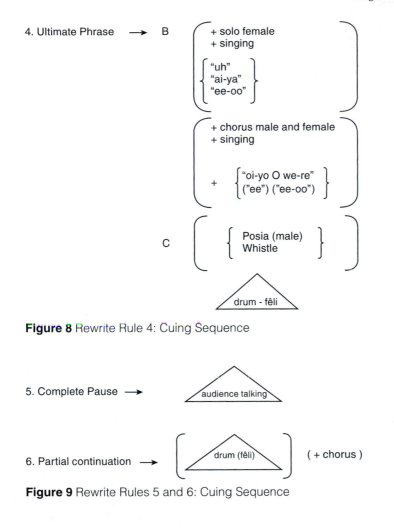

Figure 8 Rewrite Rule 4: Cuing Sequence

5. Complete Pause ⟶ audience talking

6. Partial continuation ⟶ [drum (fêli)] (+ chorus)

Figure 9 Rewrite Rules 5 and 6: Cuing Sequence

7. Pitch Specifications*

    7.1   *P ⟶ C, D$^{\uparrow\uparrow}$, F, G

    * = transposed ½ step down

Figure 10 Rewrite Rule 7.1: Cuing Sequence

and pitch. Therefore, Rule 7 breaks down pitch (Figure 10). This rule indicates that of all the possible pitches, we are dealing with four: C, D that is quite a bit higher than a D in a tempered octave, F, and G. Furthermore, I have grouped the performance into pitch segments and indicated what pitches are employed for each pitch segment in Rewrite Rule 7.2. (Figure 11). Thus the two pitches that we identified as repeated F's, we now know to be two eighth notes. Another rule specifies rhythm combinations (Figure 12). These rhythmic patterns can

7.2   Cuing sequence $\longrightarrow$

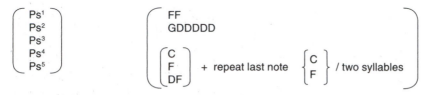

Figure 11 Rewrite Rule 7.2: Cuing Sequence

7.3 $(\,Ps^3\,)\,(\,Ps^4\,)+(\,Ps^5\,)$

Pitch segments

Figure 12 Rewrite Rule 7.3: Cuing Sequence

then be specified into eight different rhythm specifications (Figure 13). The 8/8 time segments are divided as 2 + 2 + 2 + 2 eighth notes, except in the phrase "oi-yo o were," where we have 3 + 3 + 2 eighth notes (Figure 14).

All of these rules formalize, in a kind of shorthand, the relationships between elements of the sound structure. In addition, there are social issues to be considered. If, for example, the soloist offers only one cue for a pause, her status has been enhanced relatively little. In those instances when three cues are provided to bring about a pause, the soloist's status is enhanced to a greater degree. This situation is described in Rewrite Rule 10.1 (Figure 15).

A summary of those rules can now be seen in the grammar where all of the rules are presented in sequence (Figure 16).

Reconstruction of Historic Patterns

Linguists have also applied segmentation and comparison to try and reconstruct historical patterns, attempting to discern the original pattern or prototype of music from the historical past. The problem with such an exercise is that one is not relying on direct ethnographic or historical data but on a kind of logic that may or may not provide us with an accurate view of change as it actually happened. Different examples are placed alongside one another and compared. Based on frequency of occurrence, certain elements are assumed to be more stable and therefore older. One of the few ethnomusicologists to pursue such reconstruction was Charles Boilés (1973a), who took a corpus of the Spanish romance "Don Gato" to analyze historically, using rigorous linguistic procedures.

8. Rhythm Specification

8.1 Cuing Sequence [{ $Rs^1 + Rs^2 + Rs^3 + Rs^4$ }] + [Rs^5] [Rs^6] { Rs^7 / Rs^8 }

8.2

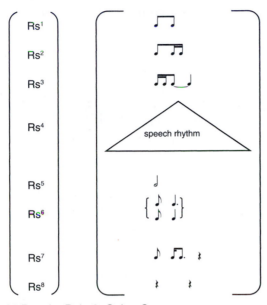

Figure 13 Rewrite Rule 8: Cuing Sequence

9.1 Meter → 8/8

9.2 8/8 → { 2 + 2 + 2 + 2 / 3 + 3 + 2 / oi-yo o were }

Figure 14 Rewrite Rule 9: Cuing Sequence

10. Status enhancement of soloist

10.1 Degrees:

[1 cue] → [Ø status enhancement]

[3 cues] → [+ status enhancement]

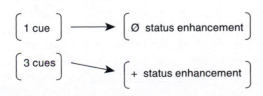

Figure 15 Rewrite Rule 10.1: Cuing Sequence

Another example, which I created, analyzes African rhythmic patterns. To understand the discovery procedures, see Figure 17, Reconstruction of Proto-Rhythmic 12/8 Pattern, which compares nine African rhythm patterns. The dotted lines indicate the segmentation that has been carried out to create the units that are then further analyzed.

Various procedures are carried out to find common elements and patterns. These procedures include determining the rhythmic order (Figure 18).

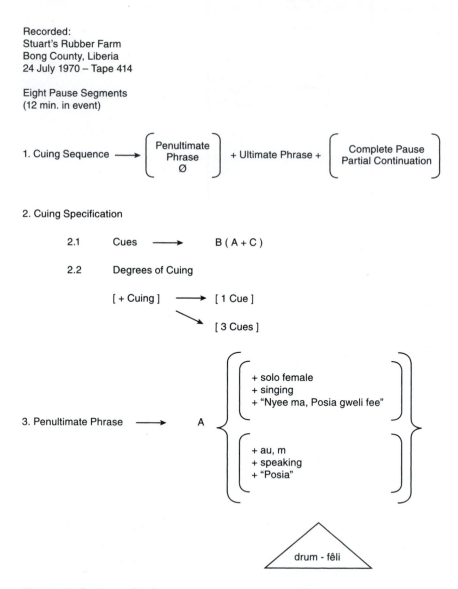

Recorded:
Stuart's Rubber Farm
Bong County, Liberia
24 July 1970 – Tape 414

Eight Pause Segments
(12 min. in event)

1. Cuing Sequence ⟶ [Penultimate Phrase / Ø] + Ultimate Phrase + [Complete Pause / Partial Continuation]

2. Cuing Specification

    2.1   Cues ⟶ B (A + C)

    2.2   Degrees of Cuing

        [+ Cuing] ⟶ [1 Cue]
                   ↘ [3 Cues]

3. Penultimate Phrase ⟶ A { [+ solo female / + singing / + "Nyee ma, Posia gweli fee"] [+ au, m / + speaking / + "Posia"] }

drum - fêli

Figure 16 Grammar for Cuing Sequence for Event Pause

4. Ultimate Phrase ⟶ B

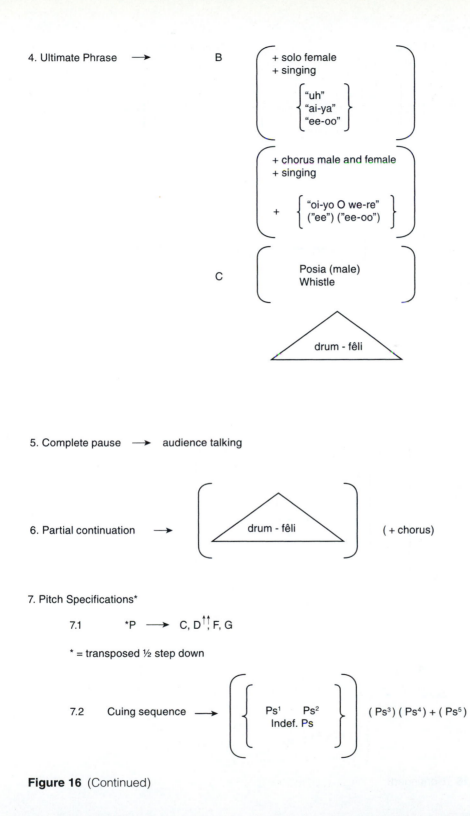

+ solo female
+ singing

{ "uh"
  "ai-ya"
  "ee-oo" }

+ chorus male and female
+ singing

+ { "oi-yo O we-re"
    ("ee") ("ee-oo") }

C

Posia (male)
Whistle

drum - fêli

5. Complete pause ⟶ audience talking

6. Partial continuation ⟶ [drum - fêli] (+ chorus)

7. Pitch Specifications*

7.1   *P ⟶ C, D↑↑∶ F, G

* = transposed ½ step down

7.2   Cuing sequence ⟶ [{ Ps¹   Ps²
                            Indef. Ps }] (Ps³) (Ps⁴) + (Ps⁵)

Figure 16 (Continued)

71

7.3   Pitch segments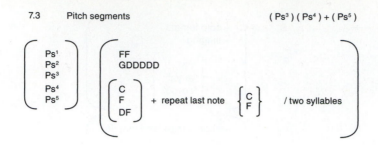

8. Rhythm Specification

8.1 Cuing Sequence

8.2

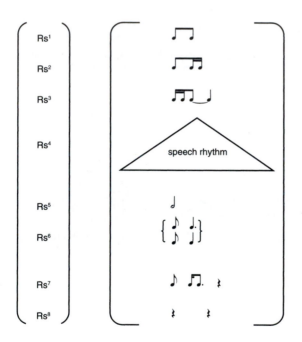

9. Meter Specification

9.1   Meter $\longrightarrow$ 8/8

$$\left\{ \quad 2 + 2 + 2 + 2 \qquad \right\}$$

Figure 16 (Continued)

72

9.2   8/8 $\longrightarrow$ 3 + 3 + 2 / oi-yo o were

10. Status enhancement of soloist

    10.1   Degrees:

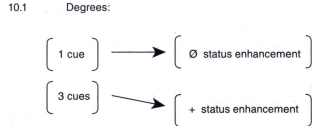

Key to symbols:

+   boundaries of symbols within a string; within brackets a positive specification of analysis.

$\longrightarrow$ rewrite as …

( )   optional

( ) ( )   choose at least one

{ }   choose one

[   ]   may indicate abbreviation of two or more rules pertinent to strings different
            and identical in the same place; also when used in feature specification,
            contain a positive specification of analysis

Ø   null

   shows degrees in a multivalued feature.

△   encloses an element not to be analyzed further in this particular grammar

Figure 16 (Continued)

By lining up the segments according to units that are similar, we can see that all the examples can be grouped into two basic patterns labeled I and II. We can also take the total set, without grouping them into similar units, and indicate the notes that are in common (Figure 19). (The numbers [1–12] label the units and the order in which they appear.)

The rhythmic positional structure with grouping is another way of isolating the units of similar patterns (Figure 20).

The patterns with similarity of rhythmic pattern can be constructed and labeled for immediate constituent order. These can be labeled with

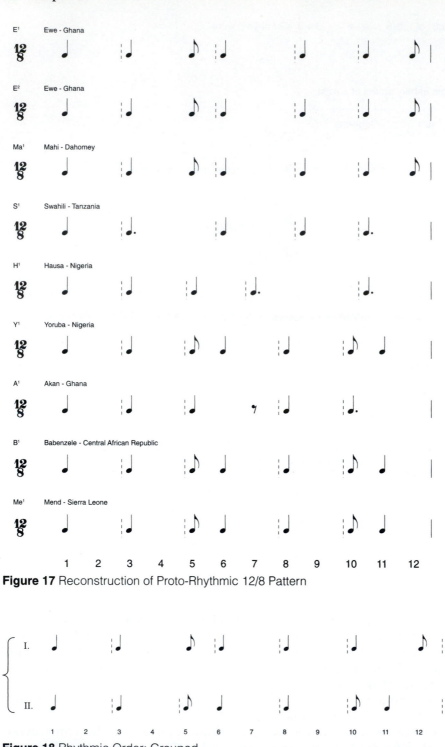

Figure 17 Reconstruction of Proto-Rhythmic 12/8 Pattern

Figure 18 Rhythmic Order: Grouped

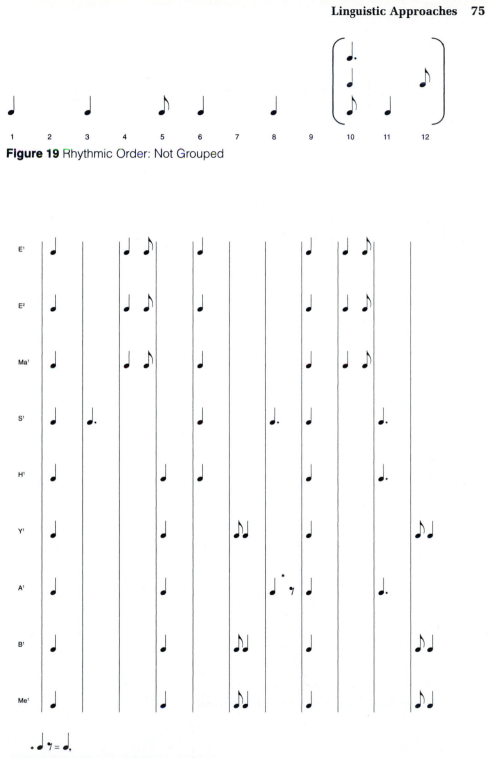

Figure 19 Rhythmic Order: Not Grouped

Figure 20 Positional Structure: Grouped

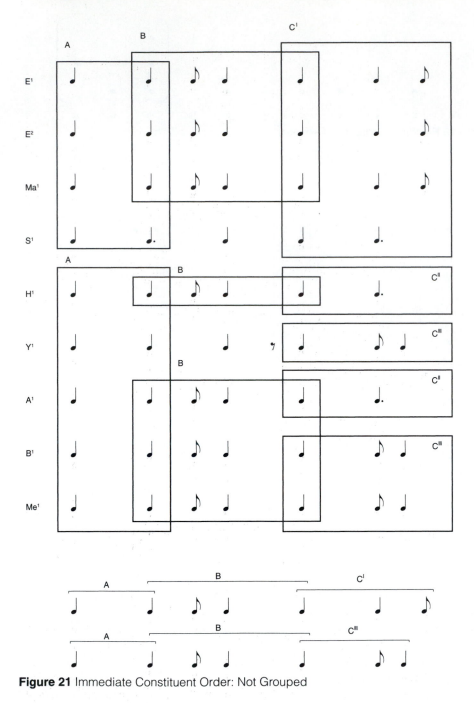

Figure 21 Immediate Constituent Order: Not Grouped

Figure 22 Rhythmic Positional Structure: Not Grouped

alphabetical letters to help indicate the relative similarity and difference of larger patterns (Figure 21).

The positional structure can be expressed without grouping, and a slightly different structure emerges. Notice that in Position 10, for example, a variety of rhythmic values occur, ranging from an eighth note to a dotted quarter note (Figure 22).

Another exercise can be a rhythmic reconstruction to determine what earlier rhythmic patterns might have been. The assumption is that common elements

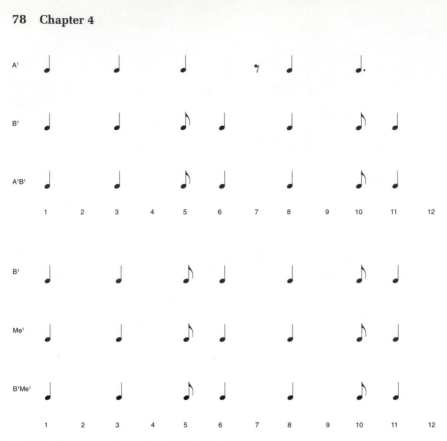

Figure 23 Proto-Rhythmic Reconstruction

are more likely to have persisted over time than elements that are not shared (Figure 23).

One can go back further in finding common elements and designate these as even earlier common patterns, which are shown in the proto-proto rhythmic reconstruction (Figure 24).

Finally, one can proceed by this process of isolating common elements to develop a proto-proto-proto rhythmic reconstruction as shown in Figure 25.

A branching tree diagram shows the presumed relationships among the patterns and how they changed and divided over the years. The top of the diagram represents the presumed oldest grouping of the pattern and then moves down the diagram through time as the patterns branch off from one another as they presumably changed (Figure 26).

Again, formal procedures provide us with a way to compare patterns even though we do not necessarily know if these patterns are understood by the people performing them to actually relate in the way we presume. Nevertheless, these are formal procedures for hypothetical exercises that can project rhythmic patterns back into the past.

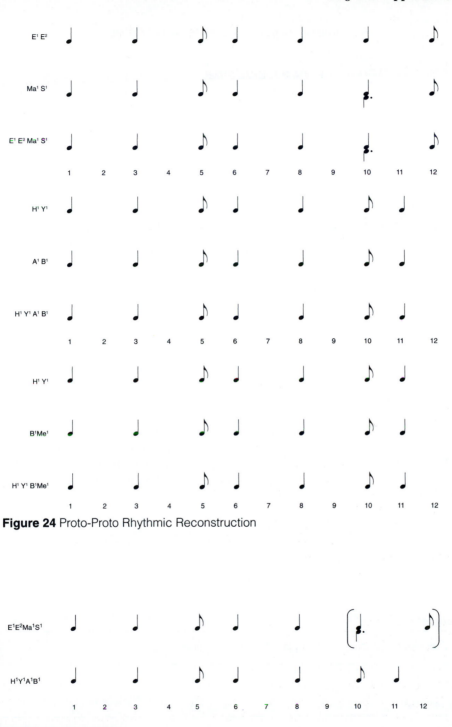

Figure 24 Proto-Proto Rhythmic Reconstruction

Note: H¹Y¹B¹Me¹ = same as H¹Y¹A¹B¹

Figure 25 Proto-Proto-Proto Rhythmic Reconstruction

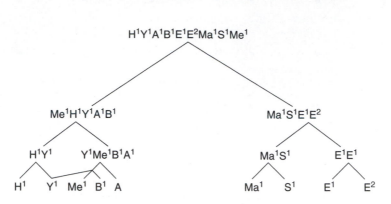

Same result in comparing $**E^1E^2Ma^1S^1$ and $H^1Y^1B^1Me^1$

Figure 26 Branching Tree Diagram of Rhythmic Reconstruction

Semiotics

Another linguistic approach used by ethnomusicologists is semiotics. Very broadly speaking, **semiotics** can be defined as the "science of signs." Building on the pioneering work of Charles S. Peirce and colleagues (1982) and Charles W. Morris (1972), semiotics has become both a field in and of itself, as well as having been incorporated in various ways into many other areas of research, including ethnomusicology.

Semioticians use a number of terms that form the basis for their understanding of the communication process. To begin, **semiosis** is the process by which something is a sign to a person. The **sign vehicle** is the physical embodiment of a sign. In music, the musical notation could constitute a sign vehicle,

Semiotics

- The science of the study of signs

Semiosis

- Process by which something is a sign to a person

Sign vehicle

- Physical embodiment of a sign

in this case a sign for an audio phenomenon. The **interpreter** is the agent of the semiosis and the one who carries out the communication process. **Designatum** is that to which the sign refers.

There are three kinds of rules, norms, or constraints that make semiosis possible. The first of these are **syntactic rules**, which deal with the relationship of one sign to another or the grammar of position and placement. (This was the concern of Chomsky and is the concern of many researchers studying Western art music form.) Thus syntactic rules could describe a musical form as being built of an A section followed by a B section with an A section concluding the work. The second are **semantic rules,** which treat the referential relationship between a sign and its designatum. When people talk about "meaning" they are often referring to the semantic dimension. For example, one might say that a semantic rule describes the relationship between a falling minor third in the A section that someone interprets to represent a tear dropping. The third are the **pragmatic rules**, which treat the uses or effect that any particular sign has on its user as well as the context or situation of the interaction. In this case, one is interested in the actual interpretation that takes place during the semiosis process.

Although semiotics has defined these three levels of analysis, most studies in the arts, and by extension, ethnomusicology, do not go beyond the syntactic.

Interpreter

- Person or agent who carries out the communication process

Designatum

- The referent for a communication process
- The thing designated by a sign

Syntactic rules

- Concern the relationship of one sign to another

Semantic rules

- Concern the referential relationship between a sign and its designatum

Pragmatic rules

- Concern the uses or effect of any sign on its user
- Concern the context of interaction

We need to note here that when a researcher does go to any level beyond the syntactic, one is automatically considering the levels below the chosen level as well. An analysis of the semantic level includes, by definition, the syntactic as well.

Assumptions

1. **Charles Peirce assumed that "man is a symbol." "My language is my sum total of myself."**

   This view, Thomas Sebeok maintained, is tantamount to assuming that man is a string of signs or a process of communication. Such an assumption, which defines a person by language, is very similar to the ideas of the ethnoscientists.

2. **Symbols grow. They come into being by development out of other signs.**

   This assumption is made by those scholars who emphasize the study of signs per se. Umberto Eco, who views semiotics as the study of all cultural processes, makes a more moderate set of assumptions. In doing so he presupposes that the process of communication is permitted by an underlying system of signification or code. These two approaches follow different methodological paths and require different approaches, even though they remain somewhat intertwined.

Application

A number of areas have received the attention of semioticians. These aspects of inquiry include proxemics (spatial relationships in human interaction), paralinguistic codes, kinesics (body movement), medical activity, architecture, music (Baest and Driel 1995; Monelle 2000; Reiner 2000; Tarasti 2002), and mathematical codes. Visual codes, such as the semiotics of film, have also been studied.

A number of scholars in the area of symbolic anthropology have relied on semiotics as they have considered culture as communication or signification in various ways. Certainly, the studies of Claude Lévi-Strauss, Clifford Geertz, David Schneider, and Victor Turner, as well as Mary Douglas and Gregory Bateson, are among those to be placed here. Each of these scholars does not necessarily make the same assumptions about people or pay the same attention to context. Yet they share a basic view that culture is a kind of communication.

Turner (1967), for example, analyzed *symbols* as molecules of ritual with 81semantic richness and depth. He pointed to the dimensions identified as positional, exegetic, and operational in symbols in his work on East African initiation rituals of social action, basing his conclusions on intensive empirical research. These terms are very similar to the syntactic, semantic and pragmatic. The positional and syntactic are similar, the exegetic and semantic bear resemblance, and the operational and pragmatic are parallel.

In another variation, James A. Boon, anthropologist, substituted the term *cultural operators*—defined as "the succinct and orderly conjunction of diverse elements" (1973:10) for symbols, which Turner used. Cultural operators may or may not possess clearly articulated boundaries such that we might find in a symbol. Boon's interest is not so much in the cultural operator as a unit but in the interconnections made possible by that operator.

Semiotics in Ethnomusicology

Just as semiotics ranges widely, so do the studies we would include under the broad heading of semiotics in ethnomusicology. One of the early sources for interest in this area must be recognized as Charles Seeger. In his article "Music as a Tradition of Communication, Discipline, and Play" (1962: 156–63), he proposed the following questions and answers:

Why do people make music?

To communicate.

What do they communicate?

A discipline.

How do they communicate it?

By play.

Although Charles Seeger was not a semiotician in the strict sense, he certainly viewed music as a communicative system. Other ethnomusicologists have directly and indirectly drawn on semiotics, including David McAllester, Alan Lomax, and Alan Merriam. But in 1971, at a meeting of the Society for Ethnomusicology (SEM), Charles Boilés directly addressed semiotics in a paper entitled "Semiotics of Ethnomusicology." Because this was my first SEM meeting as a graduate student, I vividly remember sitting and listening to the paper, understanding little but seeing Seeger perched in the front row. I wondered who this elderly gentleman was. I was struck when he posed a question and the audience gave him rapt attention.

Boilés (1982) translated Charles Morris's terms into the ethnomusicological world. He pointed out, for example, that according to Colin McPhee's data on Balinese theater, different scales accompany different types of actors. *Tembung* accompanies leading characters; *baro* is used for the entrance or subordinate characters. Each scale, Boilés maintained, was a sign vehicle for which the designatum is a kind of actor or action. Furthermore, it may be said that the Balinese listener immediately takes account of the character types involved with the action at various points (1973b:35).

Nahoma Sachs, in a dissertation written in 1975, "Music and Meaning: Musical Symbolism in a Macedonian Village," was interested in identifying musical symbols, particularly the process of birth, existence, and death that a symbol undergoes.

Beyond these scholars, we need to point to Jean-Jacques Nattiez (1977), who put musical semiotics on the map. Working from his base at the University of Montreal, where he was a colleague of Boilés for a number of years, he developed a deep interest in this area. His book *Music and Discourse: Toward a Semiology of Music* (1990), a translation from the French version (1976), emphasizes the rigorous procedures that are possible with semiotics. He incorporates transformational-generative grammar and draws on Western art music scores for his analysis.

He writes of the three levels: poetic (production), esthetic (reception), and neutral (level of the object as heard and produced). As such, he is interested in different kinds of rules or meaning, although his categories are not quite parallel to syntactic, semantic, and pragmatic meaning in semiotics.

Another scholar who has made suggestive comments about linguistic models for ethnomusicology is Thomas Turino. He has proposed that Peircian semiotics defined the sign in a much broader sense than other scholars in structural linguistics. He notes,

> It has always been surprising to me that in the great musical semiotics boom of the 1970s, scholars chose the Saussurian line and attempted to show the similarities between music and language. A basic premise in my work is that the most important theoretical insights about the social power of music will be derived from outlining the *differences* between propositional, semantico-referential language, and non-propositional sign modes such as music and dance. (1999:222)

He goes on to say, "Music involves signs *of* feeling and experience rather than the types of mediational signs that are *about* something else" (1999:224). Turino—like Feld and Fox—is pointing to music as a communicative medium that is in many respects different from language, even if some of the linguistic theories have value for ethnomusicological analysis.

Critique

Despite the contributions of semiotics, a number of criticisms have also been made of semiotics.

1. **Semiotics has emphasized product to some exclusion of process.**

   Like a number of other theoretical orientations, semiotics has not attended to the temporal dimension in a significant way. Because of this, the critique arises that there is a tendency to focus on product without attending to issues of process.

2. **Semiotics has not shown great interest in the context of the performance.**

   Semiotic analyses tend, although not exclusively, to extract the data from the situation of production. Sharing some of the assumptions of structural linguistics, context is less important because of assumptions of shared mind structures.

3. **Semiotics has often equated language with music.**

The tendency to assume that language and music operate in a similar manner, which in some studies draw on semiotics, can prove problematic.

Contribution

In the end, semiotics has made contributions that have rippled through research in ethnomusicology. These can be summarized as follows:

1. **Semiotics has provided formalization, particularly in the issues of meaning.**

The use of semiotics has provided further formalization of the intricacies of meaning and communication. Thus it has created a model in an area where there previously has been little attention, particularly to semantic dimensions.

2. **Semiotics has differentiated syntactical, semantic, and pragmatic levels of meaning.**

These various kinds of meanings have been widely adopted and used by a variety of scholars in interpreting the communicative process. They label and differentiate important aspects of meaning.

On balance, semiotics has illuminated an area of knowledge and provided us with some formal ways for investigating meaning in musical communication, particularly semantic meaning. Research in ethnomusicology has been enriched in the long run by the discoveries of semiotics.

Ethnomusicology Examples

The Chica Genre in Peru

Thomas Turino provides us with an application of semiotics to explain how the *cumbia* musical genre in Andean Peru represents an emergent social identity. He maintains that those Andeans who migrated to Lima developed this genre in a manner that was somewhat out of awareness. The musicians integrated certain musical structures from the highland music together with the rhythm from the urban *cumbia,* thus indexing both Andean highland identity and urban identity in the present *cumbia* performance. Into that mixture, they added the third perspective of electric instruments to stand for youth and modernity. Today, "Peruvians themselves recognized that *chicha* performance serves as a logical sign for the identity of second-generation Andean migrants in Lima." This is a performance that can simultaneously incorporate the highland, urban, youth and modernity aspects because different musical aspects represent those different perspectives. "The genre

organically fused indices that mirrored their ambiguous social position"
(1999:247).

The Pause Sequence from the Kpelle of Liberia

The Kpelle example from Liberia of transformational-grammar of the pause
cues, from my own research, discussed earlier in the chapter, can be extended
semiotically. To reiterate, in rewrite rule 2.2, I indicated there could be one
or three cues given for every pause occurrence. What semiotics can help
explain is the significance of one versus three cues. As mentioned earlier,
when there is one cue, there is often a partial continuation of the performance
and not a complete pause. That explains what happens syntactically. When
the master of ceremonies as well as the soloist and the chorus all indicate
pauses, they are reinforcing the soloist, relaying her message, because it
originated with her, and perhaps, most important, enhancing her status.
These multiple cues to stop can be explained as signifying status
enhancement. Thus, semiotically, one cue means relatively little enhancement
of status. Three cues, given by different performers, mean relatively high
enhancement of status. So multiple cues mean higher importance for the
soloist in semiotic terms. Multiple people relaying the soloist's cue add
importance to her message and give credibility to what she is doing. This
example has parallels elsewhere in Kpelle society in Liberia. For when a
chief gives an order, he does not issue it to the people himself. Rather, he
relays it to his linguist or spokesperson, who then relays it to the intended
recipient. Such repetition of the message, like the repetition of the cue,
enhances his status.

The meaning we have derived semiotically here goes beyond just understanding structure to further exploring the significance of the structure. Rather
we are connecting the signs to other aspects of culture in order to understand
the significance of these symbols for people's lives and the way they live those
lives.

Conclusion

Linguistic models have had enormous influence on the way ethnomusicologists carry out research. The formalism of linguistics was instantly appealing to
scholars who had been trained to pay attention to musical form. The parallels
between language and music, at first glance, were apparent and important. The
developments of linguistics, integrated with communication theory developments, all contributed to a very significant area of interest for ethnomusicologists. Although models were not necessarily adopted exactly, the basic
premises of some of these perspectives continue to influence ethnomusicological research in important ways.

References

Adams, Charles R. 1974. "Ethnography of Basotho Evaluative Expression in the Cognitive Domain Lipapali (Games)." PhD diss., Indiana University.

Asch, Michael. 1972. "A Grammar of Slavey Drum Dance Music." Paper presented at the annual meeting of the Society for Ethnomusicology, Toronto.

Baest, Arjan Van, and Hans Van Driel. 1995. *The Semiotics of C. S. Peirce Applied to Music: A Matter of Belief.* Tilburg: Tilburg University Press.

Bahr, Donald M., and J. Richard Haefer. 1978. "Song in Piman Curing." *Ethnomusicology* 22(1): 89–122.

Bartók, Béla, and Albert Lord. 1951. *Serbo-Croatian Folksong.* New York: Columbia University Press.

Becker, Judith, and Alton Becker. 1979. "A Grammar of the Musical Genre Srepegan." *Journal of Music Theory* 24(1): 1–43. (Reprinted in *Asian Music* 14(1):30–73 with original pagination preserved.)

———. 1983. "A Reconsideration in the Form of a Dialogue." *Asian Music* 14(1): 9–16.

Besmer, Fremont E. 1974. *Kídan dárán sállà: Music for the Eve of the Muslim Festivals of 'Id Al-Fatir and 'Id Al-Kabir in Kano, Nigeria.* Bloomington: African Studies Program, Indiana University.

Blacking, John. 1995b. "Music, Culture, and Experience." In *Music, Culture, and Experience,* ed. Reginald Byron. Chicago: University of Chicago Press, 223–42.

Bogatyrev, Petr. 1971. *The Functions of Folk Costume in Moravian Slovakia.* Translated by Richard G. Crum. The Hague: Mouton.

Boilés, Charles L. 1967. "Tepehua Thought-Song: A Case of Semantic Signalling." *Ethnomusicology* 11(3): 267–392.

———. 1973a. "Semiotique de l'ethnomusicologie." *Musique en Jeu* 10: 34–41.

———. 1973b. "Reconstruction of Proto-Melody." *Annuario Interamericano de Investigacion Musical* 9: 45–63.

———. 1982. "Processes of Musical Semiosis." *Yearbook for Traditional Music* 14: 24–44.

Boon, James A. 1973. "Further Operations of 'Culture' in Anthropology: A Synthesis of and for Debate." In *The Idea of culture in the Social Sciences, edited by Louis Schneider and Charles Bonjean, 1–32. Cambridge: Cambridge University Press.*

Chenoweth, Vida, and Darlene Bee. 1971. *"Comparative-Generative Models of a New Guinean Melodic Structure." American Anthropologist* 73: 773–82.

Chomsky, Noam. 1957. *Syntactic Structures.* The Hague: Mouton.

Crafts, Susan, Daniel Cavicchi, and Charles Keil. 1993. *My Music: Explorations of Music in Daily Life.* Hanover, NH: Wesleyan University Press.

Feld, Steven. 1974. "Linguistic Models in Ethnomusicology." *Ethnomusicology* 18(2): 197–217.

———. 1981. "'Flow Like a Waterfall': The Metaphors of Kaluli Musical Theory." *Yearbook of Traditional Music* 13: 22–47.

———. 1982. *Sound and Sentiment: Birds, Weeping, Poetics, and Song in Kaluli Expression.* Philadelphia: University of Pennsylvania Press.

———. 1984. "Sound Structure as Social Structure." *Ethnomusicology* 28(3): 383–409.

———. 1988. "Aesthetics as Iconicity of Style, or 'Lift-Up-Over Sounding': Getting into the Kaluli Groove." *Yearbook of Traditional Music* 20: 74–113.

———. 1991. "Sound as a Symbolic System: The Kaluli Drum." In *The Varieties of Sensory Experience: A Sourcebook in the Anthropology of the Senses,* ed. David Howes. Toronto: University of Toronto Press, 79–99.

———, and Aaron Fox. 1994. "Music and Language." *Annual Review of Anthropology* 23: 25–53.

Goodenough, Ward H. 1957. "Cultural Anthropology and Linguistics." In *Report of the Seventh Annual Roundtable Meeting on Linguistics and Language Study,* ed. Paul L. Garvin. Georgetown University Monograph Series on Language and Linguistics, No. 9. Washington, D.C.: Georgetown University Press, 167–75.

Herzog, George. 1934. "Speech Melody and Primitive Music." *Musical Quarterly* 20: 452–66.

———. 1945. "Drum Signalling in a West African Tribe." *Word* 1: 217–38.

Hughes, David W. 1988. "Deep Structure and Surface Structure in Javanese Music." *Ethnomusicology* 32(1): 23–74.

Kaeppler, Adrienne L. 1972. "Method and Theory in Analyzing Dance Structure with an Analysis of Tongan Dance." *Ethnomusicology* 16(2): 173–21.

Kant, Immanuel. 1955 [1952]. *The Critique of Pure Reason.* Translated by J. M. D. Meiklejohn, Thomas K. Abbott, and James C. Meredith. Chicago: Encyclopaedia Britannica.

Keil., Charles. 1979. *Tiv Song.* Chicago: University of Chicago Press.

Lerdahl, Fred. 1983. *A Generative Theory of Tonal Music.* Cambridge, MA: MIT Press.

Lyons, John. 1970. *Chomsky.* London: Fontana.

Malinowski, Bronislaw. 1922. *Argonauts of the Western Pacific; An Account of Native Enterprise and Adventure in the Archipelagoes of Melanesian New Guinea.* London: G. Routledge.

———. 1965 [1935]. *Coral Gardens and Their Magic.* Bloomington: Indiana University Press.

Monelle, Raymond. 2000. *The Sense of Music: Semiotic Essays.* Princeton, N.J.: Princeton University Press.

Morris, Charles W. 1972. *Writings on the General Theory of Signs.* The Hague: Mouton.

Nattiez, Jean-Jacques. 1977. "The Contribution of Musical Semiotics to the Semiotic Discussion in General." In *A Perfusion of Signs,* ed. Thomas A. Sebeok. Bloomington: Indiana University Press, 121–42.

———. 1990. *Toward a Semiology of Music.* Princeton: Princeton University Press.

Peirce, Charles S., Max Harold Fisch, and Christian J. W. Kloesel. 1982. *Writings of Charles S. Peirce: A Chronological Edition.* Bloomington: Indiana University Press.

Propp, Vladimir Akovlevich. 1958. *Morphology of the Folktale.* Edited with an introduction by Svatava Pirkova-Jakobson; Translated by Laurence Scott. Bloomington: Research Center, Indiana University.

———. 1984. *Theory and History of Folklore.* Translated by Ariadna Y. Martin and Richard P. Martin. Minneapolis: University of Minnesota Press.

Reiner, Thomas. 2000. *Semiotics of Musical Time.* New York: Peter Lang.

Robertson, Carol E. 1979. "'Pulling the Ancestors': Performance, Practice, and Praxis in Mapuche Ordering." *Ethnomusicology* 23(3): 395–416.

Sachs, Nahoma. 1975. "Music and Meaning: Musical Symbolism in a Macedonian Village." PhD diss., Indiana University.

Sapir, J. David. 1969. "Diola-Fogny Funeral Songs and the Native Critic." *African Language Review* 8: 176–91.

Saussure, Ferdinand de. 1966 [1916]. *Course in General Linguistics.* Translated by Wade Baskin. New York: McGraw-Hill.

Seeger, Charles. 1962. "Music as a Tradition of Communication, Discipline, and Play." *Ethnomusicology* 6(3): 156–63.

Stone, Ruth M. 1982. *Let the Inside Be Sweet: The Interpretation of Music Event among the Kpelle of Liberia.* Bloomington: Indiana University Press.

Sturtevant, William C. 1968. "Studies in Ethnoscience." In *Theory in Anthropology: A Sourcebook*, eds. Robert A. Manners and David Kaplan. New York: Aldine, 475–500.

Tarasti, Eero. 2002. *Signs of Music: A Guide to Musical Semiotics.* Hawthorne, N.Y.: Mouton de Gruyter.

Turino, Thomas. 1999. "Signs of Imagination, Identity, and Experience: A Peircian Semiotic Theory for Music." *Ethnomusicology* 43(2): 221–255.

Turner, Victor. 1967. *The Forest of Symbols: Aspects of Ndembu Ritual.* Ithaca, N.Y.: Cornell University Press.

Tyson, Lois. 1999. *Critical Theory Today.* New York: Garland.

Zemp, Hugo. 1978–1979. "'Aré 'aré Classification of Musical Types and Instruments." *Ethnomusicology* 22(1): 37–67; 23(1): 5–48.

Chapter 5

Paradigmatic Structuralism

Paradigmatic structuralism, which bears similarities to the structuralist linguistic models, arose in the mid-twentieth century in a climate of rationalist thought. Generated by Western European scholars, structuralism owed much to theorists such as René Descartes (1596–1650), who "conceived of the thinking human being as inherently rational, and thus the determining locus of knowledge and truth" (Tunstall 1979:51). Even more specifically, philosopher Immanuel Kant (1724–1804) assumed similar mind structures, in which case cultural context was much less important in understanding cultural forms such as music. Historical background and social interaction receded as sources of explanation.

Claude Lévi-Strauss, a French anthropologist, followed the linguist Ferdinand Saussure and developed a broad-based approach to structuralism. He proceeded in the late 1950s to apply a structuralist analysis to a number of cultural systems, including "totemistic practices, kinship conventions, and myth repertoires" (Tunstall 1979:54). In the course of this work, he discovered that structures within one system were similar to those found in another system. This was not surprising given the assumption of similar mind structures.

His fieldwork in the Matto Grosso and Amazonian rain forest in Brazil offered evidence to support his idea. In studying Indian myths, he found strong connections between what had first been unrelated aspects. He saw oppositions between honey and tobacco, between the raw and the cooked, between nature and culture. These oppositions were ultimately connected through the process of transformation and then formed the building blocks of his analysis.

Lévi-Strauss interpreted myths for their use of natural phenomena to explain the world and thus provide a system of logic. Among his best known works explaining these analyses are *Tristes Tropiques* (1955), *Totemism*

Paradigmatic structuralism

- Approach to structuralism that assumes similar mind structures
- Built on a system of oppositions
- Oppositions mediated through transformations
- Surface structures much less important than underlying deep structures

---

(1963), *The Savage Mind* (1966), *The Elementary Structures of Kinship* (1969a), and *The Raw and the Cooked* (1969b). The categories within these various systems were those possessed by a group of people. Any of the phenomena within a culture could reveal this structure.

Paradigmatic structuralism is based on several fundamental assumptions. They form the foundation for the work of researchers who are conducting studies in this area.

Paradigmatic Structuralism: Assumptions

1. **All human experience is governed by a limited number of operational categories inherent in the structure of the mind.**

   All of the researcher's data can be elegantly reduced to a few constructions that define how the human mind works. For example, a culture might use the colors red and green for traffic signals. These are surface appearances that represent the ideas of "stop" and "go," which lie at a deeper level in the mind.

2. **These categories are mainly binary or oppositional.**

   These structures can be viewed as existing in pairs that are opposites of one another. The meanings of the two terms are contrastive in the extreme: black/white, raw/cooked, stop/go, and one category excludes the other category.

3. **These oppositions are mediated through transformations.**

   The paired statements also contain a logical middle point between them. If, for example, you have a red light and a green light, these exist in binary opposition to one another. These opposites are connected by the intermediary yellow light, which is part of the transformation from red to green: red–yellow–green.

4. **Surface structures are much less important than the underlying deep structures or base of the pattern.**

   The details of human behavior, which constitutes the surface, are not of concern. Rather the structures that generate this behavior are considered much more important by paradigmatic structuralists.

Paradigmatic Structuralism: Critique

1. **Paradigmatic structuralism isolated logical units outside of their cultural context.**

   There was little concern for the context in which behavior took place. Rather, the structure took precedence over the behavioral setting.

2. **Paradigmatic structuralism focused on ideal rather than enacted human behavior.**

The emphasis in much fieldwork that was carried out with this orientation was on the ideal as people talked about it or as the researcher inferred from various evidence. Less emphasis was placed on interpretation about the details of a particular situation or behavior.

Paradigmatic Structuralism: Contribution

1. **Paradigmatic structuralism contributed an analysis of some elegance.**

With structuralism came a certain economy of analysis, a stripping away of nettlesome ethnographic detail. The formalism of structural linguistics is also evident in paradigmatic structuralism.

2. **Paradigmatic structuralism provided a powerful orientation for making connections within the broader social system.**

It is not surprising that parallel structures exist within a society. Paradigmatic structuralism offered some insight into plotting those connections within broader systems.

Paradigmatic Structuralism in Ethnomusicology

The early 1970s was a period of considerable interest in structuralism in ethnomusicology as well as other areas of scholarship in music (Scott 2000). Numerous conference papers and journal articles explored the approach in the field of ethnomusicology.

Lévi-Strauss (1971) himself explored a structural analysis of Ravel's *Bolero*, although this was an example drawing on a thoroughly Western example of music. Pandora Hopkins (1977) commented that Lévi-Strauss, "has made it possible to compare classificatory systems (and therefore patterns of thought) that have traditionally been considered . . . not comparable. . . . Thus Lévi-Strauss' concepts are liberating" (259). And these concepts found "music as a particularly apt demonstration of the basic ordering processes of the mind" (Tunstall 1979:62).

John Blacking showed a strong inclination in his work to paradigmatic structuralism while always having some reservations about totally divorcing the contextual. His book *How Musical Is Man* (1973) displayed a structuralist bent as he compared the structure of music to the structure of other cultural phenomena. The book shared with structuralist thought an ultimate interest in the implications of musical structures for human cognitive structures (Tunstall 1979:60). Thus Blacking, like Nattiez who uses linguistic models of structuralism, urged the development of more abstract analysis as a goal for ethnomusicology. He said further, "Music may express the quintessence of a society's socio-conceptual structure and hence serve as a kind of litmus paper for structural analysis" (1972a:6).

Steven Feld's work (1982) among the Kaluli in New Guinea demonstrated a strong tilt to structuralism as well. For he, like Lévi-Strauss, looked to myth and compared the structures he found in myth with structures in the music. His goal, similar to that of Blacking, was to discover basic structures that explained the organization of the creative process. He also emphasized ideal structures elicited from questioning the Kaluli rather than describing musical performances and the detail of the actual unfolding events.

Paradigmatic Structuralism in Ethnomusicology: Assumptions

1. **All musical performance is governed by a limited number of operational categories inherent in the structure of the mind.**

   Analysis of music can be boiled down to a few essential categories, which are indicative of basic structures of the mind. For example, one might determine that all musical instruments are male and female. Pitches might also be divided into male and female. Even timbres might be male or female.

2. **These musical categories are mainly binary or oppositional.**

   To take the previous example, instruments exist in oppositional categorization, and male is the complete opposite of female, just as a high pitch is the complete opposite of a low pitch.

3. **These oppositions in music are mediated through transformations.**

   A high pitch exists in relation to a low pitch through a middle point or middle pitch. This transformation relates the high point to the low point.

Paradigmatic Structuralism in Ethnomusicology: Critique

1. **Paradigmatic structuralism in ethnomusicology isolated logical units outside of their cultural context.**

   With the assumption that people share similar mind structures, the cultural context became less important and was not of paramount concern.

2. **Paradigmatic structuralism focused on ideal rather than enacted human behavior.**

   Paradigmatic structuralism in ethnomusicology focused on the ideal musical performance and not so much with observing and recording the contextual details of individual performances.

Plate 15 Bruno Nettl, Courtesy of Bruno Nettl.

Paradigmatic Structuralism in Ethnomusicology: Contribution

1. **Paradigmatic structuralism contributed an analysis of some elegance for ethnomusicologists.**

   These structures could be appreciated by ethnomusicologists acquainted with form and analysis in Western music theory. In addition, Bruno Nettl (1958:37–41) saw the rearrangement of data into levels as providing greater objectivity in musical analysis.

2. **Paradigmatic structuralism in ethnomusicology provided a powerful orientation for making connections within the broader musical system.**

   Feld (1982) made the connection between Kaluli myth and the broader musical system. Such a connection allowed ethnomusicologists to move beyond the sound of the music and relate it to the broader social and cultural system within which it existed.

Paradigmatic Structuralism and Music Theory

We also need to take a small detour and acknowledge the influence of structuralism in the field of Western music theory, particularly in the work of Heinrich Schenker (1945, 1977). His terms to distinguish the different levels of abstracting in music—background and foreground—can be compared to Lévi-Strauss's deep structure and surface structure. Schenker's middle ground is the equivalent of transformation for Lévi-Strauss (Tunstall 1979:284–85). And, like Lévi-Strauss, Schenker's approach to music analysis emphasizes a base structure that then generates surface structures.

Paradigmatic structuralism has profoundly influenced Western music theory analysis and remains a strong underlying orientation in much work today. Many studies continue to reflect the paradigmatic structuralist approach most prominently set forth by Heinrich Schenker.

A Kpelle Example Employing a Structuralist Analysis

The charter Kpelle myth, which the Kpelle say summarizes their culture, is embedded in the Woi epic, which in turn includes a number of other folklore genres. This myth of the superhuman hero Woi describes how he moved across the land with his extended family, meeting obstacles in the form of superhuman enemies. This superhero always conquered the enemy and moved onward following each victory (Stone 1988).

Although this myth on certain levels describes a world of spirits and humans, it also represents the very visible history of the Kpelle people who, over the past three hundred years, moved from the grasslands area in Mali toward the Guinea coast. They traveled during some periods and stopped during others as they confronted their enemies and fought them. As they moved on, they met yet further opposition to their forward movement and were continually faced with new challenges.

In Lévi-Straussian terms, this myth shows the fundamental opposition of movement and pause mediated by confrontation. It is confrontation that brings a halt to the forward movement and results in the pause. The opposition that structures this myth looks like this:

Movement   Confrontation Pause

Given the assumption that this opposition is a deep structure, a paradigmatic structuralist could argue that such a pattern is also fundamental to much of Kpelle musical performance because rhythmic and melodic segments are characterized by movement, action, and a lively sense of energy. A dancer, for example, launches a solo dance segment. After a short time, she confronts the drummer and pauses. She then begins another movement, only to stop yet again as she and the drummer communicate and confront one another. The dancer and drummer often challenge one another kinesthetically and sonically to achieve synchrony. The structure is built by the opposition of motion and pause—precisely the pattern created in the charter myth.

The base structure of movement/pause generates surface structures like the genre of the Woi myth or of recreational dancing where young women dance *loking*, *kenema*, or *sokokpa* dance steps. These ethnographic manifestations of deeper structural patterns transcend any single media and range from verbal art to dance.

We can even see the pattern in ordinary greeting behavior in which speakers alternate turns, starting and stopping frequently as they fit their speech one to another. A greeting sequence might proceed in this fashion:

SPEAKER 1:	Are you awake?	Movement
SPEAKER 2:	Hm, Keema.	Confrontation
SPEAKER 1:	Hm.	Stop
SPEAKER 2:	Are you awake?	Movement

Structural pattern of movement/pause is widespread and pervasive in Kpelle society. It characterizes a fundamental way of structuring activity and creating music and dance as well as greeting behavior. This pattern underlies much of Kpelle life, and as we discern it we see images of the society that other theories might not capture.

Paradigmatic Structuralism: Conclusion

Paradigmatic structuralism helps us classify and explain data extending over both time and space. The approach accounts for multiple levels of analysis and elucidates complex details. Ethnographic detail recedes in this approach as does concern for individual interpretation of that ethnographic detail.

References

Blacking, John. 1972a. "Deep and Surface Structures in Venda Music." *Yearbook of International Folk Music Council* 3:91–108.

———. 1973. *How Musical Is Man?* Seattle: University of Washington Press.

Feld, Steven. 1982. *Sound and Sentiment: Birds, Weeping, Poetics, and Song in Kaluli Expression.* Philadelphia: University of Pennsylvania Press.

Hopkins, Pandora. 1977. "The Homology of Music and Myth." *Ethnomusicology* 21:247–62.

Lévi-Strauss, Claude. 1955. *Tristes Tropiques.* Paris: Plon.

———. 1963. *Totemism.* Boston: Beacon Press.

———. 1966. *The Savage Mind.* Chicago: University of Chicago Press.

———. 1969a. *The Elementary Structures of Kinship.* Boston: Beacon Press.

———. 1969b. *The Raw and the Cooked.* New York: Harper & Row.

———. 1971. "Boléro du Maurice Ravel." *L'Homme* 11(2):5–14.

Nettl, Bruno. 1958. "Some Linguistic Approaches to Musical Analysis." *Journal of the International Folk Music Council* 10:37–41.

Schenker, Heinrich. 1945. *Challenge to Musical Tradition: A New Concept of Tonality.* Edited by Adele T. Katz. New York: Knopf.

———. 1977. *Readings in Schenker Analysis and Other Approaches.* Edited by Maury Yeston. New Haven: Yale University Press.

Scott, Derek B., ed. 2000. *Music, Culture, and Society: A Reader.* New York: Oxford University Press.

Stone, Ruth M. 1988. *Dried Millet Breaking.* Bloomington: Indiana University Press.

Tunstall, Patricia. 1979. "Structuralism and Musicology: An Overview." *Current Musicology* 27:51–64.

Chapter 6

Marxist Explanations

Marxist theory arose in the 1950s and bore a clear connection to paradigmatic structuralism. The "oppositions" of structuralism were replaced by "dialectics"—statements and their antithesis—in Marxism. One of the differences was that Marxist theory foregrounded the economic aspects of culture.

"For Marxism, getting and keeping economic power is the motive behind all social and political activities" (Tyson 1999:50). Economics is the base on which the superstructure the society is built. Society is based on **historical materialism**—that is, material things exist independent of the mind and have a reality. Of primary interest to Marxist theorists are differences in social classes, the most significant groups being the proletariat (lower class or working class) and the bourgeois (upper or wealthy class). The superstructure is the ideology that develops above the materialistic/economic base.

Marxist theory, of course, is built on the thinking and writing of Karl Marx, who was troubled by the rise of capitalism and industrialism in the mid-nineteenth century. He was concerned about the trend of people who were forced to sell their labor to factories as these replaced individuals working at home (Tyson 1999:58). He postulated that this change would create alienate workers from their work and ultimately be negative for society. His ideas were

---

Marxist theory

- Research framework that draws on ideas of Karl Marx
- Built on system of dialectics
- Economics is the base on which the superstructure of society is built
- Differences in social class of interest to Marxist theorists

---

Historical materialism

- Theoretical approach derived from Karl Marx and Frederich Engels
- Material world has a reality separate from the mind

---

elaborated in his well-known book *Das Kapital (Capital)* that has been was translated and published in many editions since the latter part of the nineteenth century (1967 [1867]).

Assumptions

Scholars who rely on Marxist theory for research make a number of interrelated assumptions that bear explication.

1. **All human structures have specific material/historical causes, and these causes need to be understood.**

   Concrete conditions in the world need to be explored to provide understanding. The explanations typically lie in material and historical causes. Marx claimed that the current distribution of economic resources should not be taken as natural, but that we should examine the historical reason why society is organized as it is economically.

2. **Marxist analysis focuses on relationships between socioeconomic classes both within a single society and among societies.**

   The dynamics of economic power among these classes is of central concern to Marxists. These differences in class are critical to dividing people and prove more significant, from a Marxist perspective, than do issues such as religion, race, gender, and ethnicity (Tyson 1999:50). The material causes can be traced to class differences, which are important to explore.

3. **Ideology is a belief system resulting from cultural conditioning.**

   Repressive ideologies, by falsely appearing as natural, prevent us from understanding the historical circumstances that create an uneven distribution of material resources. The study of these causes is no way straightforward or easy. In fact, because of ideology it may be nearly impossible to understand the root causes of certain aspects of a culture.

4. **One goal of Marxist theorists is to identify the ideology at work in cultural productions.**

   One can then determine how the particular ideology reinforces or undermines the system in which the cultural production plays a role. Ideology is pervasive and crucial to anything an ethnomusicologist is studying.

5. **Another concern of Marxists is commodification—the practice of relating people or things on the basis of their exchange value or sign-exchange value.**

   A commodity is any thing or service that is exchanged or sold. This might range from a musical composition to wheat or oil. A commodity's value, in

---

Commodification

- Act of turning a thing or an activity into a commercial entity

the capitalist system, or so Marxist theorists maintain, lies in the money or things for which it can be traded, that is, the exchange value. Alternatively, value derives from the social status that the commodity brings to its owner.

6. **Capitalism is continually requiring new markets, and this search for new places to sell goods and get materials is the cause of imperialism.**

Countries create colonies through the extension of their influence. All of these conditions can lead to what Marxist scholars have called the colonizing of the consciousness, carried out through a variety of routes and in a number of venues.

7. **Ideas are frequently framed in terms of dialectics or propositions and their antitheses.**

The concern with *dialectics* is very reminiscent of the *opposition* that was a building block of structuralism. Marxism shows a clear relationship to paradigmatic structuralism. The difference is the emphasis in Marxism on history and the potential to overthrow the system within the dialectical order.

The 1970s brought a flowering of Marxist theory, which permeated humanities and social science research. This ascendancy followed on the heels of structuralism and a search for alternative avenues of theory. In some cases, scholars such as Maurice Godelier (1977) combined Marxist theory with that of structuralism. Because Marxism, like paradigmatic structuralism, delineated base structure and superstructure, these models shared some ground on the issue of levels.

Anthropologists also extended certain Marxist concepts in their work. Arjun Appadurai (1988:5) noted that commodities are central to the concerns of archeologists, economic anthropologists, exchange theorists, and even social anthropologists.

Appadurai focuses on the "social life" of commodities, arguing that commodities are things with "a particular type of social potential" and it is productive to "regard commodities as existing in a wide variety of societies (though with a special intensity and salience in modern capitalist societies)" (1988:6–7). He notes that Marx himself at times argued for this more broadly based notion of commodity where it was not so inextricably tied to the circulation of money (Marx 1973). "Politics (in the broad sense of relations, assumptions, and contests pertaining to power) is what links value and exchange in the social life of commodities" (Appadurai 1988:57).

Regula Qureshi (2002) identifies three broad strands of Marxism that have relevance to ethnomusicology:

1. A "culturalist Marxism" with "a commitment to the cultural centrality of music" (Norris 2000; Solomon 1974)
2. A political economy-centered Marxism
3. "Activist" or "state" Marxism

Plate 16 Regula Qureshi. Courtesy of Regula Qureshi.

The culturalist Marxism was developed by the Frankfurt School during the years between the two world wars and was made visible more recently in the United States by Frederic Jameson (1971, 1990), who drew on the work of Theodor Adorno. Jameson brought to his Marxist analysis the orientations of semiotics and poststructuralism (Qureshi 2002:xvi).

The British introduced yet further variation in the Continental-American reading of Marxist theory. They centered on a "Marxist focus on class conflict to the theorizing of popular culture and popular music" (Shepherd et al. 1977 and Garofalo 1987, as cited in Qureshi 2002:xvii). The political economy-oriented Marxism appeared in the work of anthropologists, sociologists, and historians in the 1970s. The work was "centered in studies of political economy that addressed structures of capitalist domination and differential economic-political power across societies (Qureshi 2003:xvii). Scholars such as Godelier (1977), Maurice Bloch (1975), and Pierre Bordieu (1995) worked in this area. In this approach, theorists distinguish between the *center* and *periphery*. Power is exercised at the center, a colonial or national capital, for example, whereas the periphery is the place affected by the exercise of that power, such as the rural area where people produce goods for trade (Barnard 2004:89).

More recently, a "neo-Marxist approach using the concept of flexible accumulation" treats the "increasingly differentiated global capitalist practices, including the music industry and its global decentering, which are most immediately relevant for popular music studies." (Blim 2000; Krims forthcoming; Qureshi 2002:xvii). The blossoming of world music has contributed to this trend. Qureshi points to another "decentering initiative" that attempts to critique a Marxism focused on Europe (Chakrabarty 2000; Chaudhury 1995; Qureshi 2002:xvii).

Finally, the state Marxism associated with Soviet ideology, as well as ideology in other states such as China, was the setting where music, as one of the humanities, "was seen as a tool for shaping communist society and abolishing class hegemony" (Qureshi 2002:xviii). This meant that music became something to be manipulated for the purposes of solidifying state control.

Marxist Theory: Critique

1. **Marxist theory relies on the perspective of the analyst.**

   The disadvantage of the approach is that Marxist theory does not necessarily allow for indigenous interpretations but rather applies a top-down type of explanation.

2. **Marxist theory emphasizes a system in which the individual has little control or ability to act.**

   Just as structural functionalism originated in the climate and period of colonialism and necessarily must be understood within that broader framework, so Marxist theory emerged in the context of centralized control. Communism in the former Soviet Union and Marxism theory were not identical. Nevertheless, Marxist theory arose in a particular cultural and historical environment, one in which individuals were limited in agency.

Marxist Theory: Contribution

1. **Marxist theory addresses the economic aspects that are sometimes omitted from explanations provided by other theories.**

   Marxism begins from the assumption that all cultural and social forms are secondary to the material needs to eat and possess shelter. This starting point led Marxist theorists to seek explanations of economic conditions that gave rise to behavior in culture or that sustained certain processes and forms.

2. **Marxist theory attempts to account for historical conditions.**

   In a number of other models that have been considered, such as structural functionalism and structuralism, historical conditions were largely ignored. Scholars who employed Marxist theory found new possibilities for analyzing these areas of musical performance and production.

Marxist Theory in Ethnomusicology

Marxist theory has been used by a number of ethnomusicologists, particularly those working in the area of popular music. Most ethnomusicologists who rely on Marxist theory do not necessarily label their work as Marxist per se. A number of key assumptions can be derived about Marxist theory in ethnomusicology.

Marxist Theory in Ethnomusicology: Assumptions

1. **Musical structures have specific material/historical causes, and these causes need to be understood.**

   Ethnomusicologists working from a Marxist perspective show a concern for economic aspects to a degree that they might not otherwise be concerned. This might include an interest in the economics of the popular music industry, for example.

2. **Marxist analysis by ethnomusicologists focuses on relationships between socioeconomic classes both within a single society and among societies.**

   Such concerns can be manifest in terms of power between performers and classes of performers or performers and their audiences or producers, for example.

3. **Ideology in musical performance settings is a belief system resulting from cultural conditioning.**

   The ethnomusicologist is then interested in uncovering the causes of a particular ideology and the conditions under which it arises.

4. **Another concern of ethnomusicologists using Marxist theory is to consider commodification—the practice of relating people or things on the basis of their exchange value or sign-exchange value.**

   The concern for ethnomusicologists becomes the exchange value of performance, measured in economic or social terms.

5. **Marxist ethnomusicologists frequently frame ideas in terms of dialectics or propositions and their antitheses.**

   These dialectics are similar to the oppositions of structuralism, with the exception that historical conditions are important in Marxist dialectics.

Marxism in Ethnomusicology: Critique

1. **Marxist theory relies on the perspective of the ethnomusicologist.**

   Because of the assumption that participants are influenced by ideology, there is little value placed on the ideas of the musicians and audience members in creating interpretation. Such a situation places the researcher in a dominant position for creating analyses.

2. **Marxist theory emphasizes a system in which the musicians and audience members have little control or ability to act.**

   The issue of agency for music participants becomes problematic in a system in which they are envisioned as dominated by a hegemonic system.

Marxism in Ethnomusicology: Contribution

1. **Marxist theory addresses the economic aspects that are sometimes omitted from explanations provided by other theories.**

   A valuable consideration for ethnomusicology is the economic dimension, which is given attention in Marxist theory. Previous approaches have not emphasized economics, which are placed center stage in Marxist theory.

2. **Marxist theory attempts to account for historical conditions in ethnomusicological research.**

   The emphasis on historical conditions is also a dimension that has been understudied in some of the earlier ethnomusicological studies. Marxism provides a way of addressing these historical conditions.

Marxist Examples in Ethnomusicology

A number of ethnomusicologists have employed Marxist theory for their research, often in conjunction with other approaches. Christopher Waterman in his 1990 book *Jùjú* hints at his reliance, in part at least, on Marxist approaches. He says, for example, "My interpretation of modern Yoruba music history is based upon the assumption that adaptive strategies are always played out within the limitations of world view and *material* circumstance" (7; emphasis added). A little later he comments, "I want to suggest that an effective analysis of musical practice must concern itself at some level both with the analytical *distinction* between the cultural and social and with their *necessary interdependence*; and, further, that this dialectic is essential to an understanding of *music history* [emphasis added] (1990:7). Here he speaks of the material and historical issues, essential concepts to a Marxist analysis. Waterman spends considerable effort in analyzing class differences, another area of importance for Marxism. Speaking of music, in particular, he says,

> Jùjú simultaneously legitimates inequality and argues that all actors may become wealthy and powerful, a kind of African Horatio Alger ideology. In the face of widening disparities in wealth, education, and health, music plays a role in the reproduction of hegemonic values. (1990:227)

Waterman's work differs from other popular music scholars who rely on Marxist theory, for many of the other popular music researchers have seen popular music as protest of a kind to the dominant hegemony. He finds that in the multiple ways *juju* may be interpreted, one possibility is for the sustenance of class differences. (Also note that Waterman did not conduct his study in a society that was ruled by a Marxist government. Rather Nigeria was ruled by Britain in the colonial period and derives much of its outside models of rule from the United Kingdom.)

Tim Rice (1994), who writes of music in Bulgaria from quite another viewpoint, comments on Marxist theory at certain points in his analysis. "But music was more than simply an over-determined aspect of the superstructure, as Marxist theory might suggest: it also played an active role in the ideology which dialectically sustained the economy" (163). Later, he goes on to say, "Although economic ideological and musical practice worked dialectically to reinforce one another and their age- and gender-based hierarchies, song and dance were also arenas in which those at the bottom of the hierarchical ladder, especially women and the young, expressed their feelings and contested and negotiated their inferior status" (164).

In Rice's field setting, Marxist theory was part of the political context, which also impinged on his study, for he tells us,

> In Bulgaria after 9 September 1944, a Marxist theory of change became a matter of state policy. . . . [T]he practice of music is shaped by both economic and ideological factors . . . Under Communism a fiddler could feed a household, and musicians became one kind of specialized laborer in the building of communism and communist ideology. (1994:170).

Peter Manuel (1987), studying popular music of Cuba, commented on how state Marxism related to the music of Cuba:

> First of all, in spite of the prodigious vitality of the Cuban music scene today, it is clear that twenty-five years of socialism in Cuba has not produced revolutions or even dramatic changes in the *styles* of music popular there. Rather, the Revolution has contributed to a general and dynamic evolution and sophistication, within the broad framework of the stylistic forms inherited from the pre-revolutionary period. (175)

Although Manuel and Rice are addressing somewhat different issues, Rice points to the invariable influences of a Marxist government on the music and the context of production, and Manuel concludes that the politically oriented Marxist government has not dominated the shape of the music scene, a complex mixture of internal and external genres.

Marxist theory in ethnomusicology is also aligned with theoretical thinkers who work in music more broadly. Jacques Attali (1985), whose work *Noise: The Political Economy of Music* has provided ideas for scholars in popular music and related areas, notes, "If it is deceptive to conceptualize a succession of musical codes corresponding to a succession of economic and political relations, it is because time traverses music and gives meaning to time" (19). Attali is attuned to the political and economic issues that affect music. In a related way, Keith Negus (1996) in *Popular Music in Theory* comments on the relation between production and consumption of music. Negus points to Marx in observing that people do not create history "under circumstances chosen by themselves, but under circumstances directly encountered, given and transmitted from the past" (138).

Ethnomusicologist Regula Qureshi's book, *Music and Marx: Ideas, Practice, Politics* (2002), is centered on but not limited to essays from the remarkable confluence of music scholars at the University of Alberta who approach the study of music through Marx: Regula Qureshi, David Gramit, Henry Klumpenhouwer, and Adam Krims. As Qureshi outlines in the introduction, these essays approach music and Marx from four perspectives by problematizing the following:

1. Commodification and fetishism as it relates to music
2. "Poetics of musical form and genre as socially mediated by capitalism"
3. Economic processes as related to music making
4. "Musicological and music practices" as related to "Marxist state policies" (Qureshi 2002:xv)

The book provides widely divergent views on how Marxist theory relates to music, ranging from ethnomusicology to many other approaches to the study of music. It is the most comprehensive look at Marx and the study of music for the ethnomusicologist presently available.

A Kpelle Example of Marxist Orientation

In the course of my fieldwork in Liberia, I worked with Moses Woni and John Woni, who formed a musical ensemble to perform and create a new kind of Kpelle music. When I arrived to conduct fieldwork in 1975 in central Liberia, I found them living near Salala where they performed in a circuit of rubber camps, particularly on days when the workers had just been paid. Their music texts were laced with English phrases as well as East African popular music sounds they had heard on Nairobi records. This period was important in their career for they were on the cusp of commodifying their music. They were attempting to get recordings made of their music so they could then sell them and make a living without relying on other forms of labor.

The group tried to take advantage of the money that flowed into the rubber camps on payday. They relied on a patron to invite them to a particular camp. That patron sponsored the performance and paid them a token amount of money. But most of their earnings came in the form of gifts made by the audience members when the music moved them to be generous. As the performance proceeded, audience members who wanted to present a gift approached the master of ceremonies to call for a pause. As the performers halted, the donor stepped forward to present a token amount of money and to underscore it with an elaborate speech. He said, "I'm Saki, I come from Zotaa. Here is $100 to wet the skin of the drum. You playing thank you, thank you." His speech first established who he was and where he came from as a way of establishing his credibility to speak. Then he used exaggeration to indicate how much money he was paying. He gave one dollar, which he inflated to

$100 in his speech. The money would be used to buy beer and "wet his tongue," which was being compared implicitly to the skin of the drum.

To echo Appadurai's observation on commodities, this exchange was not new in Kpelle society. Performers had long received gifts for their performance, and they had long performed for the token gifts. In this new order, however, in the rubber camps, ordinary workers now had the power to take part in the economy of music. The substantial gifts were no longer limited to wealthy patrons and pooled family resources. So a new class of people had resources at their disposal, and Moses and John Woni appeared in the camps at particularly advantageous monthly times when they knew their possibilities for receiving money and beer were optimal.

In other subtle ways the Woni group offered their audiences value. They promised indirectly to show them what was fashionable and of the moment. In the 1970s, they signaled this in their dress: they wore Afro haircuts, bell-bottom trousers, and dark sunglasses.

Young people, especially, flocked to hear them, hungering for those aspects of contemporary life that they deemed high value—songs of unrequited love, confrontations with urban life, "hip" English terms, and rhythms of world popular music. Young people saw the possibility of enhancing their own presentation of self by learning from and experiencing the music of the Woni group. For suddenly the songs emphasized the individual solo singer as a star performer.

Even the length of the Woni group's songs became commodified. One particular evening, we came to a scheduled performance at the home hamlet of the Wonis. As we set up recording equipment and the crowd gathered, a friend of John Woni stood dangling a watch. What, I asked, was the significance of the watch? John said that he and Moses had realized that in the Nairobi records, they had heard songs much shorter than the way the Woni group played theirs in the rubber camps. So John wanted to perform in a manner that would make

Plate 17 Moses and John Woni viewing a video playback of their performance, Photo by Verlon L. Stone

their songs more like what they admired on the East African records. He instructed his friend, holding the watch, to signal him when three minutes had elapsed. The Wonis were consciously shaping their songs to conform to models on recordings they knew were commodities. They were shaping their music to increase the exchange value.

The Wonis lived at the intersection of two worlds: they took steps to enhance their possibility of entering the urban music scene while at the same time they took advantage of their indigenous roots. They drew on the Kpelle language but then transformed text to also be intelligible, in some sections of their songs, to English speakers. The Woni group anticipated entering the popular music economy and were positioning themselves for this change (Stone 1982:40–46). I was privileged in 1975 to witness the initial steps in this process of commodification.

Conclusion

The world societies as Marx envisioned have not really unfolded. Furthermore, a narrow construction of Marxist theory is outmoded. Nevertheless, as Raymond Firth (1984) asserts,

> What Marx's theories offer to social anthropology is a set of hypotheses about social relations and especially about social change. Marx's insights—about the basic significance of economic factors, especially production relations; their relation to structures of power; the formation of classes and the opposition of their interests; the socially relative character of ideologies . . . embody propositions which must be taken for critical scrutiny into our body of science (52–53).

A number of scholars, including Henry Klumpenhouwer (1998), see a future for Marxist theory in music studies. He writes, "Marxist criticism offers the only possibility for sustained and successful critique of our current mode of production," and he calls for the development of "a Marxist poetics of music" (290–91).

We need also to acknowledge the contribution Marxist concepts can make to the world of ethnomusicology, recognizing that it will, no doubt, be adapted to a changing environment and altered circumstances even while supporting the idea of basic material necessities in all cultures.

References

Appadurai, Arjun, ed. 1988 [1986]. *The Social Life of Things.* Cambridge: Cambridge University Press.

Attali, Jacques. 1985 [1977]. *Noise: The Political Economy of Music.* Translated by Brian Massumi. Minneapolis: University of Minnesota Press.

Barnard, Alan. 2004. *History and Theory in Anthropology.* Cambridge: Cambridge University Press.

Blim, Michael. 2000. "Capitalism in Late Modernity." *Annual Review of Anthropology* 29:2–38.

Bloch, Maurice, ed. 1975. *Marxist Analyses and Social Anthropology.* London: Malaby Press.

Bordieu, Pierre. 1995. Randal Johnson, ed. *The Field of Cultural Production: Essays on Art and Literature.* New York: Columbia University Press.

Chakrabarty, Dipesh. 2000. *Provincializing Europe: Postcolonial Thought and Historical Difference.* Princeton, N.J.: Princeton University Press.

Chaudhury, Ajit. 1995. "Rethinking Marxism in India: The Heritage We Renounce." *Rethinking Marxism* 8(3): 133–43.

Firth, Raymond. 1984 [1975]. "The Sceptical Anthropologist? Social Anthropology and Marxist Views on Society." In *Marxist Analyses and Social Anthropology*, ed. Maurice Bloch. London: Tavistock, 29–60.

Garafalo, Reebee. 1987. "How Autonomous Is Relative: Popular Music, the Social Formation and Cultural Struggle." *Popular Music* 6(1): 77–92.

Godelier, Maurice. 1977. *Perspectives in Marxist Anthropology.* Cambridge: New York.

Jameson, Fredric. 1971. *Marxism and Form: Twentieth-Century Dialectical Theories of Literature.* Princeton, N.J.: Princeton University Press.

———. 1990. *Late Marxism: Adorno or the Persistence of the Dialectic.* London and New York: Verso.

Klumpenhouwer, Henry. 1998. "Commentary: Poststructuralism and Issues of Music Theory." In *Music/Ideology: Resisting the Aesthetic*, ed. Adam Krims. Amsterdam: G and B Arts International, 289–310.

Krims, Adam. Forthcoming. "Popular Music Studies, Flexible Accumulation, and the Future of Marxism." In *Popular Music and Social Analysis,* ed. Allan Moore. Cambridge: Cambridge University Press.

Manuel, Peter. 1987. "Marxism, Nationalism and Popular Music in Revolutionary Cuba." *Popular Music* 6(2): 161–78.

Marx, Karl. 1967 [1867]. *Capital: A Critique of Political Economy.* New York: International Publishers.

———. 1973. *Grundrisse: Foundations of the Critique of Political Economy.* New York: Vintage Books.

Negus, Keith. 1996. *Popular Music in Theory: An Introduction.* Hanover and London: Wesleyan University Press.

Norris, Christopher. 2001. "Marxism." *The New Grove Dictionary of Music and Musicians.* 2nd ed. London: Macmillan Press.

Qureshi, Regula. 2002. *Music and Marx: Ideas, Practice, Politics.* New York: Routledge.

Rice, Timothy. 1994. *May It Fill Your Soul: Experiencing Bulgarian Music.* Chicago: University of Chicago Press.

Shepherd, John, Phil Verder, Graham Vulliamy, and Trevor Wishart. 1977. *Whose Music? A Sociology of Musical Languages.* London: Latimer New Dimensions.

Solomon, Maynard. 1974. *Marxism and Art: Essays Classic and Contemporary.* New York: Knopf.

Stone, Ruth M. 1982. *Let the Inside Be Sweet: The Interpretation of Music Event among the Kpelle of Liberia.* Bloomington: Indidana University Press.

Tyson, Lois. 1999. *Critical Theory Today.* New York: Garland.

Waterman, Christopher. 1990. *Jùjú: A Social History and Ethnography of an African Popular Music.* Chicago: University of Chicago Press.

Chapter 7

Literary and Dramaturgical Theories

Literature and drama have offered models and analytic devices that ethnomusicologists have found to be useful tools. Among the most pertinent are metaphor, dramaturgical, and deconstruction theories. All derive from the humanities and are attractive for certain kinds of ethnomusicological studies. They are also significant because, in this book, the theories presented have borrowed from anthropology, biology, and linguistics. In metaphor, we see a model that emerges, in part, from literary criticism and the humanities.

Metaphor

Metaphor is "the figure of speech in which a name or descriptive term is transferred to some object different from, but analogous to, that to which it is properly applicable" (OED 1986:384 [1781]). In thinking about metaphor as an explanatory device, I want to focus on the argument for metaphor that Richard Brown (1989 [1977]) makes and the assumptions implicit in his presentation. In *A Poetic for Sociology*, he sets out an exemplar for studying human behavior that centers very specifically on metaphor. He goes on to explain that "[M]etaphor can be understood as an illustrative device whereby a term from one level or frame of reference is used within a different level or frame" (78). He quotes the sociologist Robert Park who says, "Our great cities, as those who have studied them have learned, are full of junk, much of it human." Park (1952:60) sees junk as a metaphor for people, conveying impact and connotative richness by comparing people with lots of problems such as poverty to junk, an impact not achievable with conventional description.

Richard Brown uses metaphor as a part of **cognitive aesthetics** to unite art and science. He asserts that his approach allows a unity of logical deductions and controlled research with intuitive insights and subjective understanding. Cognitive psychology and its concern for communicative issues then becomes

Cognitive aesthetics
• Research framework that unites art and science
• Emphasizes unity of logical deductions and intuitive insights
• Focuses on the lived world

relevant for scholars interested in literary issues such as metaphor. Implicit in his assertions are a number of assumptions.

Metaphor: Assumptions

1. **Social theory must be both objectively and subjectively meaningful.**

   Science emphasizes that the objective of research involves a prescribed method such as the scientific method, and art stresses the subjective, or the expression of individuals. If one develops a model that unites these two areas, then both the objective and subjective are important to incorporate into the model.

2. **All knowledge, whether formal or commonsensical, is symbolic construction and brings with it the possibility of multiple realities.**

   Metaphorical construction by nature points to multiple meanings and multiple perspectives for interpretation. A reality is an arena where certain rules obtain. Another reality will have other rules to which people relate. Everyday life is one reality, and dreaming or musical performance may be other realms of reality.

3. **Implicit in ordinary language analysis is the logical possibility of multiple systems of accounting for human action.**

   Following on the previous assumption, the use of metaphor produces more than one possible way for analyzing human interaction. Diverse realities are linked to produce new perspectives.

4. **There is a focus on the lived world as the framework out of which cognition emerges.**

   The system that Brown explores stresses the everyday life world as the one from which cognition develops. This is the ebb and flow of the ordinary reality that people experience as they go about their daily lives.

5. **Theory and data are both symbolic constructs.**

   Because we use language to construct theory and data, we necessarily employ words to stand for or represent the musical performance we seek to understand.

6. **The observer is subject to the same scrutiny as theory and data.**

   Because the observer is part of the total interaction, she or he must also be part of the study and be considered in the total research complex.

Metaphor: Contribution

1. **Metaphor allows for conceptual consideration of dissimilar elements in a single idea.**

   This is a particularly useful apparatus for scholars trying to bring a scientific explanation to bear on an artistic performance. Objective quantitative information can be related to subjective qualitative aspects of performance.

2. **Metaphor emphasizes the possibility of multiple perspectives for analysis.**

   Many of the earlier theories we have explored have emphasized a singular explanation. With metaphor, we enter into a period of time when scholars increasingly favor a multiplicity of explanatory possibilities.

3. **Metaphor incorporates both the subjective and the objective perspectives.**

   This approach allows the scholar to both honor individual interpretation and the need for a broader scientific explanation.

Metaphor: Critique

1. **A metaphor may overly crystallize the extent to which there is conjunction of two apparently dissimilar concepts.**

   It may be tempting to see a neatly formed metaphor where the evidence does not necessarily support such an explanation. At this point, James Boon's (1973) notion of a **cultural operator** can describe a conjunction without the formation of a distinct and enduring conceptual object.

2. **Metaphor may not attend to processual aspects of relationships and may overemphasize the static relationship.**

   An interpretation that emphasizes the clear formation of a higher level concept such as a metaphor may not account for the temporal changes that may affect such a conjunction.

Metaphor in Research

Metaphor becomes not just an organism in and of itself, but it can be placed within any other part of a system. Because metaphor emphasizes the possibility of juxtaposition, it allows us to sometimes transcend certain problems.

Cultural operator

- Succinct joining of elements that appear to be from diverse orders
- Emphasis on connection but not necessarily the product of the conjunction

By transferring ideas and associations of one system or level of discourse to another, metaphor allows each system to be perceived anew from the viewpoint of the other.

What Brown sees as the special utility of metaphor is the possibility to join things in a way that allows fidelity to the various elements of the metaphor at a specific level as well as faithfulness to both art and science at a more general level.

During the late 1970s and 1980s, increasing attention was paid to metaphor as an important conceptual tool through books by Andrew Ortony (1979), Sheldon Sacks (1979), George Lakoff and Mark Johnson (1980), Wolf Paprotté and René Dirven (1985), and Robert E. Haskell (1987). Yet in all of these works, there has been a notable lack of integration in the literature between literary theory, on one hand, representing art, and the literature in cognitive psychology, on the other hand, representing science (Shen 1992:568).

A number of scholars who have employed metaphor have found it a particularly appropriate device for explanation. James Fernandez (1986) in anthropology, for example, focused on metaphor in *Persuasions and Performances: The Play of Tropes in Culture*. In his view, metaphors enable ritual practitioners to perform, and he sought to understand how humans act in relation to these powerful images (22).

James Boon, also an anthropologist, recognized that the use of metaphor can sometimes overly crystallize the boundaries of the metaphor. He maintained that although disjunctive areas may be conjoined, the point of juncture may not be neat, tidy, or stable. He chose cultural operator to convey that looseness. Although a drum, for example, may be associated with the concept of female and carvings may exist on the drum to depict a woman, another drum within a society may carry no connection to the idea of femaleness. Thus the metaphor of drum and female is not necessarily tight and stable within a particular society.

Boon (1973) defines cultural operators as the "succinct and orderly conjunction of elements from what appear to the analyzer, to the actors, or both, as diverse orders" (10), noting that when the conjunction of elements does not appear bound, the research focus then moves to the connection between cognitive areas rather than on the nature of the higher level object (Stone 1982:3). Boon's modification of metaphor theory helps account for situations where the connection between cognitive domains may be less than distinct.

Music Metaphors

We should not be surprised that metaphors employing images of music structure are a favorite of intellectuals. Scholars from a variety of disciplines have been attracted to comparing structures or objects to music.

Brown himself, for example, uses "Coda" as a title for his last chapter. Douglas Hofstadter (1979) in *Gödel, Escher, Bach: An Eternal Golden Braid* employs musical subtitles for many of his chapters—"Three-Part Invention,"

"Two-Part Invention," "Crab Canon," and "Six-Part Ricercar"—even though he works in the area of cognitive science.

Metaphor in Ethnomusicology

The interest in metaphor became prominent in ethnomusicology in the late 1970s and early 1980s. Scholars used metaphor in a variety of ways in ethnographic study, although not necessarily as a way of uniting the intuitive and the logical at the level of disciplinary explanation as Brown advocated. Rather, ethnomusicologists have frequently used it as a way to develop explanation *within* a musical system.

Metaphor in Ethnomusicology: Assumptions

A number of assumptions have undergirded the use of metaphor in ethnomusicology:

1. **Ethnomusicological knowledge is built on symbolic constructions and brings with it the possibility of multiple realities.**

    Metaphors may be created by musicians and audience members creating descriptive statements, as well as by the ethnomusicologist who creates images to convey analytic ideas of musical performance.

2. **Implicit in ordinary language analyses of music performance is the logical possibility of multiple systems of accounting for human action.**

    There are multiple ways that different participants may use language to explain the complexities of musical performance. Metaphors by nature connect aspects that may at first appear quite different or distinct.

3. **There is a focus on the lived world such as performance as the framework out of which cognition emerges.**

    That is, the focus is on the everyday performance world as it unfolds and not the idealized world imagined by the scholar. All of the details of performance become the material for metaphorical analysis.

4. **Theory and data are both symbolic constructs in ethnomusicology.**

    Metaphor is relevant not only to the ideas of the ethnomusicologist but to the musical data as well. Symbolic construction is relevant to these various domains of ethnomusicology.

5. **The ethnomusicologist is subject to the same scrutiny as theory and data.**

    The ethnomusicologist is part of the social interaction just as much as the performers or audience are a part of this setting. And the ethnomusicologist needs to be made part of the total analytic setting.

Metaphor in Ethnomusicology: Critique

Although metaphor has brought some contributions to ethnomusicology, there are a number of criticisms of the approach as well:

1. **An ethnomusicological metaphor may overly crystallize the extent of the conjunction of two apparently dissimilar concepts.**

   If an ethnomusicologist finds a particular interval connected to a certain emotion or affect, this connection may not be permanent or constant. This conjunction might be fleeting and temporary for any number of reasons.

2. **Metaphor may not attend to processual aspects of relationships and may overemphasize the static relationship.**

   An interpretation that emphasizes the clear formation of a higher level concept such as a metaphor may not account for the temporal changes that may affect such a conjunction.

Metaphor in Ethnomusicology: Contribution

There are a number of significant contributions that metaphor research has made to the field of ethnomusicology:

1. **Metaphor allows for conceptual consideration of dissimilar elements in a single idea.**

   This is a particularly useful apparatus for ethnomusicologists trying to bring a scientific explanation to bear on an artistic performance.

2. **Metaphor emphasizes the possibility of multiple perspectives for analysis in ethnomusicology.**

   Many of the earlier theories explored earlier in this book emphasized a singular explanation. With metaphor, we enter a realm where the ethnomusicologist increasingly favors a multiplicity of explanatory possibilities.

3. **Metaphor in ethnomusicology incorporates both the subjective and the objective perspectives.**

   This approach allows the scholar to both honor individual interpretation and the need for a broader scientific explanation. Such a possibility provides for considerable scope between individual ideas and broader scholarly perspectives.

Metaphor in Ethnomusicology

Steven Feld (1982), although partially employing a paradigmatic structuralist approach, draws heavily on metaphor in his study of Kaluli music in New Guinea. As he explains, for the Kaluli, "language codes musical concepts into a lexicon whose systematic features embody cognitive arrangements, that is, classifications and categorizations socially learned and shared to differing degrees by different sectors of the community (stratified by factors like age, sex, interest, skill, experience, and social expectation)" (164). He speaks of the Kaluli mediating sound and sentiment by becoming birds as he uses aspects of Lévi-Straussian structuralism and metaphor. Thus the bird is a central metaphor and one can alternately see people as birds. Beyond this, bird voices are metaphors for spirit voices. Furthermore, myth encapsulates much about the landscape and music (Feld 1981).

Kpelle Example of Metaphor

Among the Kpelle people of central Liberia, I have discovered in my own work that *sang* is a fundamental term and concept for understanding music and aesthetic expression. *Sang* means "proverb" in one of its incarnations. It is also a metaphor that means a beautifully sung phrase with appropriate text, melody, and rhythm placed together. *Sang* is a conceptual place of conjunction, or juxtaposition, with a certain richness. In songs, a solo singer often signals that she is about to sing the favored part where verbal proverbs and rich illusory language loaded with metaphor is employed. In her text a female soloist sings, "Listen to my singing song. As I sing it, I open its net." Then follows song text that is filled with a dense multiplicity of images in sound, motion, and text. The song is here compared to a net that can be opened up to reveal aesthetic riches. And *sang* is the word used to describe this particularly rich area of performance that is revealed when the net is opened.

For the Kpelle performer, the very essence of performance, *sang,* is a metaphor, representing a conjunction of many apparently dissimilar things. And audience members delight in hearing the new and sometimes surprising, connections that are made.

Both Feld and I have found that metaphor is a mode of explanation and intellectual organization within the area of music theory as well as indigenous performance. In New Guinea in the Pacific, as well as in Liberia in West Africa, metaphor provides an important concept for theoretical explanation that may also relate to other intellectual traditions.

Because metaphor addresses the issue of bringing together apparently dissimilar elements, it may help bridge certain difficulties that we face in bringing scientific methods to the study of aesthetic performances such as music making. But the extent of that utility awaits further exploration by ethnomusicologists.

Dramaturgical Models

The images found in drama, the **dramaturgical models,** have structured certain related models of analysis for the humanities and social sciences. A number of scholars received inspiration from Kenneth Burke (1969), employing his

Dramaturgical model

- Research framework that draws on images of theatrical drama

ideas. William O. Beeman (1993) usefully reviews the research that burgeoned in this area.

Sociologist Erving Goffman articulated the dramaturgical model in a way that scholars from a number of other disciplines found useful. Goffman (1959:167) talked, for example, about distinctions between **front-stage** and **backstage behavior**. In a musical performance, backstage behavior could be the negotiation with a club manager, which was not intended for the patrons to see. Front stage constituted the performance itself. Goffman (1974) also used terms like *actor* to label the participant. Although he recognized the individual, he stressed the role that the actor was scripted to play and the constraints of a script rather than individual volition or choice.

Framing is another concept that Goffman (1974) applied to interaction events. "Frame" incorporates behaviors that are appropriate in that mode. The frame of play, for example, is quite different from the everyday life frame. And signals are often given to establish the frame of a given situation. These signals may be associated with lightning, dress, movement, sound, or rules of behavior.

Victor Turner (1986), an anthropologist working in East Africa, distinguished **social drama** from cultural drama. Life cycle rituals, festivals, and social conflicts are all social dramas. These situations all require public action.

Front-stage/ Backstage behavior

- Terms drawn from theatrical images: front-stage behavior is the performance as presented for an audience; backstage behavior is the performance that takes place primarily out of the presence of the audience

Framing

- Process of guiding the audience to what is considered essential
- Cues are often provided to help establish the frame

Social drama

- Social process arising out of conflict situations as defined by Victor Turner
- Component parts include breech, crisis, redressive action, reintegration

Music for entertainment of theatrical performances, in contrast, is an example of cultural drama. Social drama unfolds in four phases: "breach," "crisis," "redressive action," and "reintegration" (74–75). The third stage is character-ized by ritual processes. Turner (1990:11), borrowing from the anthropologist Arnold van Gennep, organized these rituals into phases of separation, transi-tion or liminality, and incorporation. He emphasized dramaturgical theory in his use of the term *drama* and in "homage to Goffman's idea that people pre-sent their selves by acting out roles in settings and scenes" (Palmer and Jankowiak 1996:237–39).

Dramaturgical Theory in Ethnomusicology: Assumptions

A number of assumptions can be made about the use of dramaturgical theory in ethnomusicology:

1. **Everyday life is analogous to dramatic enactment and musical on stage.**

   People in everyday life are like actors, and the spaces where they interact can be compared to a stage where life unfolds.

2. **Certain aspects of musical interaction are open and available to the public in a social setting.**

   These aspects may be designated as "front stage" where all the people pre-sent can observe what is going on.

3. **Other aspects of musical interaction are hidden from some of the participants.**

   These aspects may be designated as "backstage." where only some of the people present can observe what is occurring.

4. **Musical interaction is circumscribed spatially.**

   The dramaturgical model compares the spatial boundaries of musical inter-action to a stage. This is a distinct and bounded area that defines the arena of performance.

Dramaturgical Theory in Ethnomusicology: Critique

1. **Dramaturgical theory may overly emphasize the scripted aspect of music performance.**

   In this situation, the performance of musicians may be assumed to involve few decisions by individuals and considerable predetermination.

2. **There may be limitations in assuming that the social world is equivalent to a theatrical performance.**

   Among ethnomusicologists, Veit Erlmann, citing Johannes Fabian, sounds a note of caution. There is a problem with assuming there is a seamless quality for viewing the world as performance, and he calls for examining critically the use of the dramaturgical model (Erlmann 1996a:19–20; Fabian 1990:13).

Dramaturgical Theory in Ethnomusicology: Contribution

1. **The basic concepts, such as "role," "front stage," and "frame," transfer very easily and appropriately to ethnomusicology.**

   The basic concepts are very comparable to concepts in music performance and relate quite naturally.

2. **The temporal structure of theatrical performance with marked beginnings and endings fits the structure of many musical events.**

   Musical performances, like theatrical performances, are often appropriately analyzed as discrete units of time with carefully delineated starting and ending points.

Dramaturgical Theory Examples in Ethnomusicology

Many ethnomusicologists have involved Goffman's concepts for certain portions of their research, even if they have not relied solely on dramaturgical theory. Christopher Waterman (1990:162–216) described band captains in Nigeria as expert *impression managers.* Ingrid Monson (1996:17) found the idea of *frame* a valuable concept that helped explain multiple perspectives in the research setting.

The concept of **face work**—that is, collaborative sociability to maintain a consistent image of self—is also applicable in jazz and "the solidarity and emotional bonds with other musicians are emphasized when players talk about what they love best about performing" (Monson 1996:177). In this way they can manage the impression they provide to others.

Another aspect of self-presentation is the idea of *honor* in Albania, which Jane Sugarman finds that Goffman addresses: "Phrased in his terms, if demeanor is the means through which individuals present themselves as honorable, while deference is the recognition of an individual's 'honor' on the part of others, then "each individual is responsible for the demeanor image of himself and the deference image of others" (Goffman 1967:84; Sugarman 1997:217).

Face work

- Actions people take in social situations to present a sense of self that is consistent and socially acceptable

Plate 18 Jane Sugarman. Courtesy of Jane Sugarman.

Dramaturgical Theory: A Kpelle Example from Liberia

In my own research of music in Liberia, I discovered that musicians often interwove what I would regard as *backstage behavior* into the *front-stage behavior* or the performance itself. At an epic performance, for example, the lead performer chided the chorus for not singing well, told the audience they needed to ask more questions, and interwove these directions into the actual performing or "pouring of his epic."

In Liberia, Kpelle performers also sang criticism of local or national rulers. They inserted political commentary in the music event frame, which they would not be permitted to do in everyday life. The rules of public criticism were quite different in these two frames.

Within in the humanities, in literary research in particular, there are a set of theories that have some relevance. They have not been used to any great extent by ethnomusicologists, but they are worth noting, nevertheless.

Reader-Response Theory

Although reader-response theory is not a major mode of analysis for ethnomusicologists, it behooves us to fit this important literary approach into our theoretical array. In a general way, reader-response theory centers on taking account of how readers respond to literature. Within this general definition are a number of specific approaches. **Transactional reader-response theory**, as practiced by scholars such as Louise Rosenblatt (1978), centers on the study of the "transaction between text and reader." Her interest lies in the text in a number of senses: "the printed words on the page; a reader; and poem, which refers to the literary work produced by the text and the reader together" (Tyson 1999:58).

Following Wolfgang Iser (1978), we might refer to two kinds of meaning that every text offers: determinable and indeterminable. *Determinable meaning* is created by events in the plot and description of physical aspects. *Indeterminable meaning* refers to actions that are open to multiplicity of explanations. In Rosenblatt's terminology, the *efferent* mode of reading is a focus on information in the text. Her *aesthetic* mode focuses on "a personal relationship to the text that focuses our attention on the emotional subtleties of its language" (Tyson 1999:158).

Another form of reader-response theory is the **subjective reader-response theory**. As evidenced in the work of David Bleich (1978), the readers' responses form the text. The readers' responses are treated as a text to be analyzed, and Bleich terms the act of interpretation as resymbolization.

Social reader-response theory, associated with the later work of Stanley Fish (1980), stresses that meaning is created not by an individual acting independently but by the interpretive community of which we are a part. The point of this approach is that "no interpretation . . . can claim to reveal what's

---

Transactional reader-response theory

- Research framework in literary studies that focuses on relation between the reader and the text
- Includes determinable (efferent) meaning created by the plot and description of physical aspects
- Includes indeterminable (aesthetic) meanings that are open to a multiplicity of explanations

---

Subjective reader-response theory

- Research framework in literary studies; readers' responses are treated as the text

---

Social reader-response theory

- Research framework in literary studies; meaning created by the interpretive community
- No single interpretation can reveal what is in a text

in a text. Each interpretation will simply find what its interpretive strategies put there" (Tyson 1999:173).

The interest of reader-response analysis to ethnomusicology is related in part to the focus on the receiver of the literature. In a music performance, the audience member is analogous to the reader in literature, and reader-response theory thus assists us in theorizing how listeners help to create a performance.

Deconstruction

Deconstruction is a theory that was put forward by Jacques Derrida in the late 1960s and has had a major influence on literary studies, in particular, some forty years later (Derrida, 1998). Other disciplines have drawn on deconstruction and the emphasis it has placed on process.

Deconstruction claims that communication is not about concepts that are stable but rather about an array of signifiers that are continually changing. In the end, meaning results from "the differences by which we distinguish one signifier from another" (Tyson 1999:245). Meaning consists of a never-ending deferral of conclusion. Derrida claims that what we experience is the trace from the interplay of signifiers.

Derrida (1998) relies on the notion of binary opposition from structuralism. He adds the distinction, however, that these oppositions are hierarchical, and one of the pair in the opposition is always privileged. By finding the privileged member of the opposition, one can discern something of the operative ideology or system of value. Such a view that emphasizes an infinite number of vantage points serves to decenter the world and challenge structuralist views of the world.

Ethnomusicology and Deconstruction

Although we cannot, at this time, point to major ethnomusicological works that have centered on deconstruction as a mode of analysis, some of the central themes of this approach have influenced scholars and ethnomusicology. Deconstruction, for example, forms one of the bases of postmodernism on which many ethnomusicologists have relied.

Ethnomusicologists have employed deconstruction, although usually as part of other theoretical orientations. Benjamin Brinner quotes Jean-Jacques Nattiez (1991:12), who in turn describes the sound product that results from the give-and-take in a gamelan ensemble as a "trace" (Brinner 1995:4). Trace is the evidence that is available from a deconstruction process over time.

Legacy of Literary Theories

Although ethnomusicologists have not relied to any great extent on any of these approaches, with the exception of metaphor, they may hold some future interest. For one thing, reader-response theories come from a humanistic perspective.

Furthermore, there is considerable interest in the affective aspect in these approaches—an area that has yet to be developed to any great degree by ethno-musicologists but one that is central to the act of music making.

References

Beeman, William O. 1993. "The Anthropology of Theater and Spectacle." *Annual Review of Anthropology* 22: 369–393.

Bleich, David. 1978. *Subjective Criticism.* Baltimore: Johns Hopkins University Press.

Boon, James. 1973. "Further Operations on 'Culture' in Anthropology: A Synthesis of and for Debate." In *The Idea of Culture in the Social Sciences,* eds. Louis Schneider and Charles Bonjean. Cambridge: Cambridge University Press, 1–32.

Brinner, Benjamin. 1995. *Knowing Music, Making Music: Javanese Gamelan and the Theory of Musical Competence and Interaction.* Chicago: University of Chicago Press.

Brown, Richard. 1989 [1977]. *A Poetic for Sociology: Toward a Logic of Discovery for the Human Sciences.* Chicago: University of Chicago Press.

Burke, Kenneth. 1969. *A Grammar of Motives.* Berkeley: University of California Press.

Derrida, Jacques. 1998. *Of Grammatology.* Translated by Gayathi Chakravoity Spivak. Baltimore: Johns Hopkins University Press.

Erlmann, Veit. 1996a. *Nightsong.* Chicago: University of Chicago Press.

Fabian, Johannes. 1990. *Power and Performance: Ethnographic Explorations through Proverbial Wisdom and Theater in Shaba, Zaïre.* Madison: University of Wisconsin Press.

Feld, Steven. 1981. "'Flow Like a Waterfall': The Metaphors of Kaluli Musical Theory." *Yearbook of Traditional Music* 13: 22–47.

———. 1982. *Sound and Sentiment: Birds, Weeping, Poetics, and Song in Kaluli Expression.* Philadelphia: University of Pennsylvania Press.

Fernandez, James W. 1986. *Persuasions and Performances: The Play of Tropes in Culture.* Bloomington: Indiana University Press.

Fish, Stanley. 1980. *Is There a Text in This Class: The Authority of Interpretive Communities.* Cambridge, Mass.: Harvard University Press.

Goffman, Erving. 1959. *The Presentation of Self.* New York: Doubleday Anchor.

———. 1967. *Interaction Ritual.* New York: Doubleday Anchor.

———. 1974. *Frame Analysis.* New York: Harper & Row.

Haskell, Robert E., ed. 1987. *Cognitive and Symbolic Structures: The Psychology of Metaphoric Transformation.* Norwood, N.J.: Ablex.

Hofstadter, Douglas R. 1979. *Gödel, Escher, Bach: An Eternal Golden Braid.* New York: Basic Books.

Iser, Wolfgang. 1978. *The Act of Reading: A Theory of Aesthetic Response.* Baltimore: Johns Hopkins University Press.

Lakoff, George, and Mark Johnson. 1980. *Metaphors We Live By.* Chicago: University of Chicago Press.

Monson, Ingrid. 1996. *Saying Something: Jazz Improvisation and Interaction.* Chicago: University of Chicago Press.

Nattiez, Jean Jacques. 1991. *Music and Discourse: Toward a Semiology of Music.* Trans. Carolyn Abbate. Princeton: Princeton University Press.

Ortony, Andrew, ed. 1979. *Metaphor and Thought.* Cambridge: Cambridge University Press.

Oxford English Dictionary, The Compact Edition. 1986. 2 vols. Oxford: Oxford University Press.

Palmer, Gary B., and William R. Jankowiak. 1996. "Performance and Imagination: Toward an Anthropology of the Spectacular and the Mundane." *Cultural Anthropology* 11(2): 225–258.

Paprotté, Wolf, and René Dirven, eds. 1985. *The Ubiquity of Metaphor.* Amsterdam and Philadelphia: John Benjamins.

Park, Robert E. 1952. *Human Communities.* New York: Free Press.

Rosenblatt, Louise. 1978. *The Reader, the Text, the Poem: The Transactional Theory of Literary Work.* Carbondale: Southern Illinois University Press.

Sacks, Sheldon, ed. 1979. *On Metaphor.* Chicago: University of Chicago Press.

Shen, Yeshayahu. 1992. "Cognitive Aspects of Metaphor Comprehension: An Introduction." *Poetics Today* 13(4): 567–74.

Stone, Ruth M. 1982. *Let the Inside Be Sweet: The Interpretation of Music Event among the Kpelle of Liberia.* Bloomington: Indiana University Press.

Sugarman, Jane C. 1997. *Engendering Song: Singing and Subjectivity at Prespa Albanian Weddings.* Chicago: University of Chicago Press.

Turner, Victor. 1986. *The Anthropology of Performance.* New York: PAJ Publications.

———. 1990. "Are There Universals of Performance in Myth, Ritual, and Drama?" In *By Means of Performance: Intercultural Studies of Theatre and Ritual,* eds. Richard Schechner and Willa Appel. Cambridge: Cambridge University Press, 8–18.

Tyson, Lois. 1999. *Critical Theory Today.* New York: Garland.

Waterman, Christopher. 1990. *Jùjú: A Social History and Ethnography of an African Popular Music.* Chicago: University of Chicago Press.

Chapter 8

Cognition and Communication Theory

Cognition and communication have influenced the theoretical direction of some ethnomusicologists. The prominence of these areas for scientific research explains the prevalence of certain concepts and predilections in our discipline even if we cannot point to a significant body of contributions from these perspectives for ethnomusicology.

Cognition

Because musical performance involves cognition, it behooves the ethnomusicologist to know something of how psychologists regard this phenomenon. Cognition relies on experimental psychology, which is largely built on laboratory research. This kind of experimental investigation is very different from ethnographic research. Nevertheless, a few ethnomusicologists have skillfully blended the ethnographic and the experimental for some striking results.

Information processing theory, one of the areas incorporating ideas of cognition, emphasizes both an active and agile listener who constantly adjusts to what he or she experiences (Harwood 1976:524). Ulric Neisser, a cognitive researcher, has made major contributions in the area of naturalistic ideas of cognition. He begins with the idea of orienting schema or, as it might also be termed, **cognitive map**. Each person has a schema, which is changed continually by experience. In the process of perception, the person seeks information dynamically and is not a passive receptor (Neisser 1976:54). But Neisser goes

---

Cognitive map

- Orienting schema for perception
- Accepts information as it becomes available at sensory surfaces
- Continually changed by incoming information

---

even further to say that a schema acts as a kind of *plan* to obtain more information (Miller, Galanter, and Pribram 1960). What he proceeds to assert is that perception is a "constructive process" where the perceiver actively seeks information and is changed by information he or she picks up. This change means the perceptual schema is altered and the next action will necessarily be different. "No two perceptual acts can be identical" (Neisser 1976:57). In the end, perception is an active rather than passive process. Furthermore, Neisser sees the process as a continuously interacting or cybernating one—rather a flow of information from the "periphery to the mind" (23).

Listening

As far as listening is concerned, Neisser (1976) notes,

> The listener continuously develops more or less specific readiness (anticipations) for what will come next, based on information he has already picked up. These anticipations—which themselves must be formulated in terms of temporal patterns, not of isolated movements—govern what he will pick up next, and in turn are modified by it. (28)

Neisser suggests to us that listening is a complex, active process in which listeners are searching for sound and then constantly being changed by what information they receive. This model fundamentally challenges the idea that an audience members are passive vessels waiting to be filled with sound and musical experience. Rather, their minds are much more active and searching as they seeks the sound than would be the case with passive audience members.

Cognitive Issues in Ethnomusicology

The cognitive area has been of interest to music scholars for a very long time, going back to Hermann Helmholtz's work on perception (1863). As Carol L. Krumhansl (1995:54) notes, much of the music research since that time has centered on the topic of consonance. Then in the mid-1950s two books broadened the exchange between music theory and psychology. One of these, *Emotion and Meaning in Music* by Leonard Meyer (1956), relied on "Gestalt psychology, motivation and emotion, learning, and information theory." The second, *La Perception de la musique* by Robert Francès (originally published in 1958), explored the "perception of melody, harmony, tonality, and atonality, using a wide range of methods, musical materials, and levels of training" (Krumhansl 1995:54).

The work that followed in the 1970s, particularly by scholars such as Carol Krumhansl (Krumhansl 1979, Krumhansl and Shepard [1979]), Jay Dowling (1972, 1978), and Lola Cuddy (Cuddy and Cohen 1976; Cuddy and Miller 1979) emphasized a cognitive orientation and offered insights into listeners' schemas.

Ethnomusicologists have conducted a range of studies using cognitive orientations. One collection of these studies is found in the volume *Ethnomusicology and Music Cognition,* published as an issue of *The World of Music* and edited by Ellen Koskoff (1992).

Benjamin Brinner (1995), among ethnomusicologists, has looked to cognition in his study of central Javanese gamelan performance. He uses cognition concepts in connection with other linguistic ideas such as "competence" that have become commonplace to the vocabulary of many scholars. He asserts, "Analogy is one of the musician's most powerful tools, channeling the application of generalized music making procedures to specific frameworks according to perceived similarities between these frameworks" (28). He also extends Neisser's idea of schemata to a broader level (see also Davidson and Torff 1992). Brinner builds on Norma McLeod and Marsha Herndon's definition of competence as "an idealized conceptualization of possible rules setting a style" (1980:188). "I think it is essential to consider how competence varies in type and degree within a musical community as a result of individual motivation and ability in response to community options and demands" (1995:31). Furthermore, he sees competence as "an entity that changes throughout individual lives and over the history of a community and tradition, as something that can be grasped at a given moment as a frozen representation of a dynamic, multidimensional flow" (1995:32). He then outlines domains of competence that operate along the procedural/declarative, explicit/intuitive, and active/passive continua (1995:47). These are areas of cognitive activity that can be explored. To illustrate he notes, "Cuing and all the related procedures constitute a complex domain . . . [that] requires, for example, that players of the leading melodic instruments have active knowledge of the introductions to hundreds of pieces. Other musicians need only a passive knowledge of these introductions so that they can recognize them and join in the performance" (1995:57).

Margarita Mazo has skillfully blended ethnographic and experimental work to study Russian laments. Armed with ethnographic research on the use of laments in rural Russia, she then submitted the recorded laments to spectrographic analysis. The spectrograms of the laments helped indicate aspects of pitch contour, voice timbre, and breathing patterns (Mazo 1994: 164–211).

In a related vein, Cornelia Fales has explored the cognitive dimension that she calls "auditory illusion." Her fieldwork took place in Burundi, East Africa, where she recorded voices whispering while the very low-pitched trough zither, *inanga,* was being played. But Fales found that the listener's impression that the whispered song was pitched resulted when the listener mentally transferred the pitches from the *inanga* to the voice—thus the illusion. One could easily notice that the pitches were being played by the trough zither and the performer was whispering, not singing (1993). The cognitive activity became a point of focus for Fales in the laboratory as well, where she was able

Plate 19 Margarita Mazo. Courtesy of Margarita Mazo.

with computer analysis to discover timbral qualities that made transfer of the trough zither sound to the voice cognitively possible.

Cognition: Conclusion

Cognition theory embraces a range of approaches that emphasize analysis of the perceptual process. Over time the understanding of that process has become more and more complex. The perceptual process is assumed to be one where the mind is actively seeking data and the schema in the mind is

Plate 20 Cornelia Fales. Photo by K. A. MacDonald.

being continually updated based on experience. Although the work in psychology has emphasized experimental research, ethnomusicologists have used cognitive concepts and explored them with ethnographic as well as experimental research.

Communication Theory

Communication theory has had an important, if somewhat diffuse, impact on the ideas in ethnomusicology. Early communication theories were quite rudimentary, with a diagram often showing a listener receiving a message from a sender, illustrated by an arrow drawn between sender and listener. One could almost visualize the two individuals, each sending a message over a string from speaker to receiver. These straightforward models had considerable influence on our visualization and conceptualization process of the perceptual process.

But much more pertinent to our study is the **semiotic-cybernetic model of communication** outlined by Doede Nauta in his book *The Meaning of Information*.

It was semiotic in that it acknowledged the processing of syntactic, semantic, and pragmatic meaning. It was cybernetic in that it provided a feedback loop from receiver back to sender. This critical feedback then served to modify further the performance by the original sender.

Like Neisser, Nauta (1972:5) asserts that the cognitive map, existing in a purposeful state, is transformed as a result of the interpretation of environmental stimuli, this transformation leading to goal-directed behavior. Such ideas emphasize the active, constructive nature of cognition.

To illustrate, semiotic cybernetic communication theory could be used to analyze a performance of Kpelle music in Liberia. If the audience members especially liked what they heard, one of them might walk to the center of the performance circle and call for a pause so that he or she could praise the singer and offer a token gift. This gesture is interpreted as feedback, which the singers hear and at which they rejoice. Then the female soloist begins with even greater enthusiasm the next phase of her performance. She has modified her performance based on audience response to her initial singing. The reliance on such a model of performance prompted me (1982:8) to make the following assumption in my research of performance among the Kpelle: Music communication is a dynamic ongoing process in which participants, including performer and audience, interpret symbolic behavior.

Semiotic-cybernetic model of communication

- Framework that involves the processing of syntactic, semantic, and pragmatic meaning
- Provides a feedback loop from audience back to performer
- Feedback modifies further performance of the performer

The idea that interaction and music performance in particular is multichanneled comes also from communication theory. Thus music utilizes the audio-acoustic channel, as well as other channels such as the kinesthetic-visual channel. Multiple channels can operate at differential levels at any time and may use different codes (Birdwhistell 1970:70).

Communication Theory in Ethnomusicology

It is difficult to point to any studies in ethnomusicology that rely exclusively on communication theory. But there are some connections that should be noted. One of the most powerful concepts—feedback—was pointed out by Alan P. Merriam (1964) in the model he presented in *The Anthropology of Music*. Although he was espousing a largely structural functional model, the feedback aspect derived from communication theory has since been used by a number of ethnomusicologists (Greene 1999:476–78; Shelemay 1998:2; Stone and Stone 1981).

Another concept that has infiltrated the models of ethnomusicologists is that of multichannel communication. Thus ethnomusicologists to a great degree acknowledge that the kinesthetic channel, among other channels, is important to the total understanding of the musical performance, although they may not analyze it to any great extent. A few dance specialists, however, do analyze the kinesthetic channel in considerable detail and recognize the communication theory concepts (Kaeppler 1972).

Feedback Interview Example from Kpelle Performance

Feedback as an analytical concept implies that the researcher is focusing on the process and not merely the product of communication. One technique I have used, which centers on the feedback concept, is the **feedback interview**. This type of interview I defined as "the playback and recall of a completed event in which the participant and researcher attempt to reconstruct its meaning" (Stone 1982:52). The occasion of the feedback interview is a new interaction situation and cannot be assumed to be identical to the original event (Stone and Stone 1981). The device for triggering memory and assisting recall can be an actual instrument, a photograph, or a videotape of the earlier event that was recorded.

Feedback interview

- Playback and recall of a completed event in which the participant and researcher attempt to reconstruct its meaning
- New situation that is not identical to the original event
- Device for triggering memory that can be a videotape, audiotape, photograph, or the actual instrument that was played

At one point in my doctoral research in 1976, I showed Kpelle musicians the pictures of instruments in Hugo Zemp's book, *Musique Dan* (1971) because he had worked among a neighboring group in Côte d'Ivoire some years earlier. The photographs generated a lively discussion among the assembled musicians, and in one case talk of an instrument used in the ritual situations, which had not previously been mentioned to me in the course of my research. Without this feedback interview, I might never have known about the instrument.

At another time during my research in 1975–76, I used videotape as the memory recall device. Videotape recorded visual and aural images with far greater accuracy and speed than a researcher could do with a pen and pad. The advantage of a continuous record of iconic images was obvious. The opportunity for processual analysis was clearly important for the ethnomusicologist. Three-dimensional objects and events, for example, were encoded into electronic impulses that were later displayed as two-dimensional objects. Videotape recording abstracted iconic information far less than notes, and the iconic codes were quickly learned and perceived by people cross-culturally (Worth 1969:305; Ekman, Friesen, and Taussig 1969:240–43). The Kpelle people I worked with in the mid-1970s certainly had no difficulty viewing the videotapes and commenting on the performance they reviewed.

As Kpelle people commented about the videotape they were viewing, I recorded the verbal aspects on audiotape for later study, transcription, and translation. As one dancer, Kpete Dang, my research assistant, Yakpalo, and I watched, we recorded the followed audio exchange to a performance by the ensemble from Gbeyilataa.

RUTH STONE:	What dance is he doing?
KPETE DANG:	He is passing his feet behind each other.
RS:	That. . . what is that?
KD:	That, that is *solimo* he's dancing.
RS:	Oh.
YAKPALO:	What thing?
KD:	*Solimo*.
RS:	Oh.
KD:	Yes.
RS:	What is he imitating?
KD:	That's *Koli-gong* song's hook.
RS:	His what?
KD:	His hook.
RS:	Oh, hook.

By watching the video, Kpete Dang could isolate a specific dance step and give it a verbal label, *solimo*. This was infinitely easier than my attempt at a verbal description or my own feeble try to demonstrate the dance movement. I could then show the same tape segment to other audience members and ask them the same question.

Beyond identifying or labeling dance steps, the feedback interview also provoked more complex analysis than might otherwise emerge. In watching the same event, somewhat later in the tape, we entered a complicated analytic area:

KPETE DANG: Yes, they don't cut off the edge.

RS: What does it mean?

When a person leaves [the dance area] won't he cut the edge?

KD: He just keeps dancing . . . you just Keep dancing . . . you just keep dancing.

This description of a dance clarified for me that no ending cue was used to frame a segment when the dance is ritualistic. In Kpelle ritual, one must create a continuous structure. It was in the course of just such a feedback interview that I discovered this very fundamental principle of creating music, which had never been revealed in conversation or other types of interviews. For as Kpete Dang finally said a bit later, "You know, it's on the word of the medicine. They can't cut off the edge of the performance."

Conversely, in entertainment music, the idea was to segment the music into many short bits both over time and between parts. Furthermore, it was important to signal the end cue clearly in entertainment performance.

After questioning several people about this same segment of tape, I found unanimity about the contrast between lack of ending cues in ritual and clear ending cues in entertainment music. Thus I took a concept that was central to communication theory—feedback—and found a technique, feedback interview, to explore the feedback aspect of musical communication.

Conclusion

Cognition and communication theory are two approaches to theory that have emerged from experimental science and have found important utility in the humanities. They are distinct from earlier orientations that have been considered because of their association with psychology. As yet there is not a distinctive body of studies that have used cognitive psychology or communication theory in ethnomusicology. As a result, it is difficult to point to very many contributions in the field. Nevertheless, recent interest indicates these might be emerging approaches. If one can point to a so-called hot area in ethnomusicology today, cognition would be it. Panels at scholarly meetings show evidence of this increased interest and buzz in the field. Particularly when paired with computer analysis, it will be interesting to see to how ethnomusicology joins the ethnographic with the experimental.

References

Birdwhistell, Ray L. 1970. *Kinesics and Context.* Philadelphia: University of Pennsylvania Press.

Brinner, Benjamin. 1995. *Knowing Music, Making Music: Javanese Gamelan and the Theory of Musical Competence and Interaction.* Chicago: University of Chicago Press.

Cuddy, Lola L., and Annabel J. Cohen. 1976. "Recognition of Transposed Melodic Sequences." *Quarterly Journal of Experimental Psychology* 28: 255–70.

Cuddy, Lola L., and Janet Miller. 1979. "Melody Recognition: The Experimental Application of Musical Rules." *Canadian Journal of Psychology* 33: 148–57.

Davidson, Lyle, and Bruce Torff. 1991. "Situated Cognition in Music." *World of Music* 34(3): 120–39.

Dowling, W. Jay. 1972. "Recognition of Melodic Transformations: Inversion, Retrograde, and Retrograde Inversion." *Perception and Psychophysics* 12: 417–21.

———. 1978. "Scale and Contour: Two Components of a Theory of Memory for Melodies." *Psychological Review* 85: 341–54.

Ekman, P., W. Frieson, and T. Taussig. 1969. "II VIR-R and SCAN: Tools and Methods for the Automated Analysis of Visual Records." In *Content Analysis,* eds. G. Gerbner, O. Holsti, K. Krippendorff, W. Paisley, and P. Stone. New York: Wiley.

Fales, Cornelia. 1993. "Auditory Illusion and Cognitive Patterns in Whispered Inanga of Burundi." Ph.D. diss., Indiana University.

Francès, Robert. 1988. *The Perception of Music.* Translated by W. Jay Dowling. Hillsdale, N.J.: Erlbaum; originally published in 1958 as *La Perception de la musique.* Paris: J. Vrin.

Greene, Paul D. 1999. "Sound Engineering in a Tamil Village: Playing Audio Cassettes as Devotional Performance." *Ethnomusicology* 43(3): 459–89.

Harwood, Dane L. 1976. "Universals in Music: A Perspective from Cognitive Psychology." *Ethnomusicology* 20(3): 521–33.

Helmholtz, Hermann L. F. 1863. *Die Lehre von den Tonempfindungen als Physiologische Grundlage für die Theorie der Musik.* Braunschweig: F. Viweg und Sohn. 1954. *On the Sensations of Tone as a Physiological Basis for the Theory of Music.* Edited and translated by A. J. Ellis. New York: Dover.

Koskoff, Ellen, ed. 1992. "Ethnomusicology and Music Cognition." *The World of Music* 34(3). Includes bibliographical references.

Krumhansl, Carol L. 1979. "The Psychological Representation of a Musical Pitch in a Tonal Context." *Cognitive Psychology* 11: 346–74.

———. 1995. "Music Psychology and Music Theory: Problems and Prospects." *Music Theory Spectrum* 17(1): 53–80.

———, and Roger N. Shepard. 1979. "Quantification of the Hierarchy of Tonal Functions within a Diatonic Context." *Journal of Experimental Psychology: Human Perception and Performance* 5: 579–94.

Kaeppler, Adrienne L. 1972. "Method and Theory in Analyzing Dance Structure with an Analysis of Tongan Dance." *Ethnomusicology* 16(2): 173–21.

Laske, Otto E. 1977. *Music, Memory and Thought: Explorations in Cognitive Musicology.* Ann Arbor: University Microfilms.

Mazo, Margarita. 1994. "Lament Made Visible: A Study of Paramusical Elements in Russian Lament." In *Theme and Variations*, eds. Bell Yung and Joseph S. C. Lam. Cambridge: Department of Music, Harvard University and Hong Kong: The Institute of Chinese Studies, The Chinese University of Hong Kong, 1164–1210.

McLeod, Norma, and Marsha Herndon. 1980. *Ethnography of Musical Performance.* Norwood, Pa.: Norwood Editions.

Merriam, Alan P. 1964. *The Anthropology of Music.* Evanston: Northwestern University Press.

Meyer, Leonard B. 1956. *Emotion and Meaning in Music.* Chicago: University of Chicago Press.

Miller, G. A., Galanter, E., and Pribram, K. H. 1960. *Plans and the Structure of Behavior.* New York: Holt, Rinehart & Winston.

Nauta, Doede. 1972. *The Meaning of Information.* The Hague: Mouton.

Neisser, Ulric. 1976. *Cognition and Reality.* San Francisco: W. H. Freeman.

Shelemay, Kay Kaufman. 1998. *Let Jasmine Rain Down: Song and Remembrance among Syrian Jews.* Chicago: University of Chicago Press.

Stone, Ruth M. 1982. *Let the Inside Be Sweet: The Interpretation of Music Event among the Kpelle of Liberia.* Bloomington: Indiana University Press.

———, and Verlon L. Stone. 1981. "Event, Feedback, and Analysis: Research Media in the Study of Music Events." *Ethnomusicology* 25(2): 215–25.

Worth, Sol. "The Development of a Semiotic of Film." *Semiotica* 1: 282–321.

Chapter | 9

Performance Theory in Ethnomusicology

The term **performance theory** for an ethnomusicologist points to a range of meanings. In musicology, the idea of "performance practice" (*Afführungs praxis*) has long referred to ways of interpreting scores that are passed down in the performing culture, in contrast to details written in notation. The second focus of performance theory draws not from this musicological vision but rather from the broader sense of performance theory developed by folklorists to explain oral performance, drawing on sociolinguistics in the 1970s. Yet a third aspect of performance theory has been that used to explain theatrical performance of all kinds A fourth kind of performance theory—**cultural performance**—comes from anthropology and the work of scholars like Milton Singer, working with large-scale cultural festivals. A fifth kind of performance might encompass the concept of "performativity," which scholars like Judith Butler (1997) use to encompass everyday behavior. This final use of performance, however, is in conflict with other definitions of performance that see daily life as quite distinct and separate. Whereas the first—musicological

---

Performance theory

- Framework for analysis to explain oral performance drawing on sociolinguistics, theatrical performance, or musicology

---

Cultural performance

- Unit of analysis in large-scale societies in which people exhibit their culture to themselves and visitors
- Focus is on the performance as a totality and its relationship to the larger society
- Associated with the work of Milton Singer, among others in anthropology

focus—has tended to be much more specific, the folkloric, theatrical, and anthropological foci have been much broader. What all the performance approaches share is that they move away from the score or text as object.

Folklorists Roger Abrahams and Richard Bauman, working in the second sense of performance theory and drawing synergy from an influential essay by Dell Hymes (1975), reacted to the historic-geographic classification of texts and motifs in the discipline of folklore, in which texts were analyzed largely in separation from the context of their creation. They proposed correctives to this earlier approach and called for recognition of strategic devices employed to create a performance (Abrahams 1970, 1972, 1975). Bauman (1975) emphasized performance as a "display of communicative competence" (293). To distinguish performance from other kinds of behavior, he pointed to the following characteristics:

1. Special codes, reserved for and diagnostic of performance
2. Special formulae that signal performance
3. Figurative language such as metaphor
4. Formal stylistic devices
5. Special prosodic patterns of tempo, stress, pitch
6. Special paralinguistic patterns of voice quality and vocalization
7. Appeal to tradition
8. Disclaimer of performance (295)

Assumptions

Performance theory as developed by Bauman and his colleagues made the following assumptions:

1. *Performance enhances experience, bringing a greater intensity of communication between performer and audience.* The special characteristics of performance contribute to making performance a special arena of experience that is rich with communicative devices of many sorts.
2. *The goal of research is to study performance as a series of strategic devices that serve to structure the performance.* The strategic devices—special formulae, stylistics devices, and paralinguistic devices—help shape the process of creating the performance.
3. *The formal properties of the performance are of central interest to analysis of performance.* The scaffolding of performance is a central focus of research and forms the basis of performance study inquiry.
4. *Semiotic structures, through metapoetics, allow performers to imaginatively comment upon themselves and provide cultural self-definition.* (Bauman 1984 [1977]:29) There are multiple layers of performance, some of which provide the opportunity for reflexivity.

Performance theory, as developed by Bauman, relied heavily on the Russian formalists for many concepts. The theory went beyond Russian formalism, however, in emphasizing the emergent quality of performance, which Bauman (1977) says, "resides in the interplay between communicative resources, individual competence, and the goals of the participant, within the context of the particular situations" (38). He also maintains that verbal art terms should be understood as part of the larger "social and cultural systems organizing the social use of language" (Bauman 1986:9).

The burgeoning performance-centered studies, particularly in folklore, shifted research away from texts and text fragments that were examined for content to a careful analysis of the creative strategies that produced these texts. Naturally, such research created an emphasis on individuals rather than on anonymous producers. Repertoires of stories from tellers such as Ed Bell from Texas became the basis for an entire monograph (Bauman 1986).

Performance theory in folklore drew its inspiration largely from sociolinguistics and in many ways can be seen as an extension of the linguistic models. In the case of performance theory studies, however, data were largely ethnographic, derived from fieldwork rather than idealized as Noam Chomsky might have advocated.

Another branch of performance theory emerged, largely through the work of Richard Schechner and his students. As a director of theatrical productions, Schechner (1985, 1988) naturally relied on dramaturgical ideas to explain performance. He spoke of concepts like "rehearsals" in performance events in an approach very reminiscent of the dramaturgical explanations of Erving Goffman and Victor Turner.

Schechner (1985), drawing from both Gregory Bateson and Victor Turner, sought to explain the "ritual and cognitive underpinnings of theatrical performance in detail." He emphasized the intricate process of preparation and rehearsal that undergirds the theatrical performance. Finally, he attempted to link dramatic performances to everyday life (Beeman 1993:372). He analyzed a seance as a drama, for example, pointing out issues of performance practice on the part of the medium.

Barbara Kirschenblatt-Gimblett (1999), who has taught with Schechner in the Performance Studies Department at New York University, extended the definition of performance studies:

> By theorizing embodiment, event, and agency in relation to live . . . performance, Performance Studies can potentially offer something of a counterweight to the emphasis in Cultural Studies on literature and media and on text as an extended metaphor for culture. (1)

She also pointed out that performance studies were particularly attuned to issues of place, personhood, cultural citizenship, and equity (7).

Performance theory has also been used in yet a slightly different way by anthropologists like Milton Singer. Specializing in South Asian studies, Singer (1955:23) identified "cultural performances" as the unit of analysis in large-scale societies. In these performances he included not only concerts and plays but also rituals and festivals. Cultural performances are important, Singer maintained, because it is here that people exhibit their culture in large-scale societies to themselves as well as to visitors. They could in a sense be considered a microcosm of the larger culture. The focus here was on the performance and its relationship to the larger society, considering the implications of the performance for the society.

Performance theory has also been applied to the very process of ethnographic study because like telling a story or staging a play, ethnographic research provides meaning for experience (Kapchan 1995:483).

> Ethnography, like performance, is intersubjective, depending on an audience, a community or a group to which it is responsible, however heterogeneous the participants may be. In its concern with a self-critical methodology that takes account of its effects in the world, ethnography is first and foremost performative—aware of itself as a living script in which meaning is emergent. (Kapchan 1995:484)

Performance theory becomes an explanatory tool not just for performance that a researcher is studying but for the very process of research as a kind of meta-theory. As Kapchan presents it, this form of performance theory is highly aware of indigenous perspectives: "Such performative ethnography incorporates indigenous theory while indexing history as embodied in social practice" (1995:500, as quoted in Wong 2001:xxiv–xxv).

Critique

1. **Performance theory may but does not always stress the analyst's point of view to the neglect of that of the performer or audience member in seeking to understanding the performance.**

   Although the analyst's perspective has not been as strongly emphasized in more recent work, early performance theory relied heavily on the researcher's perspective.

2. **Although process is of concern to performance studies scholars, relatively few studies have addressed process in a detailed way.**

   One recent study by Bauman (2004) that does address processual issues explores how speakers align their oral performances with those of others and explores what he calls the "webs of intertextual resonance" (128). These webs link discursive moments that may be only a speaker away or much more separated by many speakers and many decades.

Contributions

1. **The context of creating the text gains attention because artistic performance is anchored in the particularity of its creation.**

   This breakthrough is a significant advance from considering the text to be a fixed entity to be analyzed as an object consisting of parts such as motifs.

2. **Performance theory brings an awareness of structural devices.**

   The craft of creating the text is studied here and scholars examine the devices selected to construct that text.

3. **Performance theory addresses issues of power that are evident in strategies of the various performers.**

   The consideration of the unequal distribution of power received attention in performance studies. Like Marxist theory, performance theory studied how people used power in their performance.

4. **Performance theory addresses issues of emergence and indeterminacy.**

   In its concern with the making of performance, the way performers create the story or song over time becomes a focus. Performance theory helps highlight decision points and the multiple directions that performance can move rather than simply consisting of a preformed text.

Performance Theory in Ethnomusicology

In the field of ethnomusicology, Norma McLeod and Marcia Herndon—both colleagues of Bauman at the University of Texas at the time—addressed performance theory in ethnomusicology. McLeod (1966) focused on issues of performance in her doctoral dissertation. Herndon (1971:340) went on to create a performance studies–specific definition of **occasion** as an encapsulated expression of the shared cognitive forms and values of a society, which includes not only the music itself but also the totality of associated behavior and underlying concepts. It is usually a named event with a beginning and an end, varying degrees of organization of activity, audience, performances, and location.

McLeod and Herndon (1980) also compiled a group of essays about performance entitled *The Ethnography of Musical Performance*. Aside from sharing the idea that context is critical to understanding a performance, they did not develop music performance to a depth parallel to that of the folklorists.

Somewhat later, Gerard Béhague, colleague of all of these people at the University of Texas, edited *Performance Practice: Ethnomusicological*

Occasion

- An encapsulated expression of shared cognitive forms and values
- Includes not only music but the totality of associated behavior and underlying concepts
- Usually a named event with a beginning and end
- Varying degrees of organization of activity, audience, performances, and location

Perspectives (1984), in which he pointed in the introductory essay to the importance of shifting from the somewhat narrow musicological notions and moving toward performance theory as explicated by folklorists. The contributing authors described performance in a variety of world settings without extensive reference to "performance theory" as practiced by the folklorists. The implicit theory they used was much more eclectic and sometimes closer to the idea of "performance practice" in musicology as they detailed explanation for nuances of performance.

A great number of ethnomusicologists have found the explanatory devices of performance theory in folklore, theater, and anthropology to be very compatible with their notions of how best to research music. In practice, however, there are few studies paralleling the theoretical sophistication of the folklore, theater, and anthropology works.

Performance Theory in a Kpelle Situation

A performance of the Woi epic provides us with an example that we can study from the performance theory perspective. Although the various branches of performance theory would offer many different elements to be examined, I focus in this case on the issue of the management of information (c.f. Bauman 1986:33–53).

The Woi epic centers on the superhuman hero Woi, who is traveling with his large extended family. As they move, they encounter obstacles, and Woi confronts those obstacles so he may make progress toward the coast, which lies ahead. The performance of the epic is led by the epic "pourer"—storyteller, singer, conductor. When I recorded this performance in Totota, Kulung, an itinerant performer, had come to the market day with the Gbeyilataa people. The local townspeople comprised the chorus that sings as a background to his narration and dramatization of the story. Several people also played a percussive background pattern on two beer bottles, interlocking their rhythmic patterns.

I focus my analysis on this particular performance, particularly on the third episode of pouring the epic. In episode three, as it was performed on the day I heard it, a feast was cooked for Spider, one of the living beings to which Woi's wife gave birth. Spider was brought into the world so he could play the slit drum, a hollowed-out struck log. The slit-drum music he played was intended to aid the blacksmith in pumping bellows and forging a needle so Woi's battle clothes might be sewn.

The episode opened with a tuning-in period when the fabric of the event—essentially backstage interchanges—was exhibited for all to experience. Kulung demonstrated the choral response, and the chorus then began to sing the part the pourer had shown them. Then Kulung admonished the chorus, which was simultaneously most of the audience, "Answer the song well so that my bad name doesn't remain with the woman. Because of the thing, the thing I did of old." He was exhorting them to perform so he would not feel ashamed in front of the researcher.

Once the warm-up allowed chorus and pourer to achieve a degree of synchrony, the audience member designated as the questioner asked the formulaic question: "Whose voice is that?" When he didn't get an immediate answer, he asked again, "What thing's song is that again?"

Kulung, the pourer, responded, "Spider, Father-Spider. He's the one playing the Slit-Drum." In the structuring of epic, the appropriate frame for the episode had now been established. The questioner had asked the audience, who was the dominant character for the episode, and the pourer had identified him.

One other feature that helped establish the frame was the other mini-exchange that took place between the pourer and questioner. The questioner said, "Don't lie to me here," and Kulung responded, "Very close. Lying, I lie to you? Isn't it piassava that has split over me?" The question posed about lying proved to be a way of establishing the genre that was being performed. By introducing the suggestion of lying, the questioner immediately moved us all to realize that this would be one of the imaginative forms of Kpelle expression in which exaggeration is expected and valued. The pourer confirmed that this was, indeed, one of these imaginative genres by denying that he will be lying. The audience was familiar with this formulaic questioning and denial. The pourer even drew on a figure of speech—"piassava has split over my head"—to reinforce his statement.

The breaking of piassava is an expression that indicates something important has happened. Thus the pourer is saying to the questioner, "Do you think I'd lie when something so important has happened?" And the audience knows that lying and exaggeration are part of the expectation. This formula helps clue the audience concerning what to expect.

With the leading character identified and the frame of the episode set, the third episode of the epic began to unfold. The pourer, Kulung, began,

> They cooked rice, they set it out. They cooked sweet potatoes, they set it out. They cut cassava, they set it out. They cooked eddoes, they set them out. Every kind of food they circled round him. As he eats, he plays the slit-drum.

The pourer was narrating a familiar pattern as he showed that the food fueled the slit-drum playing. And the familiar pattern of greed emerged as Spider said, "The people brought me here to play the slit-drum. Woi brought me here and the food isn't adequate." And the people responded, "Cook new rice."

At this point, the narrator switched into "deep" Kpelle to comment on the situation. The "deep" Kpelle would be understood by a knowledgeable few and not all the people. Kulung sang, "The Poro is on a person; the matter angers him. Night falls on him; the daylight bewitches him." This was a proverb with a range of meanings. But in this setting it could be interpreted as applying to Spider, who sat there without enough food to satisfy him. He was, however, obliged to play and not able to show his anger. Now if the audience didn't comprehend the point Kulung was making here, he immediately followed with another proverb to amplify his point. "The large, large rooster, the hen's voice is sweet, the rooster crows the dawn." This proverb showed yet another way of expressing the dilemma in which Spider found himself.

Even though a hen has a finer voice, it is the rooster who gets the honor of announcing the morning. The person most deserving, in this case Spider, may not always be the one rewarded. Although Spider plays well, his reward depends on the generosity of the people serving him.

An analysis of the performance to this point establishes the multiple roles played by the pourer. The epic pourer is telling a story in this epic. He is also attempting to manage the story he tells so as to plead his case as a pourer in the frame of everyday life. Rather than accent the greediness of Spider, he emphasizes Spider's servitude and dependence on the hosts. Thus Kulung, in showing the plight of Spider, assumes an unexpected viewpoint. In doing so, Kulung's motive is apparent. He can draw attention to his own dependence on the audience with allusive devices. Indirectness is his mode of managing this information.

Another clue that Kulung intends to draw a parallel to his own situation is that in between the narration he comments, "Keapee, look at me, Keapee, look at me . . . I didn't know this place." He is addressing me, the researcher and sponsor of this particular performance, as a way of making his case without directly asking for a reward for his singing.

Kulung, the pourer, takes the trickster figure and manages his presentation of Spider in a surprising way that both entertains and aligns the Spider's plight to that of an itinerant performer. The clever and strategic management of information by the epic pourer is essential to understanding the performance process and the decisions that performers make not only in the aesthetic aspects of the performance but also in the structuring of the event.

Conclusion

Performance theory, particularly as developed by folklorists and performance studies scholars, has found considerable resonance with ethnomusicologists. It has been used, along with other theories, by ethnomusicologists and helps illuminate strategic devices, in particular, in musical performance.

References

Abrahams, Roger. 1970. "A Performance-Centered Approach to Gossip." *Man* 5: 290–301.

———. 1972. "Folklore and Literature as Performance." *Journal of the Folklore Institute* 9: 75–94.

Bauman, Richard. 1975. "Verbal Art as Performance." *American Anthropologist* 77: 290–311.

———. 1984 [1977]. *Verbal Art as Performance.* Prospect Heights, Ill.: Waveland Press.

———. 1986. *Story, Performance, and Event: Contextual Studies of Oral Narrative.* Cambridge: Cambridge University Press.

———. 2004. *A World of Others' Words*. Oxford: Blackwell.

Beeman, William O. 1993. "The Anthropology of Theater and Spectacle." *Annual Review of Anthropology* 22: 369–93.

Béhague, Gerard. 1984. *Performance Practice: Ethnomusicological Perspectives*. Westport, Conn.: Greenwood Press.

Butler, Judith. 1997. *Excitable Speech: A Politics of the Performative*. London: Routledge.

Herndon, Marcia. 1971. "The Cherokee Ballgame Cycle: An Ethnomusicologist's View." *Ethnomusicology* 15(3): 339–52.

Hymes, Dell. 1975. "Breakthrough into Performance." In *Folklore, Performance and Communication*, eds. Dan Ben-Amos and Kenneth Goldstein. The Hague: Mouton.

Kapchan, Deborah A. 1995. "Performance." *Journal of American Folklore* 108(430): 479–508.

Kirschenblatt-Gimblett, Barbara. 1999. "Performance Studies." *Culture and Creativity*. New York: Rockefeller Foundation. www.nyu/classes/bkg/issues/rock2.htm (accessed October 7, 2005).

McLeod, Norma. 1966. "Some Techniques of Analysis for Non-Western Music." PhD diss., Northwestern University.

———, and Marcia Herndon. 1980. *Ethnography of Musical Performance*. Norwood, Pa.: Norwood Editions.

Schechner, Richard. 1985. *Between Theater and Anthropology*. Philadelphia: University of Pennsylvania Press.

———. 1988. *Performance Theory*. New York: Routledge.

Singer, Milton. 1955. "The Cultural Pattern of India." *The Far Eastern Quarterly* 15: 23–26.

Wong, Deborah. 2001. *Sounding the Center: History and Aesthetics in Thai Buddhist Performance*. Chicago: University of Chicago Press.

Gender, Ethnicity, and Identity Issues

Gender, ethnicity, and other identity issues affect all theoretical orientations in significant ways. They are, however, of a somewhat different order than other theories we have previously considered. Each of these issues frequently becomes enfolded and incorporated into various other theories. For we cannot eliminate issues of gender, for example, when we undertake a structuralist study or a postmodernist study. Therefore, the issues in this chapter have a kind of overarching influence on the theoretical orientations in this book, although they are in some cases and by some scholars identified as "theories."

Gender/Feminism

Gender treats issues associated with cultural concepts of maleness and femaleness that ultimately affect both the performance and analysis of music. Furthermore, because the researcher is part of the social situation of fieldwork, the researcher's gender and orientation to gender becomes a relevant issue, specifically the researcher's own interpretation of self. For example, when planning research in a West Asian society, the researcher must carefully ascertain how he or she will be received. In some areas, a proposal by a female researcher to conduct a study of men's singing may result in little face-to-face study of the performance. Concomitantly, if a male researcher proposed to study women's wedding parties, he would hardly find much access to the performances he chose to analyze. But there are research situations in which a female researcher might be granted a kind of gender-neutral status and be allowed to participate in situations that would ordinarily be inaccessible. The gender issues are interpreted by the people who are being studied, and these issues influence what access the host community is willing to grant the researcher. Such negotiations can be very complicated.

If we look at the history of ethnomusicology, there are a number of factors that impinge on issues of gender. In the early years, in particular, the discipline was male dominated, although in recent years more women have been obtaining advanced degrees. How has this affected the studies that have been done? Intellectual historians of our field have yet to examine these issues in detail, although Charlotte Frisbie conducted an analysis of women's participation in the Society for Ethnomusicology from 1952 to 1961. Although she noted that women were welcomed into roles as officers, these women did suffer discrimination in "their personal and professional lives" (Frisbie 1991:257).

The Society for Ethnomusicology, as a major professional organization, has a committee for gender as well as a committee for gay, lesbian, and bisexual issues. The members who proposed the formation of these committees in the 1990s deemed it important to collaborate on topics related to gender for academic presentations as well as for mutual support.

Under the broad rubric of gender, feminism has been a topic and focus of both researchers and the broader public. There are some assumptions that undergird **feminist theory**, granting that there is a broad range of interpretation possible under the heading of gender and feminism.

Feminist Theory: Assumptions

1. **According to feminist theorists, a patriarchy is a self-perpetuating ideological system that keeps men and women in gender roles in which male dominance prevails.**

   One version of this assumption holds that male dominance prevails in many societies around the world. Women, this assumption maintains, are dominated by men in a great number of places across the globe.

2. **A woman in these contexts is marginalized and is "othered" in that she is defined by how she deviates from male norms.**

   Women are interpreted as a deviation from the standard norms, defined by male standards for behavior. Thus they are considered to be outside the mainstream.

Feminist theory

- Research framework that focuses on gender politics, gender inequality, and sexuality

---

Patriarchy

- A social situation in which male members of a society predominate in positions of power whether as individuals or as a collective

3. **Western civilization, and some would maintain all cultures, are deeply grounded in a patriarchal ideology.**

   The male dominance runs deep in societies in the West as well as—according to some views—in all cultures, permeating daily life and how people interact with one another.

4. **Culture shapes gender and the behavior associated with it.**

   The focus here is on the dominance of men in a broad range of situations, resulting in the effect that women are sidelined and not regarded in any kind of equal or equivalent position.

A dominant emphasis in the early years of feminism was that the theoretical work of scholars should include an activist approach to make substantial changes in the society within which people live and work. Although some feminists continue to hold to this goal, others do not articulate such an emphasis.

One of the highly visible scholars in recent years has been Judith Butler. She has questioned some of the very foundations of feminist thought, beginning most notably in her book *Gender Trouble* (1990) and continuing in *Bodies That Matter: On the Discursive Limits of "Sex"* (1993). She espoused a performative theory of gender in which gender is not simply a fixed category but is rather repetitively enacted, producing the illusion of a stable concept of gender. She questioned the degree to which people have real agency in the enactment and to what extent their acts are coerced. Her main focus, however, has been in challenging a static gender binary. Butler (1988) says,

> Regardless of the pervasive character of patriarchy and the prevalence of sexual difference as an operative cultural distinction, there is nothing about a binary gender system that is given. As a corporeal field of cultural play, gender is a basically innovative affair, although it is quite clear that there are strict punishments for contesting the script by performing out of turn or through unwarranted improvisations. (531)

Critique

The disadvantage to applying feminist ideas to research in a wide range of societies is that definitions of maleness and femaleness may be widely divergent in different parts of the world. Feminist assumptions as formulated in Euro-American contexts may have little or a great deal of relevance to other parts of the world where we are conducting research. The critique of first-wave feminism was that it created a universal identity of "woman" that did not take into account issues of race and class. But this has largely been remedied.

Gender/Lesbian Issues

Although lesbianism shares with feminism the assumption of patriarchal oppression, lesbianism has layered onto it an added issue. Lesbianism holds that research must also address the problems of **heterosexual privilege** (Tyson 1999:323). That is, lesbians have an added burden of not sharing heterosexuality with feminists. Some have tried to emphasize a common denominator, "woman," and thus feminists and lesbians have not necessarily stood together to support the oppression of all women. And because feminism and lesbianism have been largely middle-class movements, working-class lesbians and those of color have been even further marginalized (Tyson 1999:324).

Contribution

A feminist perspective acknowledges structures of power that have deeply influenced our studies of music making around the world. It brings to the fore attitudes and behaviors that have sometimes been taken for granted. For that reason, feminist perspectives call our attention to issues that can be vital to the research we are conducting.

These concepts of gender are centered primarily in Western societies, and research around the world will no doubt reveal a broader range of views toward gender. In the study of music, ethnomusicologists will be in an optimal position to address a range of approaches toward gender within the music-making situation and beyond to the larger society.

Gay Issues

Gay issues revolve around definitions of the sexual desire of one man for another as well as sexual relations between men (Tyson 1999:330). Again, these are definitions that will no doubt be embellished by research in other societies. In literary research situations, gay critics "attempt to determine a gay poetics, or a way of writing that is uniquely gay; to establish a gay literary tradition; and to decide what writers and works belong to that tradition" (Tyson 1999:333).

Heterosexual privilege

- Production of heterosexual relationships as the normal, natural, taken-for-granted sexuality

Queer Theory

Queer theory is an approach built on deconstructionism, which addresses the issues surrounding the systematic discrimination against gay men. Queer theory has been an attempt to use a label for a theory, which employs a term earlier used as a derogatory name. Now that term—*queer*—is being reclaimed. The term *queer* is also being adopted as an inclusive category by some lesbians and gay men, "referring to a common political or cultural ground shared by gay men, lesbians, bisexuals, and all people who consider themselves, for whatever reasons, non-straight" (Tyson 1999:336). "Queer theory defines sexuality as a fluid, fragmented dynamic collectivity of possible sexualities" (Tyson 1999:337). As Philip Brett (1994) points out, "A lesbian and gay musicology will want to interrogate both terms unceasingly as it re-searches our history, proposes new theories of music, and devises a pedagogy (23).

Gender Issues in Ethnomusicology

Gender issues in ethnomusicology first received concerted attention in the collection of essays edited by Ellen Koskoff: *Women and Music in Cross-Cultural Perspective* (1989). In that volume, Koskoff pointed to the central questions addressed by the essays: "First, to what degree does a society's behavior affect its musical thought and practice? And second, how does music function in society to reflect or affect inter-gender relations? (1). The authors analyzed various musical practices around the world and questioned how those practices relate to gender concepts, particularly of women:

- Greek women use music as a "vehicle both for catharsis and commentary in response to their position in a male-dominated society." (Auerbach 1989:25)
- The public, professional female musician in Tunisia has not yet succeeded in being regarded as fully respectable. (Jones 1989:80)
- Women musicians in India have moved from a period of high respect to one of being forced to compete in an ever diversifying field of musical genres. (Post 1989:107)
- The female solo singer in the Javanese gamelan performance has emerged as an increasingly prominent individual, much like a Western star performer. (Sutton 1989:111)
- Temniar singers in Malaysia invert the normal male-female differentiation and in ritual they are co-creators in the re-distribution of roles. (Roseman 1989:146)

Queer theory
• Framework of analysis that studies sexuality • Views sexuality as socially constructed, fluid, fragmented

Plate 21 Ellen Koskoff. Courtesy of Ellen Koskoff.

- Singers in the ritual performances of the Kalapalo of Brazil communicate between the sexes and provide control over forces that are considered dangerous. (Basso 1989:174)

Carol Robertson, in a summary in the Koskoff volume, outlines several assumptions about the relationship of gender, social power, and performance:

1. The display and mediation of power (control over others) permeate all human transactions, both at the private and public levels.
2. In all human contexts, power and gender are linked through assumptions about the nature of sexuality, the attributes associated with each gender, and the need to control access to the decision-making process.
3. Any culture recognizes a particular power within music.
4. These associations of power with gender and music link these phenomena so closely as to provide an ideal forum for the exploration of performance as a universal key to social values and the processes through which gender roles fluctuate between stasis and change.
5. Power, gender, and performance interlock on a complex and ever-changing continuum. (Robertson 1989:226)

In exploring gender, Robertson asserts one is necessarily exploring issues of power and issues of authority within a society. These are critical problems to be explored by ethnomusicologists, for gender and power fit tightly together in the music-making context.

In the latter half of the 1990s, several ethnographies directly addressed issues of gender. These works shifted the emphasis from analysis of the variety of women's contributions through musical performance to a more explicit examination of gender definition and its relation to music making. In these newer studies there has been a questioning of earlier assumptions that social groups are constituted of a fixed and uncomplicated gender binary: men and their opposite—women.

Jane Sugarman (1997) noted, "We need to focus on the capacity of musical traditions not merely to reinforce gender relations within other domains, but to actively *engender* those individuals who participate in them" (32). She found that weddings in Albania are frequently a significant location for creating ideas of gender. All of these weddings took place against a backdrop of polyphonic singing by separated groups of men and women as they led to the high point—the taking of the bride. At the same time, she argues, "Any Prespa wedding may thus be seen as one point in an ongoing process through which community members actively constitute, reinscribe, challenge, or incrementally renegotiate the terms through which they are connected as a community" (3).

At the beginning of the twentieth century, a flood of works addressed, challenged, and questioned gender in the context of music, using phrases in the titles like "music and gender," "women's voices across musical worlds," "music, gender and identity," "gender politics," "a pedagogy of gender, race, and class," "gender maneuvering," "queer episodes in music and modern identity" and "disruptive divas." (Bernstein 2003; Burns and Lafrance 2002; Chuse 2003; Fuller and Whitesell 2002; Magrini 2003; Malott and Peña 2003; Moisala and Diamond 2000; Ramsey 2003; Schippers 2002). Gender topics and issues emerged prominently in the scholarly literature.

Historical musicology concerned itself as well, to a considerable degree, with issues of gender (Barkin and Hamessley 1999; Cook and Tsou 1994; Macarthur 2002). John Shepherd (1989), for example, asserted,

> "Classical" music is founded on a notational control of pitch and rhythm which in turn implies an androgynized sense of self as expressed through pure and standardized timbres. . . . The qualities of sound which speak so strongly in various "popular" music genres reinforce to a sense of individual identity therefore achieve little but a reinforcement of the traditional gender types that both result from and serve to reproduce an essentially masculine view of the world. (171)

Susan McClary (1989) pointed out the necessity of understanding Johann Sebastian Bach within the context of his time, particularly with respect to gender issues:

> Put quite simply, the soul here [Cantata 140, *Wachet auf*] is a nagging, passive-aggressive wife, insecurely whining for repeated assurances of love and not hearing

them when they are proffered (Movement 2, mm. 8–18) . . . Yet underlying Bach's musical metaphors is an analogy: just as a husband patronizingly puts up with a complaining mate because he knows that her insecurity stems from her emotional dependence, so God tolerates (uni-sex) us and our frailties. (54–55)

Marcia J. Citron (1993) explored gender for the composers and the creative processes, including composition, performance, and reception. She addressed the question of why music composed by women is so marginal in the standard repertoire of so-called classical music. She also studied the practices that have "led to the exclusion of women composers from the received 'canon' of performed musical works" (i).

In the discipline of ethnomusicology, scholars are just beginning to ask fundamental questions about gender concepts and discovering that the issues are not as cut and dried as male versus female. Furthermore, the very definitions of maleness and femaleness are wide ranging from one world area to another.

Ethnicity and Identity Issues

Ethnicity

Another area for analysis centers on **ethnicity**. Although structural functionalists often portrayed traits and patterns of behavior as across society, later scholars realized that within a region various identity markers are important in understanding human behavior. Gender is one form of identity that informs people's behavior. Ethnicity is another kind of identity that affects interaction. Certainly ethnicity has relevant links to gender issues and the construction of a complex human identity.

In the introduction to a collection of essays on ethnomusicology, Martin Stokes (1994) points out, "Ethnicities are to be understood in terms of the construction, maintenance and negotiation of boundaries, and not on the putative social 'essences' which fill the gaps between them" (6). According to Stokes and other scholars, ethnic boundaries define and maintain social identities, which can only exist in the "context of opposition and relativities" (Chapman, Tonkin, and McDonald 1989:17). As these scholars maintain, people attempt to define difference between themselves and other people. This difference may be violently opposed by the other group or may be used for a wide variety of

Ethnicity
<ul><li>Social groups understood in terms of the construction, maintenance, and negotiation of boundaries</li><li>Many ethnic groups exist in the context of opposition to other groups</li><li>Emphasis on differences helps define ethnicities</li></ul>

Plate 22 Martin Stokes. Courtesy of Martin Stokes.

purposes. The British in West Africa, for example, promoted "tribal" identities and the music of those groups over those of the "Creole mercantile elites" because this latter group posed a threat to British economic interests (Collins and Richards 1989, as quoted in Stokes 1994:14–15).

In the present world, where music is placed in unexpected proximity in a jumble of styles, there is clearly interest in controlling music and in turn the power of this public display. As Stokes (1994) points out, musicians often pick up musical practices, transform them, and then reinterpret them in their own terms, fitting them into their music making. In doing so, they may place them lower in complexity in a hierarchy of styles. When musicians do make this incorporation, such as Appalachian, Klezmer, and Bulgarian music creeping into Irish music, it may prove a real irritation to the purist ultranationalists of Northern Ireland. Stokes also points out the subversive potential for ethnic music in states that emphasize national unity. He says,

> Greek *Rebetika* (see Herzfeld 1987; Holst-Warhaft 1975), Turkish *Arabesk* (Stokes 1992), and Israeli Rock *Mizrahi* (Shiloah and Cohen 1983), even Andalusian *Flamenco* (Manuel 1989), celebrate an oriental "other" which is highly subversive in the context of official nationalist discourses which explicitly reject their internal "Orients" as aspects of a backward past. (Stokes 1994:16).

Daniel Reed (2003) has examined the importance of the arts as a means of generating identities and negotiating boundaries in pluralistic settings. He has

Plate 23 Daniel B. Reed. Courtesy Daniel B. Reed.

examined these issues through an ethnographic study of the roles of music and mask performance in the lives of the Dan people in the ever-changing setting of the Côte d'Ivoire, West Africa. The Dan perform with masks to enact their religious as well as ethnic identity, addressing issues that range from Christianity and Islam to the federal judiciary.

Gender and ethnic identity become intertwined issues in the work of some scholars. This is evident in Aparicio's (1998) ethnography *Listening to Salsa: Gender, Latin Popular Music, and Puerto Rican Cultures*. Gender definitions and other aspects of identity all integrate in complex, changing ways to impact our analysis and understanding of genres such as salsa.

Rural-Urban Identity

Some scholars of identity have also focused on the phenomenon of **rural-urban identity**. With the fluid movement of peoples back and forth between the capital city and the rural areas in many countries, complex relationships have developed.

Rural-urban identity
• Complex social relationships that develop from the fluid movement back and forth between the village and the city

Plate 24 Daniel Avorgbedor. Courtesy of Daniel Avorgbedor.

As Daniel Avorgbedor (1998) writes, voluntary youth associations in Ghana, West Africa, provide social structures with ties to the home village and performance reminiscent of the village music. These groups also perform and sing about the difficulties of moving between the urban and rural worlds. In an *agbadza* song, the singers satirize the plight of a woman trying to go from Senchi, a ferry port to the capital Accra (Gê).

> She wants go to Gê, but problem of the fare.
> She wants to go to Gê, but problem of the fare.
> There is no money for fare; prostitute is left at Senchi. (391)

The music provides a forum for reflecting on these issues of movement between the world of urban and rural and the identity aspects of being associated with either location.

The issue of identifying people as purely urban or purely rural is complex, for people move constantly between these areas with strong ties maintained. I remember visiting the University of Ghana on several occasions and realizing that the campus regularly emptied of faculty and staff on weekends as people returned to their home villages to attend funerals or dispatch other social obligations. When a relative of Kofi Anyidoho died, he invited me to attend a wake in Accra. That wake in the city was followed by a weekend funeral in the home village. This university professor attended a life cycle commemoration for the deceased relative both in the city and at home in the village a day or two later.

National Identity

People identify with nation-states, and this **national identity** is frequently intertwined with music performance in addition to the identities mentioned earlier. These national identity ideas are rooted in the romantic nationalism of scholars such as Georg W. F. Hegel.

Nations were the expression of a national character, and each nation had its own national genius of which music was an important aspect. Benedict Anderson (1983) emphasized the notion of nation not as a fixed physical entity but as a symbolic construct. Closely associated were the ideas of "imagined community" and "print capitalism." Eric Hobsbawm and Terence Ranger (1983) coined **invented tradition** to describe the constant social shaping that affects rituals and symbols.

In some cases, national bureaucracies have promoted the idea of a nation with music performance. In the Dominican Republic, for example, Hector Bienvenido Trujillo consciously employed radio and television to broadcast performances of the dance form merengue as a way of promoting the nation (Austerlitz 1997:77). In fact, merengue became associated with Caribbean dictatorships and a symbol of them, expressing the national genius to which Hegel referred (Averill 1989:134, as quoted in Austerlitz 1997:77).

In Tanzania, Kelly Askew (2002) describes "national identities as rooted in shifting national identity formation not unlike identity formation in individuals who are constantly at work to define themselves" (271). She focuses on *taarab*, "the genre of sung Swahili poetry that inserted itself into Tanzanian cultural policy through popular force and interrupted a nationalist discourse that continually tripped and fell over its unruly citizenry" (271).

National identity

- Social grouping of people associated with particular nation-states
- Symbolic construct for Benedict Anderson

Invented tradition

- Constant social shaping that affects rituals and symbols
- Coined by Eric Hobsbawm and Terence Ranger

Transnational Identity

Identities are also an issue for the ethnomusicologists in cases where people live in **transnational settings**. Cynthia Schmidt (1998) examines the Kru mariners who worked on ships that sailed the west coast of Africa:

> The Kru settlements spread from their homeland in Liberia to Freetown Sierra Leone where they worked in 1793 on British naval and trading vessels. By the mid-1800s they extended down the coast to Fernando Po, Nigeria, and Ghana. They even worked in the Congo, Angola, Namibia and South Africa. These seamen moved to Jamaica, Trinidad, and the Guianas as well as Martinique. A number traveled to Liverpool, England and never returned to Africa. (373–74).

Their complex identities drew on aspects of each place where they settled but were in many respects transnational, bridging a number of nations.

Ethnomusicologists face theoretical complexities as they try to understand the performance strategies of musicians in these transnational settings. Jane Sugarman's (1997) study of Albanian weddings examines them not only in Prespa but also in North America. She concludes,

> Some of the practices that they are choosing to incorporate into community events, such as elements of the standard Euro-American wedding ritual and the repertoire of pop songs that is often associated with it, are structured in accord with older, patriarchal assumptions about social relations . . . [I]ndividuals and families experiment within the realm of cultural forms by altering such practices as ritual sequences, music and dance repertoires food, dress, and household décor. (343–44)

Kay Shelemay (1998) studies the *pizmonim* repertoire of Jews who left Syria and settled in New York, Mexico, as well as elsewhere in the Americas. She follows their transnational movement and studies the resulting songs that reflect a complex history, which today places more Jews outside of Syria than in Aleppo or Damascus combined.

The fluidity of diaspora communities helps shape identities that extend beyond national boundaries and become entangled in the global circulation of people and musical practices.

Transnational identity

- Social conception of people that spans multiple national boundaries

Racial Identity

Ethnomusicologists have also addressed issues of **race** that have been integral to the understanding of music making. Race focuses on identities based on perceptions about skin color. These distinctions are socially constructed categories used in most cases to establish hierarchical structures and to discriminate against or exclude certain groups of people from certain social, political, religious, and other settings.

The way these definitions operate can prove surprising. A number of years ago when my husband and I lived in New York City, he was a teacher at P.S. 68 in Harlem, a public school with nearly all African American and Hispanic students. As a light skinned, blond descendant of Swedish and English parentage, to most people in the neighborhood on West 127th Street where he taught, Verlon was acknowledged to be "white." One Saturday he took a number of his students on a field trip to Staten Island. As they drove along, one of the kids said, "Look at that bicycle sitting outside. They better put it in the house or some white child will steal it." Another kid poked the first and said, "Hush, don't you know Mr. Stone is white." "No," retorted the first, "He's not white; white people are bad." Thus the variations in conception of "black" and "white" and how people socially constructed those definitions were laid bare in this trip to an unfamiliar borough of their own city.

The history of America, nevertheless, has produced discourse that a "pure" white race must be maintained, and any mixture constitutes a degradation. In the world of jazz performance, some of these racial distinctions are invoked:

> If jazz is one of the few cultural activities in which being African American is evaluated as "better" or more "authentic" than being non-African American, a white musician's appeal to a colorblind rhetoric might cloak a move to minimize the black cultural advantage by "lowering" an assertive African American musician from his or her pedestal to a more "equal" playing field. It is this use of colorblind rhetoric that often provokes African Americans to take more extreme positions on ethnic particularity. (Monson 1996:203)

Ethnomusicologists studying jazz are thrust quickly into issues of racial identity and often find it necessary to weave some discussion of these issues into their analyses. It would simply be irresponsible scholarship to ignore them.

Race

- Social conception of people based on a number of factors
- Skin color, genetic makeup, or a person's own identification

Plate 25 Mellonee V. Burnim. Courtesy of Mellonee V. Burnim.

The politics of race are closely intertwined with the realities that people construct of performance in jazz. As a result, "Black performers identified by African Americans as major jazz figures were omitted from or treated as footnotes in many early accounts of the genre" (Burnim and Maultsby 2006:18). Mellonee Burnim and Portia Maultsby bring a comprehensive set of essays together that addresses issues of race in music in a central way (Burnim and Maultsby 2006). Even more importantly, contemporary jazz ownership was historically a point of contention in a way that carried racial overtones.

> While ignoring bebop and its derivative hard bop style, jazz critics heralded these new styles as markers of a new era in jazz. Their writings, based primarily on musicological analysis of transcribed recordings, tended to reduce jazz to intellectual discourse. Countering this form of appropriation, African American musicians drew elements from Black vernacular and popular forms to reclaim jazz as Black cultural expression. (Burnim and Maultsby 2006:22).

Laying claim to the achievements of African American musicians, one set of scholars appropriated the creative genius of another group of people. Concepts of racial identity have been employed to provide an ethnomusicological analysis of the relevant issues.

Plate 26 Portia K. Maultsby. Courtesy of Portia K. Maultsby.

Identity Issues in Kpelle Performance

When I conducted doctoral dissertation research in the mid-1970s in Liberia, one of the performance groups that I followed and observed closely was the Woni group. They were a duo composed of vocal soloist and goblet drum (*feli*), player, Moses Woni, and supporting drummer and backup singer, John Woni (no relation), who played the two-headed cylindrical *gbung-gbung*. Various friends or acquaintances who constituted the chorus at their performances surrounded these two "stars" as "groupies." The Wonis lived in a small hamlet aloong the main highway from Monrovia to Totota where they made their living as musicians.

They consciously identified themselves with Kpelle culture by singing in the Kpelle language and drawing on Kpelle images and proverbs for their texts. They also took Kpelle melodies and transformed them to suit their other identifications.

At the same time, they also constructed their performance to identify with East African popular music, the "Nairobi sound" as they called it. They simplified rhythmic patterns, typical of Kpelle performance practice, to sound more like what they heard on popular music recordings. They shortened their songs to conform more closely to recorded cuts. They transformed the close-paced call-and-response pattern of Kpelle singing to longer solo verses and extended chorus interludes, again imitating East African popular songs.

Even as they identified with East African popular music, the Wonis also attached themselves to African American culture. They sported huge Afro hairdos and wore bell-bottom trousers—dress that was in fashion in the United States but quite unknown in Liberia. Sunglasses frequently completed the costume they wore for performances.

In striking ways, the Wonis straddled Kpelle, East African, African American, and Western cultures. Some of their song phrases were cleverly designed to be ambiguous so they could be understood as either Kpelle or English when sung for an audience. They sang, for example, "A li long ya," which could be interpreted as either, "He is going to buy a child" if one is decoding from the Kpelle-language perspective or "Alleluia" if one is listening from an English-language viewpoint. Thus they could draw in a variety of people who heard the same set of sounds but interpreted them from differing linguistic and cultural codes.

The very conscious attempt of the Wonis to embody differing identities simultaneously and reveal them in performance differentially, depending on the audience member, is not dissimilar from strategies used by jazz musicians. Monson (1996) comments,

> Universalist and ethnically assertive points of view . . . often co-exist in the same person and are best conceived as discourses upon which musicians draw in particular interactive contexts. An individual speaking to an interlocutor who underplays the role of African American culture in music, for example, might choose to respond with ethnically assertive comments. (202)

Identity is slippery, changing, and emergent in performance and everyday life alike. It is not enough to investigate someone's identity as a Kpelle person. The Wonis subtly invoke Kpelle as well as a variety of identities around themselves. The identity they project at any one moment might be quite different from the identity of another moment, depending on who the listeners and viewers are and how they interpret the performance. And this ambiguous profile is no accident, for the Wonis delight in being able to project multifaceted identities that shift quickly and easily.

Conclusion

Gender, ethnicity, and identity in its various manifestations have all helped ethnomusicologists to consider the musicians and audience members we study in more nuanced ways. We are not just concerned with a homogeneous group of people, which we assume to all act in a monolithic fashion. All sorts of considerations, ranging from race to gender, impact how musicians and audiences create and respond to performances, or how they consider the relationship between themselves and the researcher. As these issues are being studied today, they are increasingly being researched in a fluid, shifting, dynamic way. Ethnomusicologists are no longer looking at fixed categories or essences. Rather, the social constructions of these categories are ever subject to change and revision. Individuals as well as groups of individuals may be the focus of studies that emphasize issues of identity, and these studies will continue to find gender, race, urban-rural identity, and ethnicity relevant.

References

Anderson, Benedict. 1983. *Imagined Communities: Reflections on the Origin and Spread of Nationalism*. London: Verso.

Aparicio, Frances R. 1998. *Listening to Salsa: Gender, Latin Popular Music, and Puerto Rican Cultures*. Hanover, N.H.: University Press of New England.

Askew, Kelly. 2002. *Performing the Nation: Swahili Music and Cultural Politics in Tanzania*. Chicago: University of Chicago Press.

Auerbach, Susan. 1989. "From Singing to Lamenting: Women's Musical Role in a Greek Village." In *Women and Music in Cross-Cultural Perspective*, ed. Ellen Koskoff. Urbana: University of Illinois Press, 25–44.

Austerlitz, Paul. 1997. *Merengue: Dominican Music and Dominican Identity*. Philadelphia: University of Temple Press.

Averill, Gage. 1989. "Haitian Dance Band Music: The Political Economy of Exuberance." PhD diss., University of Washington.

Avorgbedor, Daniel. 1998. "Rural-Urban Interchange: The Anlo-Ewe." In *Africa: The Garland Encyclopedia of World Music*, ed. Ruth M. Stone. New York and London: Garland, 389–99.

Barkin, Elaine, and Lydia Hamessley. 1999. *Audible Traces: Gender, Identity, and Music*. Zurich and Los Angeles: Carciofoli.

Basso, Ellen B. 1989. "Musical Expression and Gender Identity in the Myth and Ritual of the Kalapalo of Central Brazil." In *Women and Music in Cross-Cultural Perspective*, ed. Ellen Koskoff. Urbana: University of Illinois Press, 163–76.

Bernstein, Jane A., ed. 2003. *Women's Voices across Musical Worlds*. Boston: Northeastern University Press.

Brett, Philip. 1994. "Musicality, Essentialism, and the Closet." In *Queering the Pitch: The New Gay and Lesbian Musicology*, eds. Philip Brett, Elizabeth Wood, and Gary C. Thomas. New York: Routledge, 9–26.

Burnim, Mellonee V., and Portia K. Maultsby. 2006. *African American Music: An Introduction*. New York: Routledge.

Burns, Lori, and Mélisse Lafrance. 2002. *Disruptive Divas: Feminism, Identity and Popular Music*. New York: Routledge.

Butler, Judith. 1988. "Performative Acts and Gender Constitution: An Essay in Phenomenology and Feminist Theory." *Theatre Journal* 40(4): 519–31.

——. 1990. *Gender Trouble: Feminism and the Subversion of Identity*. New York: Routledge.

——. 1993. *Bodies That Matter: On the Discursive Limits of "Sex."* New York: Routledge.

Chapman, Malcolm, Elizabeth Tonkin, and Maryon McDonald, eds. 1989. *History and Ethnicity*. New York: Routledge.

Chuse, Loren. 2003. *The Cantaoras: Music, Gender, and Identity in Flamenco Song.* New York: Routledge.

Citron, Marcia J. 1993. *Gender and the Musical Canon.* Cambridge: Cambridge University Press.

Collins, John, and P. Richards. 1989. "Popular Music in West Africa." In Simon Frith, ed. *World Music and Social Change.* Manchester: Manchester University Press.

Cook, Susan C., and Judy S. Tsou, eds. 1994. *Cecilia Reclaimed: Feminist Perspective on Gender and Music.* Urbana: University of Illinois Press.

Frisbie, Charlotte. 1991. "Women and the Society for Ethnomusicology: Roles and Contributions from Formation through Incorporation (1952/53–1961). In *Comparative Musicology and Anthropology of Music*, eds. Bruno Nettl and Philip V. Bohlman. Urbana: University of Illinois Press, 244–65.

Fuller, Sophie, and Lloyd Whitesell. 2002. *Queer Episodes in Music and Modern Identity.* Urbana: University of Illinois Press.

Herzfeld, Michael. 1987. *Anthropology through the Looking Glass: Critical Ethnography in the Margins of Europe.* Cambridge: Cambridge University Press.

Hobsbawm, Eric, and Terence Ranger. 1983. *The Invention of Tradition.* New York: Cambridge University Press.

Holst-Warhaft, Gail. 1975. *Road to Rembetika: Music of a Greek Subculture: Music of Love, Sorrow and Hashish.* Athens: D. Harvey.

Jones, L. JaFran. 1989. "A Sociohistorical Perspective on Tunisian Women as Professional Musicians." In *Women and Music in Cross-Cultural Perspective*, ed. Ellen Koskoff. Urbana: University of Illinois Press, 69–84.

Koskoff, Ellen, ed. 1989. *Women and Music in Cross-Cultural Perspective.* Urbana: University of Illinois Press.

——, ed. 1992. *Ethnomusicology and Music Cognition. The World of Music* 34(3). Includes bibliographical references.

Macarthur, Sally. 2002. *Feminist Aesthetics in Music.* Westport, Conn.: Greenwood Press.

Magrini, Tullia. 2003. *Music and Gender: Perspectives from the Mediterranean.* Chicago: University of Chicago Press.

Mallott, Curry, and Milagros Peña. 2003. *Punk Rocker's Revolution: A Pedagogy of Gender, Race, and Class.* New York: P. Lang.

Manuel, Peter. 1989. "Andalusian, Gypsy and Class Identity in the Contemporary Flamenco Complex." *Ethnomusicology* 33(2): 47–65.

McClary, Susan. 1989. "The Blasphemy of Talking Politics during Bach Year." In *Music and Society: The Politics of Composition, Performance and Reception*, eds. Richard Leppert and Susan McClary. Cambridge: Cambridge University Press, 13–62.

Moisala, Pirkko, and Beverley Diamond, eds. 2000. *Music and Gender.* Urbana: University of Illinois Press.

Monson, Ingrid. 1996. *Saying Something: Jazz Improvisation and Interaction.* Chicago: University of Chicago Press.

Post, Jennifer. 1989. "Professional Women in Indian Music: The Death of the Courtesan Tradition." In *Women and Music in Cross-Cultural Perspective*, ed. Ellen Koskoff. Urbana: University of Illinois Press, 97–110.

Ramsey, Guthrie P. 2003. *Race Music: Migration, Modernism, and Gender*. Berkeley: University of California Press.

Reed, Daniel. 2003. *Dan Ge Performance: Masks and Music in Contemporary Côte d'Ivoire*. Bloomington: Indiana University Press.

Robertson, Carol E. 1989. "Power and Gender in the Musical Experiences of Women." In *Women and Music in Cross-Cultural Perspective*, ed. Ellen Koskoff. Urbana: University of Illinois Press, 225–44.

Roseman, Marina. 1989. "Inversion and Conjunction: Male and Female Performance among the Temniar of Peninsular Malaysia." In *Women and Music in Cross-Cultural Perspective*, ed. Ellen Koskoff. Urbana: University of Illinois Press, 131–50.

Sakata, Hiromi Lorraine. 1989. "Hazara Women in Afghanistan: Innovators and Preservers of Musical Tradition." In *Women and Music in Cross-Cultural Perspective*, ed. Ellen Koskoff. Urbana: University of Illinois Press, 85–96.

Schippers, Mimi. 2002. *Rockin' out of the Box: Gender Maneuvering in Alternative Hard Rock*. New Brunswick, N.J.: Rutgers University Press.

Schmidt, Cynthia. 1998. "Kru Mariners and Migrants of the West African Coast." In *Garland Encyclopedia of World Music: Africa*, ed. Ruth M. Stone. New York: Garland, 2–6.

Shelemay, Kay Kaufman. 1998. *Let Jasmine Rain Down: Song and Remembrance among Syrian Jews*. Chicago: University of Chicago Press.

Shepherd, John. 1989. "Music and Male Hegemony." In *Music and Society: The Politics of Composition, Performance and Reception,"* eds. Richard Leppert and Susan McClary. Cambridge: Cambridge University Press, 151–72.

Shiloah, Amnon, and Erik Cohen. 1983. *The Dynamics of Change in Jewish Oriental Ethnic Music in Israel*. Middletown, Conn.: Society for Ethnomusicology.

Stokes, Martin. 1992. *The Arabesk Debate: Music and Musicians in Modern Turkey*. Oxford: Oxford University Press.

——, ed. 1994. *Ethnicity, Identity and Music: The Musical Construction of Place*. Oxford: Berg.

Sugarman, Jane C. 1997. *Engendering Song: Singing and Subjectivity at Prespa Albanian Weddings*. Chicago: University of Chicago Press.

Sutton, R. Anderson. 1989. "Identity and Individuality in an Ensemble Tradition. The Female Vocalist in Java." In *Women and Music in Cross-Cultural Perspective*, ed. Ellen Koskoff. Urbana: University of Illinois Press, 111–30.

Tyson, Lois. 1999. *Critical Theory Today*. New York: Garland.

Chapter 11

Phenomenology and Experiential Ethnomusicology

Phenomenology, in recent years, has been an area to which a number of ethnomusicologists have turned for theoretical inspiration. In **phenomenology**, the researcher takes the sensations and interpretations of individuals as important and critical data. Details that to other orientations are superfluous become the very heart of investigation. Multiple meanings as they are created over time become the central concern here.

Our focus here is on phenomenological sociology rather than the whole of phenomenology because it is most relevant for ethnomusicology. Other areas of phenomenology have not been so concerned with meaning from a broad range of individuals but have rather relied on the philosopher's interpretation and contemplation of these meanings. Several areas of sociology, including symbolic interaction, have drawn on the ideas we are discussing here (Blumer 1969).

The view within this broad field is most centrally associated with the work and writings of Alfred Schutz, who was born in Vienna in 1899 and died in New York in 1959. His first and most fundamental work, published in 1932, was *Der sinnhafte Aufbau der sozialen Welt* ("The Meaningful Construction of Social Reality"). Helmut Wagner, who edited one of Schutz's books, maintained that it might well have been subtitled "Husserl and Weber," for the work of these two men, the former a philosopher and the latter a sociologist, formed the cornerstone of Schutz's thinking. Schutz's early period, in addition, reflects influences of Henri Bergson, William James, and Max Scheler. His later period reflects the ideas of John R. Dewey, George Herbert Mead, Charles H. Cooley, and William I. Thomas.

During his lifetime, Schutz attempted to create the foundations for a complete and self-sufficient system of sociological thought and procedure. Schutz's

---

Phenomenology

- Research framework that focuses on studying human experience with attention to the details of the subjective interpretations

---

theory was carried to its logical conclusion by Peter Berger and Thomas Luckmann (1967) in *The Social Construction of Reality*. The basic tenets and assumptions, as well as central concerns of Schutz, bear some examination.

Sociological Phenomenology: Assumptions

1. **Social experience must be defined as meaningful experience.**

   In this assumption Schutz is interested in the nature of meaning and agrees with Max Weber about meaning arising in the context of social interaction.

2. **There is a stream of human experience (durée) that is the ground of all experience.**

   Schutz agreed with Henri Bergson that the stream of consciousness is the basis of experience. He did not, however, see this stream as constituting meaning. Rather, meaning is created when *durée* is broken by reflection, by looking back on earlier experience, or by projecting oneself from the present into the future. Schutz then defined meaning in terms of highly conscious reflective experience.

3. **Meaning is created in "typifications" or highly shared meaningful experiences, which are commonly associated with linguistic symbols (names).**

   These shared experiences make interaction possible. The concept of "lament," for example, with associations of loss and women's voices, are familiar to people who have had social experiences that help fill in their typifications.

4. **Actions follow from the typifications constructed for the situation.**

   The socially constructed meanings help shape the actions that follow. For example, when people suffer loss, they seek laments as a way of providing catharsis through the crisis.

5. **The focus of investigation is the "life-world," the whole sphere of everyday experiences, orientations, and actions through which individuals pursue their interests and affairs by manipulating objects, dealing with people, conceiving plans, and carrying these plans out (Schutz and Luckmann 1973).**

   Phenomenologists focus on the ordinary ebb and flow of ordinary life with concern for the minute interactions in which people engage as they live their lives.

Durée

- Qualitative or inner time that is distinct from quantitative or outer time, the latter measured by a clock or metronome

6. **The critical issue within the life-world is the subjective meaning of the person's membership in his community.**

   Schutz showed that even the most stereotyped cultural ideas only exist in the minds of individuals who absorb them, interpret them on the basis of their own life situations, and give them a personal tinge.

7. **A common worldview depends on the belief of the members of a community that they share views and their use standardizes expressions and formulations.**

   In general, then, Alfred Schutz was interested in a general theory of meaning capable of explaining the process by which a person selects one meaning over another, how two or more persons share meanings, understand each other, and engage in concerted social action.

8. **There are multiple realities or realms of experience.**

   These realities include the world of dreams, fantasy and play, and music, among others. The realities are termed *finite provinces* of meaning. In these finite provinces, the way meaning is created can be quite different than in everyday life.

9. **Social science should be interpretive and describe the process of meaning establishment and meaning creation.**

   The very process by which people collectively create meanings, many only partially shared, is the research concern of sociological phenomenologists.

10. **There are three criteria for adequacy: logical consistency determined according to formal logic, subjective interpretation, and adequacy for the actor as well as for his fellowmen.**

    It may be the case that each of the criteria is developed in very different ways and these all triangulate to form the basis for adequacy. Adequacy implies that an interpretation meets the requirements of the research according to a particular theoretical orientation.

Phenomenology and Music

Alfred Schutz was an amateur performing musician who drew on that experience in several essays that he wrote on the meaning of music performance: "Making Music Together: A Study in Social Relationship," (Schutz 1971a:159–78) and "Mozart and the Philosophers" (Schutz 1971b:179–200). At the time of his death, a first-draft handwritten manuscript, *Phenomenology of Music*, was left behind. It was later edited and published (1976).

Schutz's ideas come from a philosophical scholar rather than from an empirical researcher. They are suggestive rather than definitive for the field researcher.

Assumptions

1. Music can be regarded as occurring within a "finite province of meaning."

When one is performing music, different rules and meanings are created than in the world of everyday life. This does not mean that music does not relate to the larger world, for he says, quoting Schopenhauer who he greatly admired, "[O]ne might say that music as a whole is the melody to which the whole world furnishes the text" (Schutz 1971b:180). The two worlds exist in a kind of tension with one another, and the audience and performers can move between these worlds.

2. Durée, or inner time, is the central focus of the musical experience.

Schutz explains that the study of the musical process involves the analysis of communication. There is a sharing of the other's flux of experiences in inner time through a vivid present in common which "constitutes . . . the experience of the 'We,' which is at the foundation of all possible communication" (Schutz 1971a:173). Ordinary communication takes place in a clock-time world.

Schutz asserts that we must distinguish, on the one hand, inner time and outer time, both of which are important to the music-making process. Outer time is that time marked by a metronome or a conductor's beat. It is the way that musicians synchronize their performance. Inner time, on the other hand, is not measured by metronomes. It is the time in which the quality of experience rather than the quantifiable time becomes the defining feature. The phenomenologist takes this qualitative time as a primary point of analysis for it is here that experience is at its most intense.

Once musicians are playing together and their parts mesh, they are often able to quit focusing on counting beats consciously and move to inner time, the time that Schutz considers the essence of performance. Measurable time is no longer dominant.

Ethnomusicology and Sociological Phenomenology

Ethnomusicology has turned to phenomenology to a limited extent to center on processual and constantly evolving meaning that emanates from social interaction, a scene in which the ethnomusicologist plays an active role. Music meaning from this theoretical orientation is **emergent**. That is, it is meaning that cannot be predicted but changes course as particular interactions coalesce. As performance

Emergent
• Dynamic process that is not total predictable and may produce unexpected results

proceeds, a mutual tuning-in relationship develops, and an intimacy evolves as "I" and "thou" become "we." The temporal dimension unfolds as a multiply dimensioned inner and outer time. The affective and qualitative processes are central and critical to the larger understanding of music making.

> Early Western philosophers recognized the special place of music. From the Pythagoreans, from Plato and St. Augustine to Bergson and Santayana, philosophers have concerned themselves with music as one of the ways in which man expresses the basic experience of transcendency constitutive of his place within and his attitude toward the cosmos. (Schutz 1971b:180)

Comparative Musicology and Phenomenology

Beginning with the German comparative musicologists, we can find glimpses of interests in the experiential as an adjunct to the experimental. Otto Abraham and Erich M. von Hornbostel provide a clue to this other side of their work. "Before we attempted to study Japanese music in detail, we tried to form a general impression. It is possible to eliminate all theoretical knowledge, absolute pitch, sound analysis and the like, in order to surrender entirely to the sensuous effect of the music" (Abraham and Hornbostel 1975 [1903]:64). As Stephen Blum has pointed out, "Hornbostel stressed the point that an analyst's decisions concurring scales and articulation of form do not allow us to draw reliable conclusions concerning the singer's own conception" (Hornbostel 1909:1042). Hornbostel realized that comparative musicologists would eventually concern themselves with aesthetic judgments expressed in many non-European languages (Blum 1991:3–36).

Hornbostel (1928) speculated about the source of musical meaning in his often quoted statement, "we proceed from hearing, they from motion," in characterizing African musicians through physical movement and sensation (53). And some years later, Charles Seeger (1977) commented on the role of the senses when he asserted, "Tactility holds us closest to what we try to communicate" (43).

Among the early comparative musicologists, Carl Stumpf, who followed philosopher and psychologist Franz Brentano, "postulated a rather complex theory of tone sensation with a phenomenological basis. The theory focused on cognitive functions, such as judgment and comparison, mental analysis by means of similarity or difference, attention, and memory" emphasizing the "effects of tone sensation on the listener" (Schneider 1991:294).

Furthermore, Stumpf agreed with Alexander Ellis that tempered scales existed, and such temperament resulted from *intention* (Schneider 1991:29; Stumpf 1886b:513–17). Performers made conscious decisions to play and acted on those plans.

All of this evidence of interest in the experiential and phenomenological by the Berlin School demonstrates a multifaceted and complex set of research interests in Germany. Further archival work will no doubt round out what is a tantalizing glimpse into the paradigms that guided work in Berlin.

When George Herzog moved from Berlin to New York, he found in the work of Franz Boas an emphasis on musical meaning arising from the situation. "The cultural anthropology of Franz Boas and his students . . . placed greater emphasis on style, guided by Boas' principle that context is always part of the human phenomena" (Krober 1959:vi, as quoted in Blum 1991).

The 1980s, following a twenty-year emphasis on the objective and quantifiable, brought a renewed emphasis on the existential aspects of music making with attempts to account for the ethnomusicologist in the research setting (Gourlay 1982) and to represent local points of view concerning music practices (Feld 1982; Keil 1979; Robertson 1979; A. Seeger 1987b; Stone 1982, 1988; Zemp 1978–1979), although few direct references to phenomenology appeared in publications.

My own work beginning in the middle 1970s was informed by the perspectives of Alfred Schutz, Edmund Husserl, and Hebert Blumer. At a time when a number of ethnomusicologists were looking to linguistics for answers and treating it as a kind of language, Schutz's (1971a) thoughts were instructive when he said,

> The chief interest in our analysis consists in the particular character of all social interactions connected with the musical process . . . they are founded upon communication, but not *primarily* upon a semantic system used by the communicator as a scheme of expression and by his partner as a scheme of interpretation. (159)

Although most scholars would associate the study of the experiential with an anthropological influence, I would offer another interpretation. The impetus for valuing the experiential mode derived as much from the musicologically oriented ethnomusicologists as from those drawing from anthropology. It was the scholars, coming from musicology and performance, who advocated learning to become performers in various world traditions and valued the experience of the individual. They recognized the essential components of affect and emotion and were afraid of losing these in the rush to be scientific. For example, in 1987 Tim Rice made the plea for remembering the individual in ethnomusicology and reincorporating a sense of history in the study. Anthropologists like John Blacking (1973) argued equally as forcefully that music making must become the subject of inquiry.

Sociological phenomenology, emphasizing experience as the nexus where sound and behavior meet, as the point where meaning arises, and where ethnomusicologists must legitimately focus for their conclusions, has been the specific thrust of a number of works in ethnomusicology. My own work has centered on time concepts in Kpelle epic (Stone 1988), and Steven Friedson (1996) has drawn specifically on the work of Heidegger to study music of healing in Malawi. Harry Berger (1999b) has published a study of rock musicians in Cleveland, and Linda Williams (1995) explored jazz in Zimbabwe for her dissertation research, emphasizing **radical empiricism** as advocated by Michael Jackson (1989), one of the few anthropologists who works in phenomenology (see also Jackson 1996). Tom Porcello (1998:485–510) has addressed the complications of technology in analyzing the social phenomenology of music making.

Radical empiricism

- Research framework developed by William James
- Asserts that relations between things are just as important to analysis as are the things themselves.

The approach of radical empiricism, drawing on existential phenomenology, first proposed by the philosopher William James, and more recently revived by Michael Jackson, converges from the field of anthropology where "experience includes 'transitive' as well as 'substantive' elements, conjunctions as well as disjunctions and we are encouraged to recover a lost sense of the immediate, active, ambiguous 'plenum of existence' in which all ideas and intellectual constructions are grounded" (Jackson 1989:2–3; James 1976).

Critique

The criticisms that can be made of this approach are the following:

1. **This approach is overly centered on micro-details, making generalization difficult.**

   Phenomenology is very much the jeweler's eye view as opposed to the bird's-eye view of performance and life.

Plate 27 Steven Friedson playing axatse rattle with a village drum and dance society in Ghana. Courtesy of Steven Friedson.

Plate 28 Tom Porcello. Courtesy of Simon Craven.

2. **The concepts within the literature of philosophy are not grounded or tested in empirical research.**

   The ideas to which ethnomusicologists refer have been developed by philosophers as opposed to empirical researchers. As a result, much empirical work remains to be done to understand the usefulness of these ideas.

Contributions

There are a number of contributions to the field of ethnomusicology as well as problems in applying a sociological phenomenology approach.:

1. **The emphasis on social interaction as a basis for construction of meaning stresses interaction as a point of departure for research.**

   This means the fluid meanings created in performance can be addressed at least partially with phenomenology.

2. **The attention to processual aspects of music addresses the previous imbalance of many approaches that stress product instead.**

   Phenomenologists have been very attentive to temporal aspects in contradistinction to many theorists of other persuasions.

3. **The concern with the relation of music to language and various kinds of consciousness addresses the conceptual as well as a conceptual.**

The contribution of sociological phenomenology rests on its capacity to relate music to language even when the connection is more amorphous integration rather than a bounded symbol. This approach provides for the diffuse aspects of interpretation that characterize music meaning.

Phenomenology Example: Woi Epic from the Kpelle of Liberia

The Kpelle epic in Liberia, West Africa, performed with all the elaboration of chorus, questioner, and dramatic gestures, depends on the mutual audience–performer feeling. Any episode, or, for that matter, the entire evening's performance, hangs on the excitement that develops or doesn't develop, as the case may be.

Little gifts given at intervals index the audience's feeling. These tokens—cigarettes, cane juice, palm wine, or coins—undergirded by a speech of carefully shaped oratory—indicate the level of approval. Without the continued demonstration of such audience sentiment, the pourer (teller) regretfully terminates the event at an early point. Thus it is vital to attend to the timing aspects of these rewards, the nature of these tokens of appreciation, and their significance to the dynamics of the event.

The giving of gifts also brings complications. Near the end of Episode Seven, of a particular rendition, some beer was offered to the performers. As it was presented, Kulung, the pourer asked, "Am I doing it?" and someone from the audience replied, "You are doing it well." The questioner then chimed in, "You are trying." Kulung responded, "Is that right? I told you four days," as he recalled one performance where he continued performing for four days. Someone in the audience queried, "What are you doing with it?" Kulung came back, "We were doing it. Man, give me my beer." Kulung complained to the other performers, "You have drunk yours and you say this? Stop, a person doesn't do things like that." The audience, nevertheless, was anxious to hear more of the story, and the questioner, unconcerned about sharing beer among chorus and singer, continued, "This bow that is talking with its owner, I want to hear its song." Kulung, not to be deprived of his beer, picked up a bottle and started to drink from it. "Isn't it mine?" The questioner responded, "You should just be concerned to sing songs. Yours is inside it," meaning that Kulung's greater reward will come later with a fine performance. Kulung, finally persuaded, then said, "Leave mine in the bottle," and the performance continued. The gift proved to be a complication that might have ultimately terminated the performance. After a discussion, the performance resumed.

Performers of all kinds in Kpelleland relish relating stories of when they excelled in performance and their client was so moved that he or she abandoned common sense to offer extravagant gifts: a gown or a cherished tobacco box. The music, in fact, had transformed the client to interpret the situation differently than he or she would have done in everyday life. When such an elaborate gift was given, the audience, without having originally intended to do so, gave even more elegant tokens. But such, say the Kpelle, can be the power of the music.

The very structuring of Kpelle epic chorus around the perpetual exchange of small bits of sound builds momentum and energy that fuel the spoken narrative. The Kpelle are highly aware of energy levels in performance and admire a performance that is highly energized. Music creates energy that is needed to full performance (see also Schieffelin 1985:714).

The Woi epic is created not to dwell on the coordination of the parts or of the chorus with the narrator or the coordination of the questioner with the narrator. That is only the beginning; the goal, in fact, is to move the audience to laugh at the *tuu-tuu* bird falling asleep at his job when trying to pump the bellows as they admire the bowl being carved chip by chip by the jealous woman. As they sense danger as a monster blocks the part of Woi's house, they can experience a sense of inner time. They approach that inner time by working together first in rhythmic coordination, and then, when they are able to continue that coordination on a kind of automatic pilot, they can shift to inner time. Their experience in inner time will be what they will recall and cherish if the performance moves them and affects them emotionally. It will be the kind of event that people will remember some six years later, as people did Kulung's memorable performance when I made a return trip to Liberia.

Conclusion

As Christine Skarda states, "[T]he phenomena with which the phenomenological approach concerns itself are (1) the essential structure of the experience of the listener *reflectively* grasped, and (2) the "content" of the musical work considered as the intentional correlate of musical consciousness with its particular mode of existence" (Skarda 1989:46). There was an "emphasis upon the flow of conscious life and the concept of the 'specious present'" (65).

Schutz's ideas are provocative starting points, largely undeveloped in the crucible of fieldwork. They are suggestive but not definitive, and only through grounding in ethnographic work will they become embedded in the paradigms of ethnomusicologists.

References

Abraham, Otto, and Erich M. von Hornbostel. 1975 [1903]. "Studies on the Tonsystem and Music of the Japanese." In *Hornbostel Opera Omnia,* Vol. 1, eds. Klaus P. Wachsmann, Dieter Christensen, and Hans-Peter Reinekke, The Hague: Martinus-Nijhoff, 1–84.

Berger, Harris. 1999b. *Metal, Rock, and Jazz: Perception and the Phenomenology of Musical Experience.* Hanover, N.H.: University Press of New England.

Berger, Peter, and Thomas Luckmann. 1967. *The Social Construction of Reality*. Garden City, N.Y.: Doubleday.

Blacking, John. 1973. *How Musical Is Man?* Seattle: University of Washington Press.

Blum, Stephen. 1991. "European Musical Terminology and the Music of Africa." In *Comparative Musicology and Anthropology of Music*, eds. Bruno Nettl and Philip V. Bohlman. Chicago: University of Chicago Press, 3–36.

Blumer, Herbert. 1969. *Symbolic Interactionism: Perspective and Method*. Englewood Cliffs, N.J.: Prentice-Hall.

Feld, Steven. 1982. *Sound and Sentiment: Birds, Weeping, Poetics, and Song in Kaluli Expression*. Philadelphia: University of Pennsylvania Press.

Friedson, Steven M. 1996. *Dancing Prophets: Musical Experience in Tumbuka Healing*. Chicago: University of Chicago Press.

Gourlay Kenneth. 1982. "Towards a Humanizing Ethnomusicology." *Ethnomusicology* 26(3): 411–20.

Hornbostel, Erich M. von. 1909. "Wanyamwezi-Gesänge," *Anthropos* 4: 781–800, 1033–52.

———. 1928. "African Negro Music. *African Journal of the International African Institute* 1(1): 30–62.

Jackson, Michael. 1989. *Paths toward a Clearing: Radical Empiricism and Ethnographic Enquiry*. Bloomington: Indiana University Press.

———. 1996. *Things as They Are: New Directions in Phenomenological Anthropology*. Bloomington: Indiana University Press.

James, William. 1976. *Essays in Radical Empiricism*. Cambridge: Harvard University Press.

Keil, Charles. 1979. *Tiv Song*. Chicago: University of Chicago Press.

Krober, A. L. 1959. "Preface to the *Anthropology of Franz Boas*." Edited by Walter Goldschmidt. *American Anthropologist* 61(5) part 2 (Memoir no. 89).

Porcello, Thomas. 1998. "'Tails out': Social Phenomenology and the Ethnographic Representation of Technology in Music-Making." *Ethnomusicology* 42(3): 485–510.

Rice, Timothy. 1987. "Toward the Remodeling of Ethnomusicology." *Ethnomusicology* 31(3): 469–88.

Robertson, Carol E. 1979. "'Pulling the Ancestors': Performance, Practice, and Praxis in Mapuche Ordering." *Ethnomusicology* 23(3): 395–416.

Schieffelin, Edward L. 1985. "Performance and the Cultural Construction of Reality." *American Ethnologist* 12: 707–24.

Schneider, Albrecht. 1991. "Psychological Theory and Comparative Musicology." In *Comparative Musicology and Anthropology of Music*, eds. Bruno Nettl and Philip V. Bohlman. Chicago: University of Chicago Press, 293–317.

Schutz, Alfred. 1932. *Der sinnhafte Aufbau der sozialen Welt; Eine Einleitung die Verstehende Soziologie*. Vienna: J. Springer, 1932.

———. 1971a. "Making Music Together: A Study in Social Relationship." In *Collected Papers II: Studies in Social Theory*. The Hague: Martinus Nijhoff, 159–78.

———. 1971b. "Mozart and the Philosophers." In *Collected Papers II: Studies in Social Theory*, edited and introduction by Arvid Broderson. The Hague: Martinus Nijhoff, 179–200.

———. 1976. "Fragments on the Phenomenology of Music." In *In Search of Musical Method*, ed. F. Kersten. London: Gordon and Breach.

————, and Thomas Luckmann. 1973. *The Structures of the Life-World.* Chicago: Northwestern University Press.

Seeger, Anthony. 1987b. *Why Suyá Sing: A Musical Anthropology of an Amazonian People.* Cambridge and New York: Cambridge University Press.

Seeger, Charles. 1977. *Studies in Musicology 1935–1975.* Berkeley and Los Angeles: University of California Press.

Skarda, Christine A. 1989. "Alfred Schutz's Phenomenology of Music." In *Understanding the Musical Experience,* ed. Joseph Smith. New York: Gordon and Breach, 43–100.

Stone, Ruth M. 1982. *Let the Inside Be Sweet: The Interpretation of Music Event among the Kpelle of Liberia.* Bloomington: Indiana University Press.

————. 1988. *Dried Millet Breaking: Time, Words, and Song in the Woi Epic of the Kpelle.* Bloomington: Indiana University Press.

Stumpf, Carl. 1886b. "Review of Alexander J. Ellis, 'On the Scales of Various Nations.'" *Vierteljahrsschrift für Musikvissenschaft* 2: 511–24.

Williams, Linda Faye. 1995. "The Impct of African-American Music on Jazz in Zimbabwe: An Exploration in Radical Empiricism." Ph.D. Dissertation, Indiana University.

Zemp, Hugo. 1978–1979. "Aré 'aré Classification of Musical Types and Instruments." *Ethnomusicology* 22(1): 37–67; 23(1): 5–48.

Chapter 12

Historical Research

Historical investigation centers on questions of the past. History is also an academic discipline "that studies the chronological record of events (as affecting a nation or a people), based on a critical examination of source materials and usually presenting an explanation of their causes" ("History" 2005).

Historians apply both external and internal criticism to evaluating sources. According to historian Gilbert J. Garraghan (1946), there are six inquiries that a scholar should make of a source:

1. When was the source produced?
2. Where was the source produced?
3. Who produced the source?
4. Did the source come from preexisting sources?
5. What was the original *form* of the source?
6. What is the credibility of the contents of the source? (168)

The first five inquiries are considered external inquiries—questions used to establish the authority of the source. The last area of inquiry is considered internal criticism used to establish the source's credibility.

Furthermore, Robert J. Schafer and David A. Bennett (1980) presented a series of questions to use in establishing credibility of eyewitness accounts that include the following:

1. Is the meaning of the statement to be interpreted as presented?
2. What was the author's position in being able to report? Were his language and social skills appropriate?
3. How did the author report?
   a. Did he have time, place, and adequate recording apparatus?
   b. When did the report come in relation to the observation? (157–58)

There are two major conditions for the acceptance of oral tradition sources: First, the tradition should be supported by an unbroken chain of witnesses from the first report to the present bearer of the tradition. Second, there should be parallel and yet independent witnesses corroborating the first person who reported (Garraghan 1946:261–62). More recent discussion of oral history in

Africa comes from the scholarship of Jan Vansina (1985), who paved the way for widespread acceptance of oral history as valid if done appropriately.

Ethnohistory "emphasizes the joint use of documentary materials and ethnographic or archaeological data, as well as the combination of historical and anthropological approaches, in the study of social and cultural processes and history" ("Ethnohistory" 2006). The journal *Ethnohistory* has over the years emphasized studies of Native American peoples but more recently has included work from around the world. Raymond J. DeMaille (1984), an anthropologist who conducts such ethnohistorical research, emphasizes the rich variety of sources to be consulted. In *The Sixth Grandfather: Black Elk's Teachings Given to John G. Neihardt,* he publishes not only research about oral histories that Neihardt conducted but provides verbatim transcripts on which Neihardt based his research.

The most prevalent history in the twentieth century is classified as **diplomatic history**. This form of history centers on politicians and studies national and international relations. Primary documents for studying diplomatic history are the large number of official documents that governments produce. This area of history was first associated with Leopold von Ranke, a German scholar, in the late nineteenth century (Ranke and Wines 1981).

Since the late nineteenth century, historians have also broadened their work to include areas like **social history,** which examines social trends and their causes. Historians have also produced **microhistory**, which may be the study of a small town or village, often drawing on anthropological or sociological paradigms. Some historians have worked in areas that relate to

---

Ethnohistory

- Uses documentary materials as well as ethnographic or archaeological data to study social and cultural processes.

Diplomatic history

- Study of national and international relations that focuses on politicians.

Social history

- Study of social trends and their causes that often focuses on ordinary people

---

Microhistory

- Study of history at a very specific level, often of a village or town.

other paradigms such as Marxist historiography, emphasizing issues of social class and economics. Other historians have worked in psychohistory, which is the study of psychological motivation.

A number of basic assumptions undergird the work of historians.

Historical Research: Assumptions

1. **History, by and large, is the study of nations and their relations to other nations.**

   The study object for many historians is the nation-state. Using that level of focus means that many historians focus on a much broader and more encompassing study object than many ethnomusicologists.

2. **Political leaders constitute the forces for change and stability.**

   Thus histories generally focus on analyzing the "great men." As a consequence, historians have not centered, to a great degree, on ordinary people and citizens.

3. **The primary data for histories are written records.**

   Written documents of all types are the focus of attention for historian scholars. They are so important that events that occurred before written records were used are said to occur in prehistory. Although many peoples of the world possess oral records as their primary databank of knowledge, history as a discipline has not considered that form of encoding the past to be a primary kind of repository.

4. **Chronology provides a metric for coordinating historical events.**

   Chronology is a kind of ordering of events in a *relative* sense where the events are placed in juxtaposition to other events (e.g., before the great flood). Events may also be ordered in an *absolute* sense and described in relation to a calendar: lunar, Gregorian, or Hijra, for example, depending on the particular cultural setting for the historical event.

Critique

1. **Diplomatic history to the exclusion of other kinds of history neglects individuals and classes of people that are, nevertheless, deserving of historical study.**

Chronology

- Ordering of historical events using systems such as calendars of various types.

Such a critique is particularly important to ethnomusicologists, who have long studied ordinary as well as great musicians. Many ethnomusicologists, for example, would find it difficult to study only a particular kind of class of musician. They would feel much more affinity with oral historians, who have conducted considerable research on working-class people.

2. **Chronology may have little significance in some cultures and provide an explanation that has little relevance to the people in a particular society.**

   A Kpelle woman of Liberia, West Africa, for example, might very well have no idea of the year in which she was born. The linking of one's birth to a particular year, month, and day might not be possible or hold any real significance. Gilbert Chase (1958:5) argued for recognizing these kinds of issues in writing music history of the Americas. He advocated some years ago for not relying on chronology as a universal way to understand history around the world.

Contribution

Historical research provides ways of interpreting events of the past. The advantages and disadvantages of employing an historical perspective include the following:

1. **Historical research provides a way of describing events that may have influenced what is happening at a current moment.**

   Scholars interpret the past as a way of understanding what is occurring in the present, providing a context for current events.

2. **Chronology offers a quantitative means of ordering discrete events that occurred in the past.**

   Chronology provides a valuable framework within which to make sense of many events that have happened in the distant as well as the recent past. It helps describe the position of events, including co-occurrence.

Historical Research in Ethnomusicology

What is interesting about historical research in ethnomusicology is that in the nineteenth century when comparative musicology was important, the people who wrote about history were very much part of the music research establishment, and well-accepted music disciplines were much more closely aligned than they are today (Bohlman 1987:161–62).

By the end of the nineteenth century, music historians embraced both Western and non-Western musics as objects of their study. That sort of music change now called diachronic was largely the focus of study, and . . . music histories continued to include considerable sections devoted to non-Western music several decades into the present century. (161–62).

These histories centered on ordering according to stylistic periods and the emergence of a few great men (161–62).

The dearth of historical perspective in ethnomusicology from the 1950s to the late 1980s—a period of some thirty years—is notable. This lack of historical studies in ethnomusicology was influenced, in part, by a vein of antihistorical feeling that ran through anthropology (Evans-Pritchard 1961). "Primitive" people didn't possess history, in large part because they didn't have written sources. Instead they were assumed to possess fairly fixed *traditions,* practices that were replicated nearly unchanged again and again. The focus of study for anthropology was the "ethnographic present," and ethnomusicology, particularly in the United States, adopted this approach during its early years.

The work of European ethnomusicologists has shown a stronger emphasis on history than American scholars. As Ludwik Bielawski (1958) notes,

> This trend toward an historical approach in ethnomusicology can be seen in the work of various scholars and has also found its expression in the activities of the ICTM [International Council of Traditional Music] study group, set up to investigate historical sources of folk music. (8)

Bielawski goes on to define his notion of historical research in ethnomusicology: "I should like to stress that my concept of history in ethnomusicology is very comprehensive; it includes the past of music and of music cultures covered by this discipline, no matter what sources are used, what methods are applied, or how detailed and certain the results are; whether, for instance, it is based on relative or absolute chronology" (10). Bielawski outlines five kinds of history:

1. Immediate history of local societies
2. Mythic past and tradition
3. Complete history of a given culture
4. History of mankind and evolutionary stages
5. Music (origins) anthropogenesis (10)

Timothy Rice in 1987 recognized this lack of attention to history as he called for reinstating the historical dimension in ethnomusicology. As he contextualized his formulation (1987:473), drawing on Clifford Geertz's (1973) statement that symbolic systems are "historically constructed, socially maintained, and individually applied" (363–64), Rice called for a reformulated model in which ethnomusicologists study "formative processes" and ask this basic question: "[H]ow do people historically construct, socially maintain, and individually create and experience music?" (473). This verbal statement was illustrated by a visual model (Figure 27).

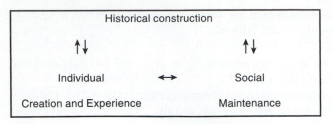

Figure 27 Model of Historical Construction

Although one might argue in another context about how the social maintenance corner of the triangle may or may not begin to resemble structural functionalism, the issue here is the renewed emphasis on the historical dimension in ethnomusicology.

Despite a lack of work regarding historical research in ethnomusicology, there *are* ethnomusicologists who have attended to historical issues. Alan Merriam (1967), the early advocate of the structural-functional approach, addressed in another context how music research could play a corroborative role in historical reconstruction. Other illustrations of historical approaches appeared in *Essays on Music and History in Africa* (Wachsmann 1971). Several works followed that focused on organological data (Epstein 1975) as well as documentary sources (Maultsby 1975; Soedarsono 1969; Stevenson 1973).

Kay Kaufman Shelemay (1980) suggested that "historical ethnomusicology" can do more than confirm already known histories. She attempted to use her musical data to provide an explanation in reconstructing Falasha liturgical history in Ethiopia. She concluded that the Falasha beliefs and liturgy emerged from influence by a "Judaized Ethiopian Orthodox monasticism" (216).

In another work, investigating Syrian Jews in diasporic communities, Shelemay (1998) showed how music performance becomes a powerful tool of remembrance—a historical device, as it were. "Memorializing individuals in song also served literally to unite early twentieth century immigrants to Brooklyn with their ancestors in Aleppo . . . The encoding of names further empowers the pizmon through linking it to a central social mechanism in the Syrian Jewish community: one in which personal names are ritually extended to a subsequent generation" (47). Thus Shelemay investigated ways that musicians use historical devices to connect the past with the present.

George Sawa (1981) pointed to continuity over time of Arabic performance practice from medieval times. Beverly Cavanagh (1982) explored continuity and change in the music of the Netsilik Eskimo. More recently, Lorna McDaniel (1994) combined research in international song repositories with interviews of culture bearers to document spirituals in Trinidad.

A number of ethnomusicological studies rely prominently on historical data even if they also contain ethnography. Gage Averill in *A Day for the Hunter: A Day for the Prey* (1997) examines popular music and power in Haiti from 1915 to 1995. Each chapter of the book focuses on a different case study, and only the period from 1986 to 1995 relies on field-researched data. Rather than emphasize the "state-populace" nexus, Averill (1997) centers on "everyday tactics of resistance . . . in which daily interactions, situations, and contexts are submerged" (9).

The Voice of Egypt: Umm Kulthūm, Arabic Song, and Egyptian Society in the Twentieth Century by Virginia Danielson (1997) centers on a single performer and her life. Although Danielson conducted ethnographic field research, she also investigated written sources. As she noted,

> A great deal has been written about music in twentieth-century Egypt. . . . Brief accounts . . . appeared frequently in the relatively large number of periodicals and columns devoted to music and theater published in Cairo. . . . Following the establishment of Egyptian National Radio in 1934, interviews with musicians were broadcast and, beginning in the 1940s, some were kept in sound archives and collected on tape by those aficionados who had the necessary equipment (5–6).

Danielson (1997) comments on the value of using historical resources when she says, "Historical resources permit comparison of interpretations of events as they occurred with later reflections on the same events and offer a view of the usages of events from the past to illustrate larger ideas or trends and to explain and shape the present" (7).

On of the more unusual works in historical ethnomusicology is Bonnie Wade's exploration of historical *visual* sources—specifically paintings from Mughal India—for the purpose of understanding music from that context. Wade's (1998) work combines ethnomusicology with art from a historical perspective. She is interested in "how Indian musicians of Hindustan encountered and absorbed music from the Persian cultural sphere in the sixteenth and seventeenth centuries" (xlix). She uses visual art, in conjunction with written sources, to interpret the historical past.

Plate 29 Gage Averill. Courtesy of Gage Averill.

Plate 30 Bonnie Wade. Courtesy of Bonnie Wade.

Eric Charry (2000), in his book *Mande Music*, provides considerable historical background to his presentation of ethnographic material—sketching the broad history of West Africa to set the scene for his present-day exploration of musical practices in the Mande area.

There are certainly other examples to be cited of ethnomusicologists using historical sources. What is clear, however, is that most of these examples have appeared toward the end of the discipline's first fifty years in the United States. Very few works written from 1958 to 1980 mentioned or emphasized history.

Assumptions

A number of assumptions are inherent in the use of history by ethnomusicologists:

1. **History in ethnomusicology centers on small groups of people or individuals and their relations.**

   Growing out of anthropology and folklore, ethnomusicologists have centered on very different kinds of individuals and groups than have historians in the

Plate 31 Eric Charry. Courtesy of Eric Charry.

discipline of history. There has been much less emphasis in ethnomusicology on "great individuals."

2. **Where history in ethnomusicology treats issues of power, it tends to look at performers who give voice to resistance rather than at the political leaders.**

The concern with power in ethnomusicology has centered on oppositional rather than diplomatic voices, for the most part.

3. **Ethnomusicological histories may focus on great musicians but more often center on ordinary musicians and their performances.**

These decisions follow from the focus in ethnomusicology, for the most part, on the ordinary and everyday. This does not imply that ethnomusicologists do not seek out outstanding performers to study, but rather that they are interested in a broad range of people who make and consume music.

4. **Chronology may or may not be included as a metric for historic events.**

Ethnographic research may reveal that chronology in a relative or absolute sense is not critical to the interpretation of history and its local understanding. An ethnomusicologist may use chronology if and when it fits with local interpretations.

Critique

There are also, however, some limitations to historical treatments in ethnomusicology:

1. **We cannot interrogate the dead, so to speak, and our abilities to derive information from documents are limited.**

   Scholars are limited in their ability to recreate events of the past from historical records. Not all of the circumstances of human interaction or musical performance in the past have been preserved, and ethnomusicologists must infer what might have taken place. They cannot interview someone who is no longer living.

2. **Chronological treatments may have relatively little significance to some people whose music we investigate.**

   Ethnomusicologists may work in situations that do not lend themselves to analysis through presentation of chronology. Rather, alternative ways of organizing and ordering data may better present an analysis that reflects the local interpretation.

Contribution

The works that have centered on historical ethnomusicology have made a number of important contributions to the field:

1. **Historical treatments provide an expanded context in which to understand present-day performance.**

   A growing number of scholars in ethnomusicology are finding that the inclusion of historical research enhances their understanding of present-day music performance. They are turning to historical sources to provide a more nuanced study of their particular issue or event.

2. **Written historic documents help corroborate oral accounts and texture ethnographic accounts.**

   Ethnomusicologists are increasingly examining archival records—including letters, posters, and newspaper accounts—and relating these written historical sources to ethnographic data like interviews, observations, and transcriptions.

3. **Ethnomusicological inquiry that emphasizes history brings historical methods to bear on topics that might otherwise be excluded from the purview of the ethnomusicologist.**

   There are a vast range of historical issues that ethnomusicologists can study that will ultimately be of interest to a broad range of scholars in the humanities and social sciences. Among these are such issues as the life career of a musician—sometimes called a life history, style changes in music performance over time, and movement of musical practices through a diaspora as people move away from their homeland over the course of time.

Historical Research: Example from Liberia

The Woi-méni-pele, an epic I have earlier mentioned as an example from the Kpelle, includes song, narration, instrumental playing, and dramatic gesture—modes by which the performers communicate to the audiences in Liberia and Guinea.

This epic first drew my attention in the mid-1970s when one Kpelle musician noted that if I wanted to understand Kpelle life, I could just listen to the Woi epic. My research assistant, John Barclay, made an even stronger claim by saying that all Kpelle life is contained within the Woi epic. Such comments were intriguing, if a bit puzzling. The Woi epic, after all, appeared to be more mythical than historical. Where were the names of rulers and their genealogies that were characteristic of the Sunjata epic (Austen and Jansen 1996)? What could this epic contribute to our understanding of history and the precolonial period for Kpelle musicians?

Wealth in Knowledge

What came from that investigation was the insight that the Woi epic is emblematic of important particularities in Kpelle history. First *a wealth in knowledge* is indexed in the epic. This wealth in knowledge as developed historically is related to what Jane Guyer and Samuel Eno Belinga (1995) have noted:

> The study of growth in Equatorial Africa in the precolonial period might be seen as, in part, a social history of expanding knowledge, and the history of the colonial era as one of loss, denial and partial reconstitution. The fact that much of this must remain inaccessible should not deter us from creating the space to envisage it. (94–95)

The Woi epic demonstrates a tremendous wealth in knowledge and accumulation that develops through historical time. The episodes that I have recorded are embedded with rich details of animals, plants, and objects of habitat. These are details that are much more extensive than required for people to subsist.

One performance of a Woi epic included the spider, *tuu-tuu* bird, anteater, *poling* bird, squirrel monkey, tsetse fly, beetle, bat, bull, and bees, among many animals. The plants, which played roles in the battles, included the *bele* tree, *koing*tree, pumpkin, and *koong* leaf. Among the objects that played a role in the battle were the bow, the arrow, a bag containing implements to help Woi, an axe, a cutlass, and a double-edged knife (Stone 1988:94).

As Jan Vansina (1990) the historian has gone on to say, "[L]ocal communities knew much more about their local habitats than they needed to know" and "such scientific knowledge for knowledge's sake was an essential ingredient . . ." of social life in the historic past in West Africa (189, 225, as quoted in Guyer

1996:5). By understanding something of the wealth in knowledge, we have a window on this period in West African history.

Movement

Beyond a wealth in knowledge in the epic, *movement* is indexed in the epic. Movement at many levels characterizes the Woi epic. At the broadest level, Woi, the superhero, is traveling with his extended family. The narrative centers on encounters Woi has along the way and the small-scale battles in which he must engage to keep moving his family. Sometimes these enemies are human, and other times they are other than human. Meni-ma-faa is a monster spirit who married Woi's sister by disguising himself as a human. The Bele tree is a supernatural plant that blocks the movement of Woi's house at another point.

The essential discovery, which I made several years after first recording the Woi epic, is that this epic symbolically represents the migration of the Kpelle people from the grasslands area of the kingdom of Mali to the forest region of the coast. Allusion and metaphor provide a view of the traces of the history of the Kpelle. These people, beginning in the fourteenth century, started their migration toward the forest region. Their history is detailed more literally in oral narratives (D'Azevedo 1962:13; Geysbeek 1994:49). This epic, however, provides a much more abstract historical presentation.

The Kpelle people, as a branch of various Mande peoples, left the grasslands area because of various pressures, and they started toward the coastal rain forest. They encountered other peoples on that long migration and fought small-scale wars to protect areas where they settled for a time. Oral history accounts detail this pattern. Peter Giting, a member of the famous Giting family of chiefs from Sanoyea, told of battles in the Kpelle area of what is today Bong County. He told me how each warring side had a musician who played before a battle to increase the warriors' courage and pump the troops up for conflict.

When the fighting ensued, musicians were immune from attack by either side. Following the battle, the winning side had the prerogative of taking the musicians belonging to the losing side. Through this practice, the musicians became a kind of war prize.

In the Woi epic, the migrations are alluded to by Woi, who is continually moving his house as battles are brewing:

Woi is ready. He said, "You singing that, Zo-lang-kee, the war is ready."

And I was in the house. I said to him, "Ee." I said to him, "Woi?"

He said to me, "Mm."

I said to him, "What war is prepared? You yourself see the Sitting-on-the-neck crowd here. Why is the war being prepared since there is no one equal to you?"

"Fine, when Kelema-ninga has pumped my bellows and they have sewn my clothes, then we will start on the war." (Stone 1988:13–14)

The moving house, filled with the extended family, symbolically represented the Kpelle people as a whole traveling toward the coast. Woi stood for the greater aggregate of the Kpelle people.

As knowledgeable Kpelle hear the epic being performed, they frequently make comments about how the Woi epic indexes the coming of their ancestors to the present area in Liberia or Guinea that they occupy, even if some have recently been displaced by the civil war that began in 1989 and lasted nearly fifteen years.

On a more specific level, movement takes place in the epic through detailed and careful labeling of various qualities of action. Kulung, the narrator, on one occasion at which I was present, dramatized Spider playing the slit drum, the blacksmith forging iron, the cowbird pumping the bellows for the blacksmith, Woi's wife carving bowls, and a group of men chopping a tree that blocked the house. The chorus echoed the visual-kinesthetic action with sound: *keng keree; keleng, keleng, zang, zang keleng; zi-zi-zi; vee, vee; bongkai, kpolong, kpolong, fee-laa; zou, zou.* The onomatopoeic words detailed the various kinds and qualities of movement.

One particular episode I have recorded is replete with movement depiction. In this episode, Woi's jealous wife gets banished to carve bowls with her voice and the text explodes with rich, variegated movement. As Woi's jealous wife engages a male client, one that she expects will reward her with an encounter in bed, she employs such onomatopoeic terms as *bongkai* (large inside), *kpolong* (thin walls), *koro, koro* (small adze strokes), *mono, mono* (shiny blackness), *fee-laa* (smooth) to describe movement. Later, as Woi's wife is approached by a female client, she shows her disgust and the movement depicted is much less varied—in fact it's quite unattractive aesthetically. She uses the sound *kpitili* (thick ugly) as the only descriptor (Stone 1988:62–63).

The rich action created by the wife with her male clients illustrates how action creates the epic in much the same way that action reveals theme and character in Xhosa narrative tradition in southern Africa. According to Harold Scheub (1970),

> Movement is vital to the tradition, action is all important, and character is revealed not by description but through action. Similarly, theme is revealed not by interpolations or preachments, but through action. (144)

The most pervasive movement of the Woi epic and one that reoccurs in each episode is that of Woi's house:

Zi, zi, zi, zi . . .

QUESTIONER: What thing's sound is that again?
NARRATOR: The house's traveling sound that is.
QUESTIONER: Oh koo. [Expression of astonishment]
NARRATOR: The house has risen into the distant sky.
             The house is going.

QUESTIONER: Woi's house?

NARRATOR: Woi's house.

QUESTIONER: Were you there?

NARRATOR: Very close, really. All things in the swamp were
               responding, "Woi, woi." Do you know the *gboto's*
               voice? There's the house they are announcing.
               Isn't it so? (Stone 1988:33)

All this action and confrontation does not lead, however, to a definitive climax. Each small crisis is resolved, and the house moves on to the next challenge.

Such patterns of multiple small crises and the lack of a single climactic scene have been noted in the narrative in other parts of Africa as well as other parts of the world. The lack of causal linear movement between episodes of the Woi epic is similar to the situation with some other African epics. It is also reminiscent of the situation that Alton L. Becker presents for *wayang kulit*, Javanese shadow theater. A *wayang* plot is built on coincidence and may begin at any point in the story temporally. In the same way, the Woi epic performance may begin on any given evening at any point in the life of Woi. Robert Plan Armstrong's (1971) textual analysis of the musical drama *The Palmwine Drinkard* from Nigeria identifies similar episodes as "sequential" rather than "consequential" in what he terms "intensive continuity," noting that "continuity can be seen as a function of the density of multiple, discrete parts" (168).

The movements that build epic performance are selected from different time dimensions as well as different space dimensions. As the audience hears, "Oh, Maa-laa, bring my voice," they are alerted to Kulung's appeal to a tutelary spirit—a supernatural being normally living in the same time but in a distinctly different space. The spirit he seeks and calls on to enhance his voice may also be the spirit of a deceased great performer who comes back to lend greatness to music making, thus originating from a different time as well as a different space.

Distributed Performance

The Woi epic's wealth of knowledge and rich depiction of movement are organized by a distributed performance pattern. In fact, the Woi epic surprised and impressed me by the way that performers divide up the parts. For example, two players play a portion each of the underlying rhythmic pattern that interlocks in the sound of struck bottles. Such distribution is reminiscent of the division of parts among the two Mangwilo xylophone players that Gerhard Kubik (1965) located in southeastern Africa. They sit opposite one another and both share in playing the same instrument. The players are referred to as Opachera (the starting one) and Wakulela (the responding one) (36).

Certain patterns appear that may have persisted from the precolonial period. In the Woi epic, the chorus is subdivided into two patterns that always fit one to another. This fundamental principle of dividing and distributing performance

Plate 32 Gerhard Kubik with a family in Disol, Nigeria, 1963. Courtesy of Gerhard Kubik.

labor—breaking parts into small bits that are then combined, not unlike a Picasso painting—is an aesthetic building principle that appears to have deep roots. It is part of a genre the Kpelle people use to index their history.

Looking beyond epic performance, Jane Guyer and Samuel Eno Belinga (1995) note for equatorial Africa:

> Collectively, knowledge was conceptualized as an open repertoire and an unbounded vista: then *within* collectivities the vista was divided up and quite widely distributed on the basis of personal capacity. Adepts were many and varied, each pushing up against the outside limits of their own frontier of the known world, inventing new ways of configuring, sorting and using what must have been an ever shifting spectrum of possibility. (93)

This principle—in which people show delight in having parts, patterns, and knowledge widely divided and distributed, and then alternatively recombined and reintegrated—resonates throughout the Woi epic. It is found in the patterning of the *konîng*, a triangular frame zither where the various parts are played in widely ranging pitch registers. The hocketing of a work cooperative that is clearing bush also shows the distributed pattern as each singer performs a one or two-note ostinato that interlocks with the other ostinatos of vocalists and instrumentalists. Guyer and Belinga (1996:7) support my contention that such dispersion is foundational in this part of Africa and essential to understanding historical developments in this region.

We can see why the Kpelle people I have interviewed are so eager to point out that the Woi epic is the embodiment of what it means to be Kpelle in a historical sense. The structuring of the epic, as well as much of its content, carries collective history with it. And this is a history, in part at least, that is brought from the grasslands area, dating from the pre-European colonial era.

This is a performance that brings the past into the present, always refiguring it in small ways. In certain respects, the Woi epic has responded to influences such as airplanes. In one version, the narrator sings of Woi moving his airplane filled with his family. But interestingly, the pace of movement and syllables used to describe the movement remain the same as when Woi moves his house, whether the family moves in a jet plane or a mud house.

There is a strong indication that the epic, unlike entertainment music, embodies continuity and an endless quality. The narrator scatters themes from different episodes throughout his performance, showing links and hinting at what possibilities for action might lie in the future. He minimizes the cutoffs and endings at the close of episodes, emphasizing the continuous flow of the work. He simply says, "Ding kpala, ke, wese." "Dried millet breaking, wese [sound of millet breaking]. After the audience responds, "Wese," he quickly launches into the next episode. Indeed, at the end of an evening's performance, the narrator doesn't reach the end of the epic. Rather, he simply stops, assuming that the next performance will take up the music and action where he left off.

The Woi epic, in conclusion, displays a wealth of knowledge that was likely the Kpelle heritage even from the time when they lived in the general area of the ancient kingdom of Mali. This richness has been handed down through the centuries and is on vivid display in the Woi epic. This heritage continues today in the moment that performers recreate and keep it as a living, portable embodiment of history.

The movement that is so replete in this form is totally antithetical to the colonial efforts to portray Africans as caught in a world of stasis and fixation. Performance of a complex distribution of parts and a rich abundance of content further counter the strong stereotypes of fixity that have been promulgated in the world of Hollywood and even sometimes in the academy.

It is critical that we take historical data seriously and build on it as we seek to better understand the performance of performers in Africa. Ethnographic study of the Woi epic has yielded rich evidence of historical issues even if they are conveyed in allusive and symbolic language.

Conclusion

Historical research in ethnomusicology was little practiced in the post–World War II years of the discipline, particularly in North America. That situation has changed considerably in the last thirty years, and an increasing number of authors are blending ethnography with historiography to find a fruitful melding of approaches. Thus the pendulum has swung back to emphasize what for a number of years was quite lacking in the field of ethnomusicology.

References

Armstrong, Robert Plant. 1971. *The Affecting Presence: An Essay in Humanistic Anthropology*. Urbana: University of Illinois Press.

Austen, Ralph A., and Jan Vansina. 1996. "History, Oral Transmission and Structure in Ibn Khaldun's Chronology of Mali Rulers." *History in Africa* 23: 17–28.

Averill, Gage. 1997. *A Day for the Hunter: A Day for the Prey: Popular Music and Power in Haiti*. Chicago: University of Chicago Press.

Bielawski, Ludwik. 1958. "History in Ethnomusicology." Translated by Ludwik Wiewiorkowki. *Yearbook for Traditional Music* 17: 8–15.

Bohlman, Philip V. 1987. "The European Discovery of Music in the Islamic World and the 'Non-Western' in 19th-Century Music History." *Journal of Musicology* 5(2): 142–63.

Cavanagh, Beverley. 1982. *Music of the Netsilik Eskimo: A Study of Stability and Change*. Ottawa: National Museums of Canada.

Charry, Eric. 2000. *Mande Music: Traditional and Modern Music of the Maninka and Mandinka of Western Africa*. Chicago: University of Chicago Press.

Chase, Gilbert. 1958. "A Dialectical Approach to Music History." *Ethnomusicology* 2(1): 1–9.

Danielson, Virginia. 1997. *The Voice of Egypt*. Chicago: University of Chicago Press.

D'Azevedo, Warren L. 1962. "Uses of the Past in Gola Discourse." *The Journal of African History* 3(1): 11–34.

DeMaille, Raymond J. 1984. *The Sixth Grandfather: Black Elk's Teachings Given to John G. Neihardt*. Lincoln: University of Nebraska Press.

Epstein, Dena J. 1975. "The Folk Banjo: A Documentary History." *Ethnomusicology* 19(3): 347–71.

"Ethnohistory." 2006. *JSTOR: Ethnohistory*. http://www.jstor.org/journals/0014180.html (accessed July 3, 2006).

Evans-Pritchard, Edward E. 1961. *Anthropology and History*. Manchester: Manchester University Press.

Garraghan, Gilbert J. 1946. *A Guide to Historical Method*. New York: Fordham University Press.

Geertz, Clifford. 1973. *The Interpretation of Culture*. New York: Basic Books.

Geysbeek, Tim. 1994. "A Traditional History of the Konyan (15th–16th Century): Vase Camera's Epic of Musadu." *History in Africa* 21: 49–85.

Guyer, Jane I. 1996. "Traditions of Invention in Equatorial Africa." *African Studies Review* 39(3): 1–28.

———, and Samuel M. Eno Belinga. 1995. "Wealth in People as Wealth in Knowledge: Accumulation and Composition in Equatorial Africa. *The Journal of African History* 36(1):91–120.

"History." 2005. *Encyclopaedia Britannica Online*. http://search.eb.com/article-9040600 (accessed October 17, 2005).

Kubik, Gerhard. 1965. "Transcription of Mangwilo Xylophone Music from Film Strips." *African Music* 3(4): 35–41.

Maultsby, Portia K. 1975. "Music of Northern Independent Black Churches during the Ante-Bellum Period." *Ethnomusicology* 19(3): 401–20.

McDaniel, Lorna. 1994. "Memory Spirituals of the Ex-Slave American Soldiers in Trinidad's 'Company Villages.'" *Black Music Journal* 14(2): 119–43.

Merriam, Alan P. 1967. "Use of Music in Reconstructing Culture History." In *Reconstructing African Culture History,* Creighton Gavel and Norman Bennett, eds. Boston: Boston University Press, 85–114.

Ranke, Leopold, and Robert Wines. 1981. *The Secret of World History: Selected Writings on the Art and Science of History.* New York: Fordham University Press.

Rice, Timothy. 1987. "Toward the Remodeling of Ethnomusicology." *Ethnomusicology* 31(3): 469–88.

Sawa, George. 1981. "The Survival of Some Aspects of Medieval Arabic Performance Practice." *Ethnomusicology* 25(1): 73–86.

Schafer, Robert J., and David H. Bennett. 1980. *A Guide to Historical Method.* 3rd ed. Homewood, Ill.: Dorsey Press.

Scheub, Harold. 1970. "The Technique of the Expansible Image in Xhosa *Ntsomi* Performances." *Research in African Literatures* 1(2): 119–46.

Shelemay, Kay Kaufman. 1980. "'Historical Ethnomusicology': Reconstructing Falasha Liturgical History." *Ethnomusicology* 24(2): 233–58.

————. 1998. *Let Jasmine Rain Down: Song and Remembrance among Syrian Jews.* Chicago: University of Chicago Press.

Soedarsono. 1969. "Classical Javanese Dance: History and Characterization." *Ethnomusicology* 13(3): 498–506.

Stevenson, Robert. 1973. "Written Sources for Indian Music until 1882." *Ethnomusicology* 17(1): 1–40.

Stone, Ruth M. 1988. *Dried Millet Breaking.* Bloomington: Indiana University Press.

Vansina, Jan. 1985. *Oral Tradition as History.* Madison: University of Wisconsin Press.

————. 1990. *Paths in the Rainforest: Toward a History of Political Tradition in Equatorial Africa.* Madison: University of Wisconsin Press.

Wachsmann, Klaus P., ed. 1971. *Essays on Music and History in Africa.* Evanston, Ill.: Northwestern University Press.

Wade, Bonnie. 1998. *Imaging Sound: An Ethnomusicological Study of Music, Art, and Culture in Mughal India.* Chicago: University of Chicago Press.

Chapter 13

Postmodern, Postcolonial, and Global Issues

The world today, some theoreticians argue, is a radically changing one in which the very ways we used to understand the world are being altered. Today's world has been labeled as "postmodern" to denote a shift to a decentered set of discourses in the information age. The Internet connects people in a global sense even as authority centers shift. Anthony Giddens (1994) describes two areas of transformation: "the extensional spread of modern institutions, universalized via globalizing processes" and at the same time "the disinterring and problematizing of tradition" (57). These shifts have brought about a "displacement and reappropriation of expertise"(58).

Modernism as a precursor to postmodernism has been characterized as the period that involved urbanization, the rise of nation-states, capitalism, and socialist movements, grand theory, and absolute values. In the late twentieth century, postmodernism emerged—a time in which people questioned ultimate truths and place an emphasis on the interconnectivity of people and cultures with multiple centers of power. The Internet itself is an apt metaphor for postmodernism with the vast web of connections and no single dominant center.

The postmodern moment becomes a time when "grand theory" that searches to explain regularities is out of favor, and scholars seek instead to point to the more chaotic dimensions of social life. Some distinctive traits of postmodern scholarship include a crisis of representation, an interest in multivocality, a focus of social power dynamics, and a concern with issues of hegemony, as well as issues about the illusion of authority on the part of the ethnographer.

In a postmodernist vein, George Marcus and Michael Fischer (1986) advocated that "A strong and distinctive practice of cultural critique by anthropologists should combine the empiricism of American documentary realism with the theoretical vision and vitality of the Frankfurt School in its early period, along with the playfulness and daring of the juxtapositions of French surrealism." Experimentation in the conduct of research and writing should be encouraged (127–28).

> It is again not entirely without paradox that postmodern theory has found its most welcoming reception and home not in France but in the United States—the nation of pragmatism, empiricism, and a much vaunted liberal consensus. . . . [I]t is among the American left, among neo- and post-Marxists, feminists, queers, and Third World and postcolonial intellectuals, that postmodernism has been most enthusiastically embraced. (Nicholson and Seidman 1995:1)

Of interest is also the curious fact that some of the people most closely associated with bringing about postmodernism—Michel Foucault and Jacques Derrida among them—would reject the association of the term with their writing (Nicholson and Seidman 1995:1).

The processes that scholars label as postmodern have their roots as far back as the 1920s, and thus the postmodern is a complex transition accomplished over a good portion of the twentieth century. The scholars associated with this movement cannot be easily grouped under a single rubric of theoretical ideas. But there have been a few theorists with widely influential ideas that are worth examining in greater depth.

Deconstruction and Jacques Derrida

Deconstruction is the approach inaugurated by Derrida that uncovers ideologies built into our language. Many of these ideas may exist without our awareness. Furthermore, "Our mental life consists not of concepts—not of solid, stable meanings—but of a fleeting, continually changing play of signifiers" (Tyson 1999:245). According to Derrida, meaning is ultimately created through differences that we grasp between one signifier and another.

Derrida borrowed and extended the notion of *binary opposition* from structuralism, arguing that one of the two terms in the opposition is always privileged. If we identify the privileged concepts in the pairs, we can then uncover the **ideology** operative in an event or production (Tyson 1999:247). For example, in a community in which racial identity is important, the concept of "black" may

---

Deconstruction

- Research framework associated with Jacques Derrida
- Emphasizes the questioning of certain ideological assumptions and exploring contradictions or language

---

Ideology

- Organized group of ideas that often relate to political or social issues

be a signifier that is opposed to "white." One of those two terms will be privi-leged, depending on the community that is considering those concepts.

Deconstruction assumes that language is the basis for understanding our world in all its dynamic and ideologically saturated nature. "Thus, deconstruc-tion is called a poststructuralist theory, not only because it emerged in the wake of structuralism's popularity but also because it constitutes a reaction against structuralism's orderly vision of language and human experience" (Tyson 1999:250). Furthermore, "There is no presence before and outside semi-ological difference" (Derrida 1982:12). The contrast in meaning between pairs of signifiers is the very bedrock of the creation of meaning. This shifts attention to the "web of social, economic, and power relationships in which a particular sort of human being is constructed" (Monson 1996:207). For Derrida, selfhood is constructed through language and the complexity of shifting meaning that arises from oppositions between signifiers.

Michel Foucault: Power and Knowledge

Another prominent scholar associated with postmodernism is Foucault. He carried out critical studies of institutions in France, centering on power and knowledge. Foucault was interested in discourse in Western thought and how it shifted. He noted that there were underlying approaches to truth in particu-lar periods (*épistème*) that changed on occasion. And his concept bears consid-erable similarities to Thomas Kuhn's notion of "paradigm" (Foucault 1972). Another area of Foucault's research centered on sexuality, and he published a three-volume history (Foucault 1976, 1984a, 1984b).

Foucault opposed a "book-centered, work-centered concept of history that treated texts and their authors as transparently obvious" (Monson 1996:207). He was more interested in "how particular statements or discourses were pos-sible rather than in the rules that governed the internal logic of any particular work" (Foucault 1972:27; Monson 1996:207). He was interested in underlying conditions that made interaction possible.

As Foucault saw it, power "circulates in all directions, to and from all social levels, at all times" (Tyson 1999:281). Power circulates through exchange of goods, taxation, charity, people, and ideas and is above all decentered.

Culture theory drew heavily on the ideas of Foucault. For culture theorists, "culture is a process, not a product; it is a lived experience, not a fixed defini-tion" (Tyson 1999:294).

Habitus and Pierre Bordieu

Pierre Bordieu (1977, 1984) is another scholar working in the postmodern vein, and his work has influenced a broad range of disciplines. He provides us with a sociology of our bodily inscribed categories—that is, habits by which we interact

Habitus
• Way of acting that has been acquired through social interaction

Schemata
• Cognitive map or mental organization that influences the processing of information

in the world. He speaks of **habitus** in terms of classificatory **schemata**, which are flexible and less fixed than categories. We might also think of habitus as "orientation" (Lash 1994:155). "Habitus . . . assumes a certain 'thrownness' into a web of already existing practices and meanings" (Lash 1994:156). People employ *habitus* as a subjective response to the larger world of relationships in which they maneuver. Bordieu found, for example, that although people, in theory, are free to choose whatever kind of music they wish for their own pleasure, certain kinds of music are favored by people in certain social positions (1984).

Culture Theory and Culture Studies

Culture studies developed in many English departments as literary scholars discovered some of the approaches that anthropologists and sociologists had long used. This movement extended to scholars in nearby film and communications departments who approached research of popular culture and areas long left to folklorists, anthropologists, and ethnomusicologists.

Drawing on Derrida, Foucault, and others, they argued for studying the process of the study object being constituted by the web of ideologies that are a necessary aspect of understanding and constituted a particular approach.

Culture theory also built on Marxist theory, even though in the 1960s cultural theory became an analytic orientation in its own right, arguing that "working class culture has been misunderstood and undervalued. As a result of its orientation, culture theory has been overtly political in studying oppressed groups. The approach makes frequent use of Marxist, feminist, and other related orientations. And for study objects, cultural theory has shown a decided preference for popular culture" (Tyson 1999:294).

Postmodernism: Assumptions

A number of assumptions guide the confederation of ideas contained in postmodernist approaches to the study of culture:

1. **Postmodernists focus on a set of decentered discourses where a single authority does not exist.**

The interest rests on a web of social, economic, and power relationships and how this set of discourses is possible within a particular setting.

2. **The goal of postmodernists is to uncover ideological issues that are often out of awareness but have important implications for understanding any particular situation.**

The researcher is charged with revealing and discerning what the particular ideologies are that influence any particular set of discourses.

3. **Language is the basis for understanding our world in all its dynamic and ideologically saturated nature.**

For a number of postmodernists, written language becomes the basis for understanding the world. The data for analysis come from printed and published texts. This is certainly the case for scholars in literary criticism, although it is important for linguistic anthropologists as well.

4. **Working-class culture has been misunderstood and undervalued.**

Postmodernists have been overtly political in studying oppressed groups. They have reacted to a focus in many disciplines, such as history and English literature, on great men and elite ideals. They have called for a turn to those who have been ignored by research in these disciplines. Some scholars, like Foucault and Bordieu, have also worked as activists in the political causes of these oppressed individuals.

Critique

Like all the theoretical orientations before, postmodernism can also be cited for some shortcomings in regard to research:

1. **Whole areas of social theory, including "institutions, social classes, political organization, political economic processes, and social movements," have been neglected by postmodernists by focusing on language (Nicholson and Seidman 1995:8).**

Areas of interest to anthropologists and sociologists, among others, in the social sciences, have been neglected. This is largely a result of the perspective of culture studies scholars.

2. **Postmodernist approaches downplay the agency of individuals, maintaining that individuals are controlled by power and hegemony, making it difficult, if not impossible, to break free.**

Postmodernist approaches, on one hand, emphasize multiple viewpoints for research. On the other hand, they deny power to individuals to make decisions, claiming that these individuals are dominated by ideologies that control their lives.

3. **Postmodernist theory emphasizes a "negative or critical aspect" (Nicholson and Seidman (1995:8).**

What is lacking is an imaginative positive orientation for alternatives to the essentialist views of which they are critical. It's easy to tear things down, and harder to build up alternatives. One suggestion for beginning to address the focus on deconstruction is "social postmodernism," which "requires a radical rethinking of the premises and language of social knowledge and politics . . . [where] intellectuals could speak to the multiplicity of oppositional movement, be attentive to their specific struggles, be coalitional, and affirm strategies and social goals that valued difference" (Nicholson and Seidman 1995:8–9). In other words, social postmodernism embraces deconstruction that attends to nuances of multiple viewpoints while at the same time adopting some of the synthesizing strategies of modernist scholars.

Contribution

A number of contributions by postmodernism to scholarship can be cited:

1. **A decentered vantage point for research provides an alternative to metanarratives that are encompassed in approaches such as Marxism, which preceded postmodernism.**

   Postmodernism acknowledges multiple possible perspectives from which to view a situation. Anthropologist Arjun Appadurai proposes that the world now is characterized by a number of "-scapes," including ethnoscapes, mediascapes, technoscapes, ideoscapes, and fin-ancescapes. These scapes are constantly shifting and help explain the postmodern world. Within the ethnoscapes, for example, are the various kinds of people that impact what goes on in the world—immigrants, tourists, refugees, and guest workers. Their movement and social practices help shape the world that is connected in new and interesting ways (Appadurai 1991:191–210; 1996).

2. **Postmodernist approaches take process on a microlevel seriously and attempt to address it.**

   Details important to ethnomusicologists now also become critical to many postmodernists who recognize the ever-shifting nature of interaction and interpretation of that interaction. Ethnomusicologists keenly attuned to the nuances of musical performances find such a focus to fit nicely with a number of their approaches.

Ethnomusicology and Postmodern Orientations

Many ethnomusicologists have found postmodernism ideas appropriate in their research. They have drawn on a number of the concepts developed by some of the major scholars in this area. These ideas give added nuance to explanations.

Jane Sugarman (1997), for example, has found Foucault's notion of "discourse" a way to organize indigenous concepts that come from a variety of settings and times. She notes,

> Much of the richness of Prespa phraseology stems from the legacy of Ottoman and Islamic discourses that Albanians share with many other communities in former Ottoman territories. By positing the existence of multiple, competing discourses, Foucault's approach also challenges the predilection of both Bordieu and interpretive scholars to characterize communities in terms of a single, monolithic culture, belief system, or set of coherent structures . . . . Such an expansion and complication of the concept of culture holds much promise for understanding the complex ways that performance forms with the traditions of long standing have served over time as sites of identity construction. (29)

Sugarman finds Bordieu's work on the nondiscursive experiential domains to be important for music. She applauds his reference to "domains of activity . . . [that are] largely 'implicit'" (27). Bordieu's ideas provide an explanation that can embrace musical activity.

Deborah Wong (2004) has drawn on postmodern conceptions of the body as a socially constructed entity with important concepts such as race expressed in performance. She describes research she conducted with a group of Asian American musicians performing a jazz composition, Jon Jang's *Reparations Now!* As she listened to a performance of the work by mostly Asian American performers with an African American friend, he commented on the competent, but "stiff" performance, characterized by a close adherence to the "metronomic sense of the beat." His conclusion was that their playing signaled they were not African American. If they had played as African Americans, they would have played with a "looser, more fluid sense of rhythm, and even timbre" (174). Wong (2004) concluded that the African American friend was hearing "the absence of an African American musicking body, and this in itself was an assertion that such a body was somehow identifiable" (174). She pointed out that "race is a constructed sign of historical injury that must be productively maintained and refashioned over time" (188). In doing so she connected her work to that of Foucault, particularly his book *Discipline and Punish* (1977).

Not all ethnomusicologists have been fully supportive of postmodernist ideas. Ingrid Monson (1996) addresses one of the critiques raised earlier and comments with concern about the theory that diminishes the "speaking subject, vernacular knowledge, and the phenomenal world" (206). And in this light Laurence Grossberg (1990) maintains that, "one cannot approach rock and roll by using anyone's experience of it, or even any collective definition of that experience. Lived experience is trivialized here in favor of its mass representations, politics, and ideologies" (113, as quoted in Monson 1996:209).

Another postmodernist scholar, Gayatri Spivak, argues that taking the speech of a person, or music, is essentialism and results in the "romanticized 'othering' of oppressed people" (Monson 1996:208; Spivak 1988:212). Speech is considered a form of phonocentrism in which Spivak, along with Derrida, would argue for writing as a "metaphor for relationality, or mediation by systems of signification" (208). Monson goes on to argue that, "This position . . . constructs a rather exalted role for the intellectual, since the scholar is absolved of worrying too much about the phenomenal world or individual agencies and is free to theorize at will" (209–10). "If all this talk of heterogeneity and diversity and empowerment is used primarily to augment the status of the academic elite and silence the 'ontologically incorrect,' I think we can expect to hear a growing crescendo of ethnic and class particularity from outside academia: 'Get real, please'" (212–13).

The troubling concern for some ethnomusicologists has proved the denigration of ethnography because the close encounter of researcher with performers as well as audience has been a hallmark of the research conducted by ethnomusicologists of many persuasions. Furthermore, with an overt political agenda of providing voice for oppressed groups and arts, one might ask how such an approach can presume to understand the "other" from afar.

John Shepherd and Peter Wicke (1997) critique the placement of music on the periphery by many in culture studies. Furthermore, they argue that music is *not* language and requires its own modes of inquiry. The body, they maintain, is the locus for music to mediate social processes. "Music's unique character therefore flows as much from its unique contribution to social processes as it does from its capacity to symbolize them. Music is an activity central rather than peripheral to people and society" (3). They argue, therefore, that postmodern theorists should consider music as a central part of social and cultural life.

Postcolonial and Global Issues

The development of theoretical issues in postcolonial and transnational studies stems from the history of domination that has characterized the history of many countries of the world. Although most postcolonial writing speaks primarily of European domination of many parts of the world, beginning in the fifteenth century, colonialism has been and continues to be a feature of the world. The Arab conquest of North and East Africa as well as southern Europe along the Mediterranean is but an earlier example that continues to influence musical practice in many parts of the world today. Colonialism was particularly significant during the height of the British Empire in the nineteenth and early twentieth centuries, which at one pointed covered a quarter of the earth's surface.

A number of scholars have studied culture from the theoretical perspectives that respond to such domination. In *Orientalism*, Edward Said (1978) critiques Western accounts of West Asia. Through **Orientalism**, he maintains,

---

Orientalism

- Representation of the cultures of the Middles East in a colonialist or exoticizing manner

outsiders render the subjects as passive and nonacting. Said notes that the language of the accounts keeps the people being described from voicing their views. Language in orientalism becomes an exercise in power by the West over the Orient in a manner paralleling colonial rule that dominated much of the area at different times. In many Hollywood movies, for example, Arab men are frequently portrayed as sneaky, greedy, and dishonest—all characteristics that serve to make them less than appealing or likable. Arab women are typically por-trayed as belly dancers, exhibiting their exotic sexuality. These qualities contribute to making them more "other" or outside of our communities. Musical themes in these movies may serve to emphasize these qualities and continually remind the audience of them.

Postcolonial theory developed in literary studies in the 1990s. This theoretical orientation seeks to understand the operations of colonialist and anti-colonialist ideologies in political, social, cultural, and psychological terms (Tyson 1999:365).

Certain musics have been heavily influenced by the colonial processes. Some ethnomusicologists find the postcolonial theory useful for their research. They realize, furthermore, that postcolonial theory can also illuminate scenes that are still colonial in character today as new colonial processes are enacted in certain areas of the globe. Colonies are not limited to named countries such as Ghana, which was colonized by England, or Côte D'Ivoire, which was colonized by France. Rather, colonies can be places of an unequal distribution of power where resources are extracted from an area, manufactured in another region, and then sold back to the first area in the form of a product at a profit to the colonizer.

Mary Louise Pratt (1992), a professor of Spanish and Portuguese, presents us with a number of key ideas for approaches to colonial ideologies. In her book, *Through Imperial Eyes: Travel Writing and Transculturation*, she introduces the concept of **contact zones**. These are "social spaces where disparate cultures meet, clash, and grapple with each other, often in highly asymmetrical relations of domination and subordination" (4). Within this contact zone one finds that subordinated or marginal groups select and invert from the materials presented to them by the dominant colonizing group in a process known as

---

Postcolonial theory

- Research framework that deals critically with colonial issues

---

Contact zone

- Social setting where cultures meet and clash

Transculturation

- Process, carried on by a subordinated group of people, in which they invert materials presented by the dominant group and in the process gain control

transculturation (6). Pratt's goal is to emphasize the "interactive, improvisational dimensions of colonial encounters" that are sometimes ignored in accounts (7).

Jean Rouch, in his documentary film, *Les Maitres Fous* (1954) showed the ritual performances of the Hauka members—immigrants from Niger who worked in Accra, Ghana. These laborers went to a rural area outside the capital on weekends where they ritually portrayed their colonial dominators and mocked them in song and dance. In this way the black subjects assumed power in a trance event. They wore military uniforms to portray the European military personnel and mocked them. The event left participants relaxed and ready to return to the tensions of the colonial work situation. Thus these marginalized people were able to invert the power situation, at least for some few hours, through the transculturation process.

Another concept in this postcolonial approach is that of **anti-conquest** whereby European bourgeois subjects seek to secure their innocence at the same moment as they assert European hegemony" (Pratt 1992:7). Pratt identifies a person she refers to as the "seeing-man"—the European male "of European landscape discourse—he whose imperial eyes passively look out and possess" (7). The domination is done in a manner that seeks to obscure the surface appearance of domination.

The third concept is **autoethnography**, that is, the "instances in which colonized subjects undertake to represent themselves in ways that *engage with* the colonizer's own terms" (Pratt 1992:7). These autoethnographies constitute a response to the dominating power and become dialogic to varying degrees. Whereas colonialism can seem like a blanket process where people are simply dominated and lose all power, autoethnography is one of the ways that colonized individuals assert agency. Some autoethnographies have been produced when the colonized have dictated their life stories and these have been recorded and later published, adhering very closely to the words of the indigenous person.

Anti-conquest

- Process whereby the dominating culture seeks to assert innocence at the very moment of asserting control over the subordinate group

Autoethnography

- Representations by the colonized subjects involving the colonizer's own terms.

Global Issues

The world that scholars face today differs in certain respects from that of earlier centuries. Movement of peoples and their interconnectedness in commerce, music, and computers makes studies of discrete self-contained villages more complicated and less useful. Stuart Hall defines **globalization** as "those processes, operating on a global scale, which cut across community, regional, and national boundaries, integrating and connecting communities and organizations in new space-time configurations" (Hall, Held, and McGrew 1992:297, as quoted in Roseman 2000:34–35). Research now requires us to account for multiple influences impinging on the music of any group of people if we are to keep up with the processes affecting the people whose music we propose to understand.

The postcolonial and global approaches are a very loose bundle of research approaches, which nevertheless display some distinctive aspects and assumptions.

Assumptions

1. **Vast portions of the world have been dominated and subordinated to colonial powers during previous centuries in ways that have profoundly affected human interaction and musical performance alike.**

   Postcolonial approaches examine issues of domination and resistance in interaction and performance. They attempt to address power imbalances that have in the past been ignored or taken for granted by researchers.

2. **There is often a denial of conquest at the very moment of asserting hegemony.**

   Such a denial is often couched in a feigned innocence of the act of hegemony.

3. **In the places where colonizer meets colonized, we find a "contact zone," or that place where subordinated or marginal groups select and invert from the materials presented to them by the dominant colonizing group in a process known as transculturation.**

   The postcolonial orientation helps us analyze the instances of where the formerly dominated seek to perform in ways that turn the domination upside down and give **agency** to the dominated.

Globalization

- Processes whereby societies and corporations are more interdependent and interconnected

---

Agency

- The ability of people to take action

4. **Colonized subjects represent themselves in *autoethnography*, that is, in ways that engage the colonizer's own terms.**

By addressing the colonizer through terms such as the printed word, the subjects can create a dialogue in the colonizer's own medium of communication.

5. **People, ideas, and music circulate in global flows that transcend national boundaries.**

These flows are prominent in diaspora communities where people have migrated, bringing their musical performance and ideas. Thus huge numbers of Liberians now live in the United States, Ghana, Côte d'Ivoire, Guinea, and Sierra Leone following the recent, extended war.

6. **Power, money, and ideas interrelate in global flows as high-speed communication facilitates the movement of these and other commodities.**

The Internet and cell phones speed the circulation of ideas on a global level. During the recent Liberian war, I received a cell phone call from the son of a drummer, Kao, with whom I had worked. Amos Kao reported his father's death to me very shortly after it occurred. I was able, through the Internet, to send money via Western Union within the hour to contribute to the death feast. Amos Kao simply reported to one of the many offices in the capital city, Monrovia, and by giving the password I had given him via cell phone–"feli," the name of the drum his father played—was able to obtain the transferred currency.

Plate 33 Kao Gibii. Photo by Verlon L. Stone.

Critique

A number of criticisms can also be made of studies in the area of postcolonial and globalization studies.

1. **Generalizations about overarching processes on a large scale may be difficult to prove.**

   Scholars in these studies may make sweeping conclusions about broad movements or changes that are not easily anchored in ethnographic data. Such ideas do not necessarily derive from a close examination of data but are rather inferences drawn by the scholar that are hard to anchor in data.

2. **Research may focus on processes that may portray very little agency on the part of individuals.**

   When a researcher is looking at large-scale global movements, it is easy to portray individuals as fairly powerless. Individuals may be given little role in the scenarios that researchers present.

Contribution

A number of contributions can be discerned for the postcolonial and globalization studies that are emerging.

1. **These perspectives try to account for the complex flow of people, goods, and interaction that is taking place.**

   Although people have always traveled and moved over vast distances, whether on pilgrimage or migration, the rate of circulation today is ever swift and complex.

2. **These perspectives address issues of domination and the consequences of that domination.**

   Postcolonial and globalization theories directly study situations where people live under the subjugation of colonial powers. Concepts and ideas have developed from these studies to describe the various turns such domination may take over time.

Postcolonial and Global Studies in Ethnomusicology

A number of ethnomusicologists have studied music, using postcolonial and globalization theoretical orientation approaches. They have discovered a number of interesting phenomena. Gage Averill's (1997) study of Haitian music shows interesting results in a postcolonial independent country. He describes the *Koudyay*, an event that survived from the colonial military regime. The term, which comes from the French *coup de jalle*, meaning a "spontaneous bursting forth," is the name for celebrations of military and political victories.

Today it is a street celebration sponsored by an important person that resembles a carnival. The purpose of these performances is varied: "to intimidate opponents, to take people's minds off of problems, to demonstrate electoral or grassroots strength" (13). The poor people of Haiti flock to such celebrations because an opportunity to celebrate is all too rare. "The sponsors of these events find, however, that the allegiance and support the poor show are fleeting" (13). Furthermore, in the exuberance of such an event, the crowd may band together in making fun of the elite who have replaced their former colonial rulers.

Monson (1999) addresses the global and local music dialectic as she argues that "riffs, repetition, and grooves—as multilayered, stratified, interactive, frames of musical, social, and symbolic action—might be helpful in thinking through some of the more challenging issues in contemporary critical thinking, including cultural hybridity, economic domination, agency, and the specific cultural complexities of the African diaspora" (32). Monson is seeking is "a way to think about socially produced fields of action" (47). She juxtaposes her view with Mark Slobin's concept of "micromusics," in which he contrasts superculture, interculture, and subculture and Veit Erlmann's "global ecumene," drawn from Frederic Jameson's notion that "the production of difference is inherent in the logic of capitalism itself" and based on Marxist interpretations (Erlmann 1996b:472, as quoted in Monson 1999:48; Jameson 1971; Slobin 1992). All of these ethnomusicologists are concerned with the global complexities. Each comes at the analysis from a slightly different perspective: Monson is emphasizing layered processes that are social constructed, Slobin is interested in interlocking worlds of musical meaning, and Erlmann is stressing power differentials.

Marina Roseman (2000) points out that the Temniar who live in the Malaysian rain forest also participate in globalization:

Plate 34 Mark Slobin. Courtesy of Mark Slobin.

Plate 35 Marina Roseman. Courtesy of Marina Roseman.

> The Temniar world is one in which the constituting of self and community is based on a never-ending dialectical incorporation of that which is outside, be that spirits, other humans, neighboring forest peoples, non-foresters, or colonials. This process of dialectical incorporation, negotiated musically, destabilizes and decenters as much as it controls and contains. (54)

Her analysis of the situation points out that the Temniar make sense of their world, employing musical processes that contribute to the dialogue that is ongoing with the world beyond. She interprets this situation to be one more multiple center of power rather than a single focal power.

A Postcolonial Example

Over the course of fourteen years, I spent several months at a time in the Middle East, studying how expatriates create music as part of recreating home. When I arrived there for the summer in the early 1990s, I discovered an event that was destined to provide American women expatriates with a glimpse into local life. The Western and Middle Eastern women lived together in an extended contact zone as they developed plans for an imaginary wedding. The Women's Group of Oil Camp (a pseudonym) had asked a wife of a company vice president to help present a fashion show. As the Middle Eastern organizer developed her program, she decided to stage a wedding in as much realistic detail as possible and to enlist a range of women to create the event cooperatively.

A Preserver of Local Life

Najad Al-Ghamdi (pseudonym) was well known throughout the region for her interest in preserving local culture. Although Najad was thoroughly Middle Eastern, she had also lived in Europe for a number of years and knew much of life in the West. As a result, although she went out in public with her hair covered, she steadfastly refused to cover her face, and thereby showed her unwillingness to totally adopt the most conservative dress of the area. She was of the Middle East, but she also showed a measure of independence from the expectations.

Life in the Middle East in this particular oil compound was normally very compartmentalized. Little socializing or intermingling of local people occurred with the American and European expatriates who had moved there. The plan of staging this wedding promised to create a demarcated space and time where interaction could take place and people could experience one another in an intimate manner.

Learning through Practice

A group of women had assembled to practice the dances for the wedding, for the second time, when I first joined the group. They were dominated by American and British women, with three Arab friends who were brought by Najad to coach the other women. Najad brought her "boom box," put on her loose dance dress over her other clothes, and started moving to the music. The assembled women imitated her movements, lacking any explicit verbal instructions. Najad clearly loved dancing and appeared to focus inward. She moved with a smile on her face as she shifted and turned the fabric of her dress in front of her. The other women also seemed mostly oblivious to those around them. After a long period of dancing, the music stopped and Najad paused. Ann Jones (pseudonym), the president of the women's group, attempted to draw Najad out in order to understand how the women were going to create the formations, the movement between formations, and other details. Those queries brought a bit of clarification but not a lot of explicit step-by-step instruction. Rather, Najad had the women practice the several types of dance that she said they would perform at the wedding. After nearly two hours, people were hot and exhausted.

Some women stayed, and some time later, Najad began coaching the women who were selected to impersonate men and do the sword dance at the wedding, using the large heavy ceremonial swords. Such an assumption of men's roles by women is not unknown in Middle Eastern engagement parties. This served the purpose of not allowing men to invade women's space, and it provided some element of fun and surprise.

Constructing a Time Flow and Surprise

Ann Jones had planned to present the guests at this event with a printed program, indicating the sequence of events that they could expect as they unfolded. As the afternoon wore on, it became clear how difficult it would be to present such a linear progression. One discussion catapulted to another like billiard balls on a pool table. Sequential order was not easily discerned. Who would walk in the procession for the wedding night? What would follow what? Finally, Najad said that she didn't want the program passed out until *after* the event because the evening was to be a surprise. As a result, the very flow of time became an issue for discussion in this contact zone. And it was clear that the time flow for the some of the women was quite different than for other women. The women discussed how the Bedouin band that would accompany the dance at the performance should be treated. One woman said the band could eat first. "No," said Najad. They should be treated well, but they would eat away from the guests. She had no intention of giving them a table on the floor where the rest of the guests would be seated. Their lower class position was not to be inverted. They would remain in the stage area, for they were not guests. She also warned the planning committee that they must be prepared for the band to fail to appear. Even though they were being paid US $1,300, bands were often temperamental and prone to missing engagements.

The tense relationship engendered by class differences became apparent. The band offered services that were highly desired by women's gatherings, and the band members were able to command a high price. But even for that kind of money, the band might demonstrate that they too had their pride and never let their clients think that they could absolutely count on them showing up. So the element of anticipation remained as to whether the band would actually come to perform for these women who clearly outranked them socially and materially.

Another issue was the kitchen and catering staff. Concerned about the sensitivities of men and women in the same place, one American woman suggested that the food could be put out and women in *abayas*—black cloaks that cover the body from head to foot—could go first to the buffet when it was clear that no male waiters would be needed to refill serving dishes. Najad countered with the idea that she would bring four female maids to help so it would not be necessary for the men ever to appear where the women were situated. She explained that at a real Middle Eastern wedding, the food is set out on tables, then picked up at the end of the wedding, with many people not even really bothering to eat. Here the meal was to be a part of the evening, and people were going to socialize and eat as they waited for the event to continue.

Cultural interchange in this contact zone of the women's club house was rich as the pace of the wedding planning increased. Things that were normally done without thinking became problematic as women from different backgrounds sought to work together. Local women learned about practices that they clearly intended to imitate. Americans wanted recipes of some of the food to make for their own occasions. Sometimes these secrets were willingly shared. Other times they were carefully guarded.

At one of the next dance rehearsals, Jonie Smith (pseudonym) came to help direct the dance rehearsal. Najad recruited this American because she realized that the American women dancers needed explicit instruction that she was not prepared to give. Jonie had been born and raised in the Middle East, married a second-generation oil man, and was often called a Bedouin by the other Middle Eastern women. She was able to mediate between the two groups. She had discussed Najad's wishes and then presented the directions to the dancers in a very linear fashion. Jonie, wire thin, irrepressible, and wearing about sixteen or more gold bangles on her arm, seemed able to tack, like a sailboat crossing a lake, between the two worlds with her wacky personality.

My daughter returned to the Middle East for summer vacation in time for the last dance rehearsal. She and several other returning students were recruited to dance in several of the numbers. Their rehearsals for the sword dance on the "wedding" night were supervised by Jonie out of sight of the other performers, for their dance was to be another surprise for the evening. Their dresses and dance overdresses were to also be a surprise and not to be seen until they appeared on the stage.

Wedding Rehearsal

The day of the imaginary wedding evening dawned on a Thursday,. The day-light hours focused on a major dance rehearsal and the decorating of the wedding space. As we went in the morning to the community building where the event was set, mildly ordered chaos ensued. A contractor's crew was present to set up tables and lay Oriental carpets. Najad had discovered a six-inch difference between the height of the stage and the runway that jutted out in a "T" shape to meet the stage. She was trying to solve the problem. Women were draping cloths to decorate the walls. The florist arrived with bouquets. The cake decorator brought the cake. And the caterer had brought the glassware and china to set tables that were not yet in place. Amid all of this, a dress rehearsal of dance numbers was to take place at 9 A.M.

Close to noon, when no rehearsal had yet occurred, several dancers indicated that they would not be available later for rehearsal, and Najad paused in her supervision of preparations to hold the rehearsal. Although this was to be the last rehearsal, many aspects of the event were not practiced because there were to be surprises, and they must not be revealed yet. In contrast, other women regarded this wedding as overplanned and overstructured, based on their previous experience.

Flow for the Wedding

The temporal structuring of the wedding night, like that of the dance rehearsals, reminded me more of my experience in West Africa than my experience in the United States. Clock time was not the operative coordinating force. Social momentum instead dominated, and the event moved according to the social cohesion or dragged when that cohesion faltered. Slated to start at 5 P.M., when I arrived a promptly, the tables were filled with eager guests anticipating this unusual event. Although rehearsals in the morning had lagged according to clock time, the gathering momentum of the event now dictated that things begin because of the eagerness of the guests who were all assembled in their excitement. Najad and her female advisers formed a receiving line at the door to greet the guests. They were dressed in glittering sequined dresses that flowed in silks and satins. Large necklaces of gold complemented the costumes.

Although the night held certain aspects of a Middle Eastern wedding flow, it also catered to the clock-conscious Americans. For it ultimately ended near midnight, several hours short of the usual local wedding. Thus there was the tug between clock time and social time as the dominating flow of the evening.

Establishing Positions and Views

The Bedouin band was ensconced to one side at the rear of the stage. Their penetrating voices were amplified to the limit as they played frame drums as well as a cylindrical two-headed drum. The band had prerecorded some background tracks and sometimes let those play as instrumental accompaniment. The latest amplification equipment supported this band of the desert.

The band was dressed mostly in fashionable clothing; for the most part bell-bottom pants predominated. One singer had a black jacket to go with her pants, cut very low in the front. She also wore a large brooch with her photo laminated to the button. In the corner sat the cylindrical-drum player, clad in black *abaya* and a black face mask, revealing only her eyes to the world. The presentation of self of this latter player sent a message. To her clients who regarded themselves as superior, this Bedouin performer was covering her face as an assertion of her status. Whereas she might, in other contexts, be accused of being lower class by her willingness to uncover, she was reversing the process and showing that she was not familiar with these women and that she was protecting her honor with this covering. The walls of containment were purposely erected to distinguish and delineate women from one another. And here it was being played out once again in ways that I had first noticed in the mid-1980s.

To be a singer or musician was to risk being considered promiscuous. These women took measures to protect themselves in the company of other women even as they produced the sounds that led to a kind of intimacy among all of those present at the wedding.

To See and Not to Be Seen

Honor was an important issue throughout the event. The recording of the imaginary wedding touched on many issues of honor. I was asked by the Women's Group to videotape the event because no woman with professional skills could be located. I was to make the one and only "private" video account of the event. Karen Poe (pseudonym), the official still photographer of the Women's Group, was to take the only still photos of the evening. I had chosen a jacket and skirt of Indian design with a sari-type shawl attached so I could cover my head and back and be as unobtrusive as possible. As I began setting up the tripod at the end of the runway extending from the stage, a local woman in the audience walked up to me and specifically asked that I never point the camera at her. I replied that if she didn't go up on stage to dance, she would not be picked up on the camera. She went on to explain that if her husband got a copy of the videotape, he would use it against her, and she was fearful that such a scenario might take place. I assured her once again and continued setting up.

Flash cameras began going off as women mingled, taking pictures of their friends in front of the decorations. The control on filming appeared nearly gone until Ann Jones announced once again that people were not to take photographs and the official photographs were to be made available to those who had attended. From that point on, people were very careful to include only their friends in the pictures. And they kept the cameras under wraps until the end of the event.

The paradox of picture taking was apparent. Most women wanted a way of remembering the event, and they wanted their pictures. But they didn't want others to be able to take pictures and potentially embarrass them. The Bedouin band made a specific request, once pictures were being taken, that they did not want to be photographed. They wanted to protect their honor. But shortly after the announcement was made about not taking pictures, the band began photographing each other. Thus pictures were highly valued, but who took them and who used them was a highly controversial point. Memories were valued, but danger lurked if people used pictures to damage honor and reputation.

The Henna Night Unfolds

The Henna Night—the first part of this event—began as the dancing women came from both doors to the main room and moved up the runway to the stage. As they reached the stage, smoke from a smoke machine and bubbles from a bubble machine added a sense of mystery and magic to the scene. Najad danced with the group as did Ann, the president of the Women's Group. They set the scene for the henna night and the procession by the henna "bride." Here were the elite women from various cultures now engaged in dance in the contact zone. Then Najad walked back to supervise the procession of the lantern maidens, carrying little kerosene lanterns, as well as the rosewater maiden. Finally, in came the henna bride—a young unmarried girl, dressed in green and gold, sporting a big garland of basil on her neck and walking with the women of her family.

This mock wedding portrayed primarily the dancing portion of the Henna Night, for the application of henna had occurred two days before this recreation. The henna bride, with her bare feet in front of her on a pillow, displayed the henna art that had been applied earlier by the artists. Punctuating the unfolding drama on stage, Najad invited the audience to dance on the stage and runway. Young women, in particular, flocked to show their skills. Their dancing, like any women's party, was an occasion for the older women to assess and view them as potential candidates for future marriage arrangements. And for these songs, we arranged that the video camera be turned off so people could dance with less inhibition. To emphasize that I was not filming at those moments, I pointed the lens to the ceiling and walked away from the tripod.

Conspicuous Display

Food appeared in the middle of the festivities, and people lingered over the banquet dinner. Abundance of all kinds of Middle Eastern dishes was evident everywhere. The Filipino maids from Najad's household presided over the buffet lines, dressed in pink satin uniforms with white aprons, anklets, and shoes for the occasion.

Thousands of dollars had been spent to present the evening and to create this experience in the contact zone for these women who had come from many nations for this performance. Fresh flower arrangements appeared on every table. Walls were draped in special fabrics. The stage was also decorated with fresh flowers. Dancers and participants all dressed in lavish dresses for the occasion. Each person who attended had paid about US $40 for her evening's ticket, in addition to her expenditures for an appropriate costume. Such obvious display of clothing and food was characteristic of both local life in general and the oil company life in particular. People clearly enjoyed exhibiting their wealth and sharing that public effect. Women carefully watched one another.

The local organizers of the evening had two outfits for the evening, changing during the banquet intermission to the wedding proceedings. Even Ann Jones's dress was upstaged by the local women's penchant for lavish dressing.

The Wedding Night

Later that evening as the Wedding Night ceremonies approached, the excitement in the room was tangible. The usual multinight festivities were placed into a single extended event. The ululation increased in frequency as women anticipated the high point of the evening. The wedding procession began as four young women entered to perform the traditional sword dance, a dance usually performed by and associated with men. The young girls, including my daughter, wore special loose dancing dresses of variegated colors over their other long dresses. The smoke and bubble machines were placed in high gear. Mystery swirled on the stage.

First in the procession came the incense maidens, little girls carrying smoking incense in their tower-shaped holders. The flower maidens followed, two little girls in dresses especially sewn by Najad's seamstress that sported plastic foam teddy bears in the net overskirts. Finally, the "bride," a close relative of Najad, escorted by the "groom" (played by Linda Nussbaum [pseudonym]), came in a sequin- and pearl-encrusted dress. She conformed closely to the perfect bride as touted in a poem printed in the program and given out at the end of the evening:

> Her hair black as the feathers of the ostrich,
> Eyes black like a gazelle's.
> Nose straight and finely modeled,
> Cheeks like bouquets of roses.
> Mouth small and round,

Teeth like pearls set in coral,
Lips small and colored like vermilion,
Neck white and long.
Shoulders broad,
Hands and feet small,
Manners agreeable,
And laughter delicate.

The bride held the arm of her "groom," as the long and elaborate train of the dress was managed by the hovering women, who constantly straightened and adjusted it for the best visual effect. The white dress, indistinguishable from a Western wedding dress, except perhaps for the unusually large number of pearls and sequins, was referred to by several local women as a "traditional" wedding dress.

A few women knew that the groom was a woman, but a number of the guests were completely fooled and began to put on their scarves to cover their heads. Such a reaction recalled the day the women had first tried on their male costumes and applied penciled beards and mustaches. The women at Shope House had been stunned by the realistic impression they provided. Even though they knew there were women beneath the costumes, these women began to alter their behavior and to make nervous jokes about men. Najad went over to one and sat in her/his lap to great hilarity all around. Clearly the male/female issue was a sensitive one that received a great deal of attention. Using women to portray men was one of Najad's little surprises for her friends as well as the other guests, one that she clearly enjoyed springing and then watching for reactions all around.

As the bride and groom reached the stage proper, they turned and faced the guests briefly before walking to their seats at the center back of the stage. The bride and groom then sat back as a variety of dances took place. They exchanged rings, drank from a goblet, and greeted their "male" relatives. More women, dressed up like men, came up and now took up the sword dance. After the dance, Najad escorted the "men" down the runway, showing them first to the guests on one side of the runway and then the other, enjoying the reaction of women who were only now realizing these were women playing men's parts.

Another little surprise came when Jonie rushed down the runway and up to the stage in a gold lamé body suit and tissue-thin skirt to perform a belly dance. The local women were surprised by her abilities and enjoyed this expatriate woman imitating their dance style. Only Najad and the young girls doing the sword dance had known that Jonie was going to perform. But the display of sensuality by a woman for women was greeted with eager ululation and clapping.

The bride and groom then descended from the stage, walked back down the runway and to the rear of the room. There the multitiered wedding cake had been set up. The cake was cut and they shared a piece before leaving the room. Then the guests were all given pieces of cake before they began to disperse even as some dancing continued by the assembled guests.

As the departing guests approached the doors to leave the building, they pulled out their plastic bags that contained their *abayas* and head scarves. These storage bags had been given to them as they arrived, and they now donned the coverings that would hide their fashion details as they moved out of one contact zone and into another—the public arena where men could be present. Covering themselves, these women disappeared into the evening to search for their drivers in the maze of waiting cars.

As this amazing evening concluded, there was considerable talk around the camp about the unusual degree of collaboration between the women for this occasion. One woman who had lived in the camp for two years commented to me, "I didn't know local women knew how to have fun." Several days later when I attended an end-of-the-year exhibition at the women's section of the local College of Architecture and Planning, women still talked about what an unusual event the "wedding" had been.

Here in a special kind of environment, a contact zone, two contrasting cultures had taken an event that occurs in both cultures and presented an evening incorporating an amalgam of the details from both cultures as a single event. The accent of behaviors was Middle Eastern, but many other touches had been adopted and were admired in the process.

Najad Al-Ghamdi showed herself to be a unique woman in this environment. She was able to gain the trust of women from multiple cultures to create this event. She clearly enjoyed showing her friends how she had trained foreign women to do local dances. The local women were amazed at the skill of the Americans, even while they were also amused at their ineptitude in the finer points of the dance movements. All of this became even more unusual because there was ordinarily so little interaction between these groups of women. Najad was able to show her friends as well that she was able to organize a diverse group of women and get them involved in creating this Middle Eastern wedding. This gave her considerable status with both her local friends and her expatriate acquaintances. Whatever the varying motivations for these women achieving a greater degree of intimacy than they had in the past, this event served to make women feel more comfortable with each other and with alien customs. It allowed women to see the "other" and how these others create customs of their home. Alternatives to the home they knew and the practices that were so familiar to them were presented. The concept of home became expanded and widened, whether they chose to accept it as something they would like as their own or not.

Conclusion

The question we must ask is whether ethnography in face-to-face encounter still serves us in our quest for knowledge about music. How do we simultaneously give a jeweler's-eye view, a bird's-eye view, and a satellite's-eye view? How do we give voice to the people whose music we study without dominating the conversation unfairly? How do we account for the web of processes that enmesh our focus of study? How do we represent the knowledge we gain?

These and other questions are part of the moment that has been labeled as postmodern. The term *postmodern* heightens the sense of a break with the past for those proposing new approaches. The transition from the modern to the postmodern world, as I see it, is much smoother if one truly acknowledges the embeddedness of much proposed postmodern theory in past practices of the modern world.

References

Appadurai, Arjun. 1991. "Global Ethnoscapes: Notes and Queries for a Transnational Anthropology." In *Recapturing Anthropology,* ed. Richard G. Fox. Santa Fe: School of American Research, 191–210.

———. 1996. *Modernity at Large: Cultural Dimensions of Globalization.* Minneapolis: University of Minnesota Press.

Averill, Gage. 1997. *A Day for the Hunter, A Day for the Prey: Popular Music and Power in Haiti.* Chicago: Chicago University Press.

Bordieu, Pierre. 1977. *Outline of a Theory of Practice.* Translated by Richard Nice. Cambridge: Cambridge University Press.

———. 1984. *Distinction: A Social Critique of the Judgment of Taste.* Translated by Richard Nice. Cambridge: Harvard University Press.

Derrida, Jacques. 1998. *Of Grammatology.* Translated by Gayatri Chakravorty. Spivak. Baltimore: Johns Hopkins University Press.

Erlmann, Veit. 1996b. "The Aesthetics of the Global Imagination: Reflections on World Music in the 1990s." *Public Culture* 8(3): 467–87.

Foucault, Michel. 1972. *The Archaeology of Knowledge and the Discourse of Language.* Translated by A. M. Sheridan Smith. New York: Pantheon Books.

———. 1976. *Histoire de la sexualité, vol. I, La Volonté de savoir.* Paris: Gallimard.

———. 1977. *Discipline and Punish.* New York: Vintage Books.

———. 1984a. *Histoire de la sexualité, vol. II, L'Usage des plaisirs.* Paris: Gallimard.

———. 1984b. *Histoire de la sexualité, vol. III, Le Souci de soi.* Paris: Gallimard.

Giddens, Anthony. 1994. "Living in a Post-Traditional Society." In *Reflexive Modernization: Politics, Tradition, and Aesthetics in the Modern Social Order,* eds. Ulrich Beck, Anthony Giddens, and Scott Lash. Stanford: Stanford University Press, 56–109.

Grossberg, Lawrence. 1990. "Is There Rock after Punk?" In *On Rock: Rock, Pop, and the Written Word,* eds. Simon Frith and Andrew Goodwin. New York: Pantheon Books, 111–23.

Hall, Stuart, David Held, and Tony McGrew, eds. 1992. *Modernity and Its Futures.* Cambridge: Polity Press.

Jameson, Fredric. 1971. *Marxism and Form: Twentieth-Century Dialectical Theories of Literature.* Princeton, N.J.: Princeton University Press.

Lash, Scott. 1994. "Reflexivity and Its Doubles: Structure, Aesthetics, Community." In *Reflexive Modernization: Politics, Tradition, and Aesthetics in the Modern Social Order,* eds. Ulrich Beck, Anthony Giddens, and Scott Lash. Stanford: Stanford University Press, 110–73.

Marcus, George E., and Michael M. J. Fischer. 1986. *Anthropology as Cultural Critique: An Experimental Moment in the Human Sciences.* Chicago: University of Chicago Press.

Monson, Ingrid. 1996. *Saying Something: Jazz Improvisation and Interaction.* Chicago: University of Chicago Press.

———. 1999. "Riffs, Repetition, and Theories of Globalization." *Ethnomusicology* 43(1): 31–65.

Nicholson, Linda, and Steven Seidman. 1995. "Introduction." In *Social Postmodernism: Beyond Identity Politics.* Cambridge: Cambridge University Press, 1–35.

Pratt, Mary Louise. 1992. *Imperial Eyes: Travel Writing and Transculturation.* New York: Routledge.

Roseman, Marina. 2000. "Shifting Landscapes: Musical Mediations of Modernity in the Malaysian Rainforest." *Yearbook for Traditional Music* 32: 31–65.

Rouch, Jean, director. 1954. *Les Maitres Fous* ("Mad Masters"). Color; VHS; 35 minutes. Watertown, Mass.: Documentary Educational Resources.

Said, Edward. 1978. *Orientalism.* New York: Pantheon Books.

Shepherd, John, and Peter Wicke. 1997. *Music and Cultural Theory.* Cambridge: Polity Press.

Slobin, Mark. 1992. "Micromusics of the West: A Comparative Approach." *Ethnomusicology* 36(1): 1–87.

Spivak, Gayatri C. 1988. *In Other Words: Essays in Cultural Politics.* New York and London: Routledge.

Sugarman, Jane C. 1997. *Engendering Song: Singing and Subjectivity at Prespa Albanian Weddings.* Chicago: University of Chicago Press.

Tyson, Lois. 1999. *Critical Theory Today.* New York: Garland.

Wong, Deborah. 2004. *Speak It Louder: Asian Americans Making Music.* New York: Routledge.

Chapter 14

Convergence and Divergence in Theory Today

Since the early twentieth century, ethnomusicologists have focused on an array of theories to assist in their analysis of music as human experience (see Figure 28). These orientations have been used in an overlapping series for scholarly research.

These theories are not totally exclusive of one another, but they often incorporate aspects of earlier theories. For example, institutions and systems are particularly significant in structural-functionalist approaches, but they are evident as well in paradigmatic-structuralist, linguistic, Marxist, and cognitive as well as communication theory, gender, ethnicity, and other identity issues. So although, on one hand, it is possible to distinguish one theoretical orientation from another, it is also the case that there is an entangled web of connections among the theories. Structuralist and linguistic theories that stress binary oppositions, for example, are connected to Marxist and some postmodern theories, which also stress oppositions, even though the oppositions are of a somewhat different nature.

Scientific Attitude and Approach

From a broad perspective, removed from the close contact with the theories, one can examine the thematic continuities and discontinuities that emerge. The theoretical orientations as described, up to this point, emphasize different sides of the scientific attitude. A stereotyped, and rather simplistic, definition of science is that the research proceeds in a detached, objective way and attempts to predict behavior in matter, animals, or humans. Today many scientists acknowledge that much of what they study cannot be predicted, increasingly pointing to the improvisatory elements in any research project. The creative, affective accents are most apparent in phenomenology and experiential ethnomusicology. In these approaches, the nuances of individual performance are noticed and analyzed. Literary and dramaturgical theories attend, in some instances, to the creative and affective. Some oral history and ethnohistory also focus on the creative and affective aspects.

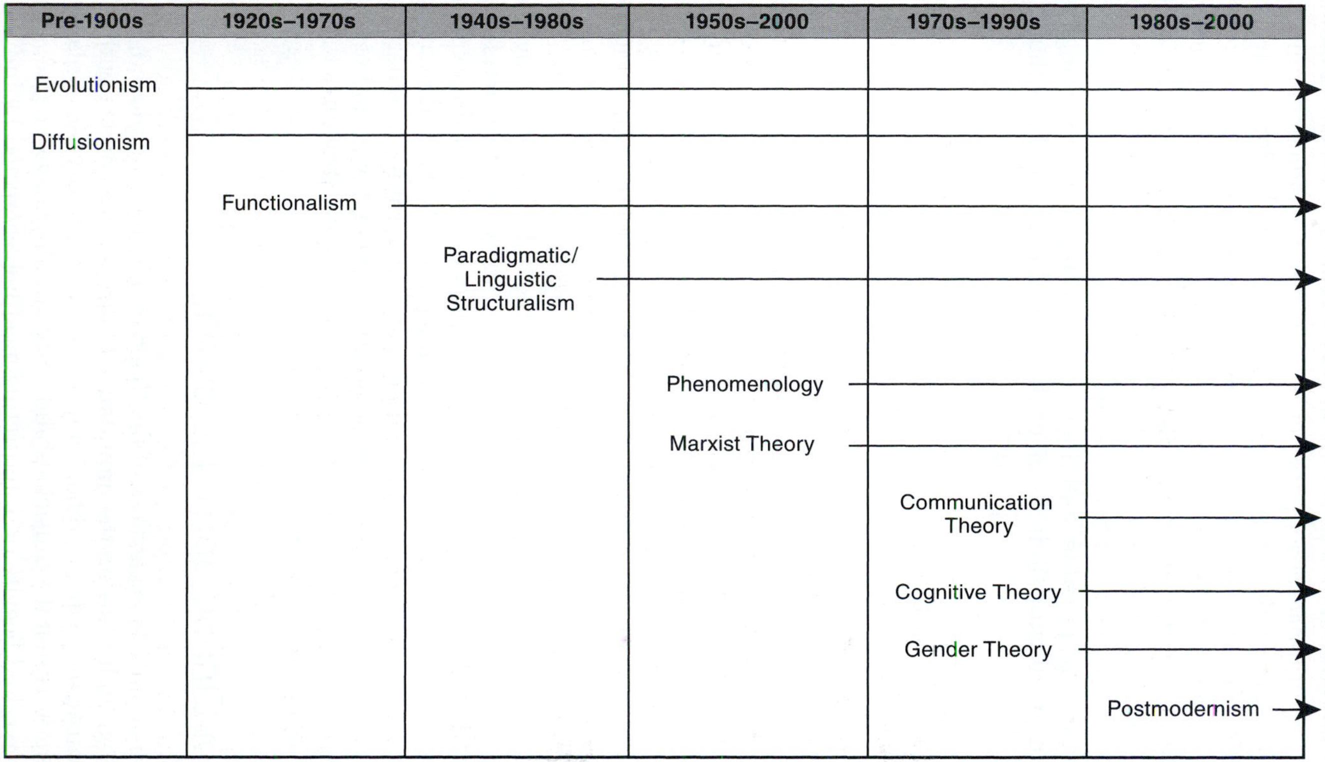

Pre-1900s	1920s–1970s	1940s–1980s	1950s–2000	1970s–1990s	1980s–2000
Evolutionism					
Diffusionism					
	Functionalism				
		Paradigmatic/ Linguistic Structuralism			
			Phenomenology		
			Marxist Theory		
				Communication Theory	
				Cognitive Theory	
				Gender Theory	
					Postmodernism

Figure 28 Succession of Theories

Structural elegance is one of the aspects that scientists consider when evaluating the power of a particular theory. That elegance is quite apparent in the linguistic and paradigmatic structuralist approaches in which large quantities of data can be reduced to simple explanatory structures. Structural elegance may also be an appropriate description for many cognition and communication theories, which share, although perhaps to a lesser extent, this formal cleanness.

Political issues—specifically power aspects—are overtly addressed in Marxist explanations, as well as in gender, ethnicity, identity, and some postmodern approaches. In fact, these are dominant areas of concern for these approaches.

Ideology is an important part of the explanatory apparatus for these theories. Yet, for some scientists, research should be detached and considered "as objective" as possible, and the concern for the overtly ideological is considered to be outside their scope of theoretical concern. For others, concern with ideology is not only appropriate but paramount.

Nature of Meaning

A significant way to distinguish approaches is to examine the locus of meaning for a given perspective. For phenomenology, meaning is created in social interaction. Meaning does not exist in and of itself outside of human and social performance. Contrast this with paradigmatic structuralism, which assumes meaning to be created by all people who share similar mind structures. For this latter group, social interaction is not critical to meaning creation—often considered insignificant details that do not point to the central issues. As a result, these two approaches contrast strongly in the way that meaning is evolved, and this has a great effect on how one employs each of these approaches.

Meaning in some other theories is shaped by underlying structures within the society, not necessarily by the agency of the individual. Ideology, for example, may be the generator of meaning creation for Marxist theory, for example. Ideology drives the analysis and shapes the parameters of the explanation in the work of many scholars working in gender, identity, and ethnicity studies.

In isolating an approach, it is important to determine whether meaning is located more in the individual and small group interaction or rather determined and strongly influenced by institutions, ideologies, and structures that are much broader and more topdown in their orientation.

Role of Ethnographic Fieldwork

Ethnomusicologists, regardless of the theories they have employed, have generally placed high value on the importance of face-to-face contact with the people whose music they have studied. They have taken seriously the explanations and interpretations that the musicians and audience alike have offered. In doing so, they have relied heavily on interpreting meaning as created by individuals and small groups.

Structuralism in linguistics and anthropology signaled that the individual voice might not be so critical, and that analysis did not necessarily depend on detailed and painstaking fieldwork because of the assumption of similar mind structures. But ethnomusicologists who have used structuralism, like John Blacking and Steven Feld, for example, nevertheless have still employed ethnographic research. Postmodern approaches, to an even greater extent, have downplayed fieldwork. Therefore, ethnomusicologists need to address how they fit with and relate to some of these assumptions and approaches, or how they incorporate fieldwork with a postmodern approach.

Level of Focus

Another way to view theories is to examine their levels of focus. Are they most interested in a jeweler's-eye view or a bird's-eye view? Phenomenology, as well as some literary and dramaturgical perspectives, has provided us, for the most part, with a jeweler's-eye view. Linguistic approaches might also focus on words and sentences as ways of analyzing an entire language. Structural approaches in paradigmatic analyses, however, are much more centered on larger study objects, seeking to neatly explain vast expanses of behavior. These contrasting levels of focus provide very different kinds of explanations, and we need to be aware of these contrastive levels of study objects.

Relationship to Social Context

The relationship of various theories to context is also very different. Context is critical to phenomenological approaches, for therein meaning resides, and it is this context from which the theorist derives meaning. For structuralist approaches, the context is much less critical in defining meaning. Rather context becomes supportive but not necessarily foundational for meaning creation. Similarity of the structure of the human mind makes concern with situational details less important than with an approach like phenomenology.

Context exists at a variety of levels, and different theories rely on different levels of context. Phenomenology, in the first place, relies on context of extreme specificity—much akin to the study object that characterizes study in this area. Cultural studies, by contrast, rely on much broader levels of context in keeping with the focus of study. Thus, when we refer to context, we need to keep in mind how different context can be for different theoretical orientations.

Role of Agency

It has become fashionable to call for attention to the individual, or *agency* as it is often termed. Now some theories are much more adept than others at addressing issues of agency or the individual. The structural-functionalist approach, with "cultural system" as its focus, shows scant attention to the individual. Likewise, many of the linguistic approaches, by assuming shared mind structures, are little concerned with individuals and the decisions they might make. Marxist theorists judge ideology to be so dominant that there is little room for the individual's decisions and actions in their explanations. Feminist theorists as well as those working in ethnic and identity studies move between the dominant ideology and individual action, giving attention to both aspects.

Phenomenology places a key emphasis on the choices of the individual, even in a highly repressive setting. The concern for individual actors has existed in theoretical thought for many years—it is not a new idea by any means. And it fits quite easily with the work of many ethnomusicologists who have long centered on the individual musician or a small group of performers.

Temporality

Time is accounted for very differently in the various theories under consideration. One of the criticisms of structural functionalism, mentioned earlier, focuses on its static quality and inability to respond to change through time. Structural functionalism developed on the heels of evolutionist theory, an approach that one might assume incorporated aspects of time. The intricacy of cultural evolution, however, was such that the time explanation was used to place other cultures further back in time and thus maintain a temporal hierarchy in which Western societies were always shown to be more advanced than the so-called primitive societies.

Communication theory, particularly of the semiotic-cybernetic variety, accounts for temporal aspects in the feedback the audience gives to the performers and the resulting adjustments they then make to their playing or singing. Postmodern theory is concerned to a degree with temporality and focuses on shifting meaning and concepts like "traces," rendering oppositions and differences as never fixed.

Likewise, in phenomenology, there is considerable attention to temporal dimensions, particularly on the microlevel. Philosophers like Edmund Husserl and Martin Heidegger brought considerable attention to temporal issues. In their wake, Alfred Schutz discussed inner and outer time in relation to music—furthering attention to music. Although more remains to be done in regard to temporal dimensions, these theories attend to time.

Questions That Theorists Find Interesting

One of the ways to compare theories is to consider what questions that theorists, employing a particular theory, find interesting and appropriate. Structural functionalists, for example, may ask, "How does music help bind individuals together in a society?" Cognitive theorists would be more interested in a question like, "How do people hear music?" Phenomenologists might ask, "How do people experience music?" Marxists would be interested in a research question like, "How does the record industry oppress the musicians?" A paradigmatic-structuralist might ask, "What base structures generate the music that people sing?" A semiotician would be interested in a question like, "What is the cultural significance of a descending minor third in a particular musical ritual?" A feminist scholar might ask, "What is the role of women in the creation of music, and how is it regarded by the men in a particular society?" As I noted earlier, there is no such thing as a *best* theory. Some theories are simply more suited for answering certain kinds of questions than others.

Conclusion

At the beginning of this book, I indicated that no single theoretical orientation had illuminated the landscape and appeared as the total solution to our quest for an analyzing framework. Ethnomusicologists have drawn on a vast array of theories drawn from the Western as well as local indigenous storehouses. Each approach has excelled in one or more areas of inquiry and shown particularly distinction in being able to help us understand an aspect of inquiry such as "temporality" or "agency."

At the end of the day, one cannot point to the best theory of the group of theories. There are ways of evaluating approaches, and depending on the research project, certain theories will be more appropriate than others. The focus of a study will help us determine what kind of theory can best illuminate our study object and research focus.

Given that many ethnomusicologists draw on multiple theories at once, it is important to understand the underlying assumptions of these theories and to determine whether overlapping theoretical approaches in our research is appropriate or not. It is up to the researcher to explain how the research apparatus is being employed. Such discussion will help other scholars understand the assumptions of the researcher and better evaluate the quality of the research.

Theory has been an important tool in ethnomusicology and can serve for future research if scholars in the discipline delineate how ethnomusicologists use it. In other words, ethnomusicologists are the ones who can best inform their scholarly audience about how they have utilized theory. By carefully weaving theory into ethnographic accounts, scholarship in ethnomusicology will be well served.

Theory is the essential complement to the rich detail of ethnographic description. Theory provides the response to "so what" when one is gathering data. In doing so, ethnomusicological explanation will be enhanced. And this explanation will be of interest beyond the discipline of ethnomusicology and link ethnomusicologists to the broader humanities and social sciences.

References

Abraham, Otto, and Erich M. von Hornbostel. 1975 [1903]. "Studies on the Tonsystem and Music of the Japanese." In *Hornbostel Opera Omnia,* Vol. 1, eds. Klaus P. Wachsmann, Dieter Christensen, and Hans-Peter Reinekke, The Hague: Martinus-Nijhoff, 1–84.

Abrahams, Roger. 1970. "A Performance-Centered Approach to Gossip." *Man* 5: 290–301.

———. 1972. "Folklore and Literature as Performance." *Journal of the Folklore Institute* 9: 75–94.

Adams, Charles R. 1974. "Ethnography of Basotho Evaluative Expression in the Cognitive Domain Lipapali (Games)." PhD diss., Indiana University.

Adler, Guido. 1885. "Umfang, Methode und Zeil der Musikwissenschaft." *Viertelsjahrsschrift für Musikwissenschaft* 1: 5–20.

Anderson, Benedict. 1983. *Imagined Communities: Reflections on the Origin and Spread of Nationalism.* London: Verso.

Aparicio, Frances R. 1998. *Listening to Salsa: Gender, Latin Popular Music, and Puerto Rican Cultures.* Hanover, N.H.: University Press of New England.

Appadurai, Arjun, ed. 1988 [1986]. *The Social Life of Things.* Cambridge: Cambridge University Press.

———. 1991. "Global Ethnoscapes: Notes and Queries for a Transnational Anthropology." In *Recapturing Anthropology,* ed. Richard G. Fox. Santa Fe: School of American Research, 191–210.

———. 1996. *Modernity at Large: Cultural Dimensions of Globalization.* Minneapolis: University of Minnesota Press.

Armstrong, Robert Plant. 1971. *The Affecting Presence: An Essay in Humanistic Anthropology.* Urbana: University of Illinois Press.

Asch, Michael. 1972. "A Grammar of Slavey Drum Dance Music." Paper presented at the annual meeting of the Society for Ethnomusicology, Toronto.

Askew, Kelly. 2002. *Performing the Nation: Swahili Music and Cultural Politics in Tanzania.* Chicago: University of Chicago Press.

Attali, Jacques. 1985 [1977]. *Noise: The Political Economy of Music.* Translated by Brian Massumi. Minneapolis: University of Minnesota Press.

Auerbach, Susan. 1989. "From Singing to Lamenting: Women's Musical Role in a Greek Village." In *Women and Music in Cross-Cultural Perspective*, ed. Ellen Koskoff. Urbana: University of Illinois Press, 25–44.

Austen, Ralph A., and Jan Vansina. 1996. "History, Oral Transmission and Structure in Ibn Khaldun's Chronology of Mali Rulers." *History in Africa* 23: 17–28.

Austerlitz, Paul. 1997. *Merengue: Dominican Music and Dominican Identity.* Philadelphia: University of Temple Press.

Averill, Gage. 1989. "Haitian Dance Band Music: The Political Economy of Exuberance." PhD diss., University of Washington.

———. 1997. *A Day for the Hunter, A Day for the Prey: Popular Music and Power in Haiti.* Chicago: Chicago University Press.

Avorgbedor, Daniel. 1998. "Rural-Urban Interchange: The Anlo-Ewe." In *Africa: The Garland Encyclopedia of World Music,* ed. Ruth M. Stone. New York and London: Garland, 389–99.

Baest, Arjan Van, and Hans Van Driel. 1995. *The Semiotics of C. S. Peirce Applied to Music: A Matter of Belief.* Tilburg: Tilburg University Press.

Bahr, Donald M., and J. Richard Haefer. 1978. "Song in Piman Curing." *Ethnomusicology* 22(1): 89–122.

Barkin, Elaine, and Lydia Hamessley. 1999. *Audible Traces: Gender, Identity, and Music.* Zurich and Los Angeles: Carciofoli.

Barnard, Alan. 2004. *History and Theory in Anthropology.* Cambridge: Cambridge University Press.

Bartók, Béla. 1933. "Hungarian Peasant Music." *Musical Quarterly* 19: 267–89.

———, and Albert Lord. 1951. *Serbo-Croatian Folksong.* New York: Columbia University Press.

Basso, Ellen B. 1989. "Musical Expression and Gender Identity in the Myth and Ritual of the Kalapalo of Central Brazil." In *Women and Music in Cross-Cultural Perspective*, ed. Ellen Koskoff. Urbana: University of Illinois Press, 163–76.

Bauman, Richard. 1975. "Verbal Art as Performance." *American Anthropologist* 77: 290–311.

———. 1984 [1977]. *Verbal Art as Performance.* Prospect Heights, Ill.: Waveland Press.

———. 1986. *Story, Performance, and Event: Contextual Studies of Oral Narrative.* Cambridge: Cambridge University Press.

———. 2004. *A World of Others' Words.* Oxford: Blackwell.

Becker, Judith, and Alton Becker. 1979. "A Grammar of the Musical Genre Srepegan." *Journal of Music Theory* 24(1): 1–43. (Reprinted in *Asian Music* 14(1): 30–73 with original pagination preserved.)

———. 1983. "A Reconsideration in the Form of a Dialogue." *Asian Music* 14(1): 9–16.

Beeman, William O. 1993. "The Anthropology of Theater and Spectacle." *Annual Review of Anthropology* 22: 369–393.

Béhague, Gerard. 1984. *Performance Practice: Ethnomusicological Perspectives.* Westport, Conn.: Greenwood Press.

Berger, Harris. 1999b. *Metal, Rock, and Jazz: Perception and the Phenomenology of Musical Experience.* Hanover, N.H.: University Press of New England.

Berger, Peter, and Thomas Luckmann. 1967. *The Social Construction of Reality.* Garden City, N.Y.: Doubleday.

Bernstein, Jane A., ed. 2003. *Women's Voices across Musical Worlds.* Boston: Northeastern University Press.

Besmer, Fremont E. 1974. *Kídan dárán sállà: Music for the Eve of the Muslim Festivals of 'Id Al-Fatir and 'Id Al-Kabir in Kano, Nigeria.* Bloomington: African Studies Program, Indiana University.

Bielawski, Ludwik. 1958. "History in Ethnomusicology." Translated by Ludwik Wiewiorkowki. *Yearbook for Traditional Music* 17: 8–15.

Birdwhistell, Ray L. 1970. *Kinesics and Context.* Philadelphia: University of Pennsylvania Press.

Blacking, John. 1969. "The Value of Music in Human Experience." *Yearbook of the International Folk Music Council* 1: 33–71.

———. 1972a. "Deep and Surface Structures in Venda Music." *Yearbook of International Folk Music Council* 3: 91–108.

———. 1973. *How Musical Is Man?* Seattle: University of Washington Press.

———. 1995a [1967]. *Venda Children's Songs: A Study in Ethnomusicological Analysis.* Chicago: University of Chicago Press.

———. 1995b. "Music, Culture, and Experience." In *Music, Culture, and Experience,* ed. Reginald Byron. Chicago: University of Chicago Press, 223–42.

Bleich, David. 1978. *Subjective Criticism.* Baltimore: Johns Hopkins University Press.

Blim, Michael. 2000. "Capitalism in Late Modernity." *Annual Review of Anthropology* 29: 2–38.

Bloch, Maurice, ed. 1975. *Marxist Analyses and Social Anthropology.* London: Malaby Press.

Blum, Stephen. 1991. "European Musical Terminology and the Music of Africa." In *Comparative Musicology and Anthropology of Music,* eds. Bruno Nettl and Philip V. Bohlman. Chicago: University of Chicago Press, 3–36.

Blumer, Herbert. 1969. *Symbolic Interactionism: Perspective and Method.* Englewood Cliffs, N.J.: Prentice-Hall.

Bogatyrev, Petr. 1971. *The Functions of Folk Costume in Moravian Slovakia.* Translated by Richard G. Crum. The Hague: Mouton.

Bohlman, Philip V. 1987. "The European Discovery of Music in the Islamic World and the 'Non-Western' in 19th-Century Music History." *Journal of Musicology* 5(2): 142–63.

Boilés, Charles L. 1967. "Tepehua Thought-Song: A Case of Semantic Signalling." *Ethnomusicology* 11(3): 267–392.

———. 1973a. "Semiotique de l'ethnomusicologie." *Musique en Jeu* 10: 34–41.

———. 1973b. "Reconstruction of Proto-Melody." *Annuario Interamericano de Investigacion Musical* 9: 45–63.

———. 1982. "Processes of Musical Semiosis." *Yearbook for Traditional Music* 14: 24–44.

Boon, James A. 1973. "Further Operations on 'Culture' in Anthropology: A Synthesis of and for Debate." In *The Idea of Culture in the Social Sciences,* eds. Louis Schneider and Charles Bonjean. Cambridge: Cambridge University Press, 1–32.

Bordieu, Pierre. 1977. *Outline of a Theory of Practice.* Translated by Richard Nice. Cambridge: Cambridge University Press.

———. 1984. *Distinction: A Social Critique of the Judgment of Taste.* Translated by Richard Nice. Cambridge: Harvard University Press.

———. 1995. Randal Johnson, ed. *The Field of Cultural Production: Essays on Art and Literature.* New York: Columbia University Press.

Brăiloiu, Constantin. 1984. *Problems of Ethnomusicology.* Translated by A. L. Lloyd. Cambridge: Cambridge University Press.

Brett, Philip. 1994. "Musicality, Essentialism, and the Closet." In *Queering the Pitch: The New Gay and Lesbian Musicology,* eds. Philip Brett, Elizabeth Wood, and Gary C. Thomas. New York: Routledge, 9–26.

Brinner, Benjamin. 1995. *Knowing Music, Making Music: Javanese Gamelan and the Theory of Musical Competence and Interaction.* Chicago: University of Chicago Press.

Brown, Richard. 1989 [1977]. *A Poetic for Sociology: Toward a Logic of Discovery for the Human Sciences.* Chicago: University of Chicago Press.

Burke, Kenneth. 1969. *A Grammar of Motives.* Berkeley: University of California Press.

Burnim, Mellonee V., and Portia K. Maultsby. 2006. *African American Music: An Introduction.* New York: Routledge.

Burns, Lori, and Mélisse Lafrance. 2002. *Disruptive Divas: Feminism, Identity and Popular Music.* New York: Routledge.

Butler, Judith. 1988. "Performative Acts and Gender Constitution: An Essay in Phenomenology and Feminist Theory." *Theatre Journal* 40(4): 519–31.

———. 1990. *Gender Trouble: Feminism and the Subversion of Identity.* New York: Routledge.

———. 1993. *Bodies That Matter: On the Discursive Limits of "Sex."* New York: Routledge.

———. 1997. *Excitable Speech: A Politics of the Performative.* London: Routledge.

Cavanagh, Beverley. 1982. *Music of the Netsilik Eskimo: A Study of Stability and Change.* Ottawa: National Museums of Canada.

Chakrabarty, Dipesh. 2000. *Provincializing Europe: Postcolonial Thought and Historical Difference.* Princeton, N.J.: Princeton University Press.

Chapman, Malcolm, Elizabeth Tonkin, and Maryon McDonald, eds. 1989. *History and Ethnicity.* New York: Routledge.

Charry, Eric. 2000. *Mande Music: Traditional and Modern Music of the Maninka and Mandinka of Western Africa.* Chicago: University of Chicago Press.

Chase, Gilbert. 1958. "A Dialectical Approach to Music History." *Ethnomusicology* 2(1): 1–9.

Chaudhury, Ajit. 1995. "Rethinking Marxism in India: The Heritage We Renounce." *Rethinking Marxism* 8(3): 133–43.

Chenoweth, Vida, and Darlene Bee. 1971. "Comparative-Generative Models of a New Guinean Melodic Structure." *American Anthropologist* 73: 773–82.

Chomsky, Noam. 1957. *Syntactic Structures.* The Hague: Mouton.

Chuse, Loren. 2003. *The Cantaoras: Music, Gender, and Identity in Flamenco Song.* New York: Routledge.

Citron, Marcia J. 1993. *Gender and the Musical Canon.* Cambridge: Cambridge University Press.

Collins, John, and P. Richards. 1989. "Popular Music in West Africa." In Simon Frith, ed. *World Music and Social Change.* Manchester: Manchester University Press.

Cook, Susan C., and Judy S. Tsou, eds. 1994. *Cecilia Reclaimed: Feminist Perspective on Gender and Music.* Urbana: University of Illinois Press.

Crafts, Susan, Daniel Cavicchi, and Charles Keil. 1993. *My Music: Explorations of Music in Daily Life.* Hanover, N.H.: Wesleyan University Press.

Cuddy, Lola L., and Annabel J. Cohen. 1976. "Recognition of Transposed Melodic Sequences." *Quarterly Journal of Experimental Psychology* 28: 255–70.

Cuddy, Lola L., and Janet Miller. 1979. "Melody Recognition: The Experimental Application of Musical Rules." *Canadian Journal of Psychology* 33: 148–57.

Danielson, Virginia. 1997. *The Voice of Egypt.* Chicago: University of Chicago Press.

Davidson, Lyle, and Bruce Torff. 1991. "Situated Cognition in Music." *World of Music* 34(3): 120–39.

D'Azevedo, Warren L. 1962. "Uses of the Past in Gola Discourse." *The Journal of African History* 3(1): 11–34.

DeMaille, Raymond J. 1984. *The Sixth Grandfather: Black Elk's Teachings Given to John G. Neihardt.* Lincoln: University of Nebraska Press.

Derrida, Jacques. 1998. *Of Grammatology.* Translated by Gayatri Chakravorty Spivak. Baltimore: Johns Hopkins University Press.

Dowling, W. Jay. 1972. "Recognition of Melodic Transformations: Inversion, Retrograde, and Retrograde Inversion." *Perception and Psychophysics* 12: 417–21.

———. 1978. "Scale and Contour: Two Components of a Theory of Memory for Melodies." *Psychological Review* 85: 341–54.

Ekman, P., W. Frieson, and T. Taussig. 1969. "II VIR-R and SCAN: Tools and Methods for the Automated Analysis of Visual Records." In *Content Analysis,* eds. G. Gerbner, O. Holsti, K. Krippendorff, W. Paisley, and P. Stone. New York: Wiley.

Epstein, Dena J. 1975. "The Folk Banjo: A Documentary History." *Ethnomusicology* 19(3): 347–71.

Erlmann, Veit. 1996a. *Nightsong.* Chicago: University of Chicago Press.

———. 1996b. "The Aesthetics of the Global Imagination: Reflections on World Music in the 1990s." *Public Culture* 8(3): 467–87.

"Ethnohistory." 2006. *JSTOR: Ethnohistory.* http://www.jstor.org/journals/00141801.html (accessed July 3, 2006).

Evans-Pritchard, Edward E. 1961. *Anthropology and History.* Manchester: Manchester University Press.

Fabian, Johannes. 1990. *Power and Performance: Ethnographic Explorations through Proverbial Wisdom and Theater in Shaba, Zaïre.* Madison: University of Wisconsin Press.

Fales, Cornelia. 1993. "Auditory Illusion and Cognitive Patterns in Whispered Inanga of Burundi." Ph.D. diss., Indiana University.

Feld, Steven. 1974. "Linguistic Models in Ethnomusicology." *Ethnomusicology* 18(2): 197–217.

———. 1981. "'Flow Like a Waterfall': The Metaphors of Kaluli Musical Theory." *Yearbook of Traditional Music* 13: 22–47.

———. 1982. *Sound and Sentiment: Birds, Weeping, Poetics, and Song in Kaluli Expression.* Philadelphia: University of Pennsylvania Press.

———. 1984. "Sound Structure as Social Structure." *Ethnomusicology* 28(3): 383–409.

———. 1988. "Aesthetics as Iconicity of Style, or 'Lift-Up-Over Sounding': Getting into the Kaluli Groove." *Yearbook of Traditional Music* 20: 74–113.

———. 1991. "Sound as a Symbolic System: The Kaluli Drum. In *The Varieties of Sensory Experience: A Sourcebook in the Anthropology of the Senses,* ed. David Howes. Toronto: University of Toronto Press, 79–99.

———, and Aaron Fox. 1994. "Music and Language." *Annual Review of Anthropology* 23: 25–53.

Fernandez, James W. 1986. *Persuasions and Performances: The Play of Tropes in Culture.* Bloomington: Indiana University Press.

Firth, Raymond. 1984 [1975]. "The Sceptical Anthropologist? Social Anthropology and Marxist Views on Society." In *Marxist Analyses and Social Anthropology,* ed. Maurice Bloch. London: Tavistock, 29–60.

Fish, Stanley. 1980. *Is There a Text in This Class: The Authority of Interpretive Communities.* Cambridge, Mass.: Harvard University Press.

Foucault, Michel. 1972. *The Archaeology of Knowledge and the Discourse of Language.* Translated by A. M. Sheridan Smith. New York: Pantheon Books.

———. 1976. *Histoire de la sexualité, vol. I, La Volonté de savoir.* Paris: Gallimard.

———. 1977. *Discipline and Punish.* New York: Vintage Books.

———. 1984a. *Histoire de la sexualité, vol. II, L'Usage des plaisirs.* Paris: Gallimard.

———. 1984b. *Histoire de la sexualité, vol. III, Le Souci de soi.* Paris: Gallimard.

Francès, Robert. 1988. *The Perception of Music.* Translated by W. Jay Dowling. Hillsdale, N.J.: Erlbaum, originally published in 1958 as *La Perception de la musique.* Paris: J. Vrin.

Friedson, Steven M. 1996. *Dancing Prophets: Musical Experience in Tumbuka Healing.* Chicago: University of Chicago Press.

Frisbie, Charlotte. 1991. "Women and the Society for Ethnomusicology: Roles and Contributions from Formation through Incorporation (1952/53–1961). In *Comparative Musicology and Anthropology of Music,* eds. Bruno Nettl and Philip V. Bohlman. Urbana: University of Illinois Press, 244–65.

Frobenius, Leo. 1898. "The Origin of African Civilizations." *Annual Report of the Board of Regents of the Smithsonian Institution* I: 640–41.

Fuller, Sophie, and Lloyd Whitesell. 2002. *Queer Episodes in Music and Modern Identity.* Urbana: University of Illinois Press.

Garafalo, Reebee. 1987. "How Autonomous Is Relative: Popular Music, the Social Formation and Cultural Struggle." *Popular Music* 6(1): 77–92.

Garraghan, Gilbert J. 1946. *A Guide to Historical Method.* New York: Fordham University Press.

Geertz, Clifford. 1973. *The Interpretation of Culture.* New York: Basic Books.

Geysbeek, Tim. 1994. "A Traditional History of the Konyan (15th–16th Century): Vase Camera's Epic of Musadu." *History in Africa* 21: 49–85.

Giddens, Anthony. 1994. "Living in a Post-Traditional Society." In *Reflexive Modernization: Politics, Tradition, and Aesthetics in the Modern Social Order,* eds. Ulrich Beck, Anthony Giddens, and Scott Lash. Stanford: Stanford University Press, 56–109.

Glaser, Barney G., and Anselm Strauss. 1967. *The Discovery of Grounded Theory: Strategies for Qualitative Research.* Chicago: Aldine.

Godelier, Maurice. 1977. *Perspectives in Marxist Anthropology.* Cambridge: New York.

Goffman, Erving. 1959. *The Presentation of Self.* New York: Doubleday Anchor.

———. 1967. *Interaction Ritual.* New York: Doubleday Anchor.

———. 1974. *Frame Analysis.* New York: Harper & Row.

Goodenough, Ward H. 1957. "Cultural Anthropology and Linguistics." In *Report of the Seventh Annual Roundtable Meeting on Linguistics and Language Study,* ed. Paul L. Garvin. Georgetown University Monograph Series on Language and Linguistics, No. 9. Washington, D.C.: Georgetown University Press, 167–75.

Gourlay, Kenneth. 1982. "Towards a Humanizing Ethnomusicology." *Ethnomusicology* 26(3): 411–20.

Greene, Paul D. 1999. "Sound Engineering in a Tamil Village: Playing Audio Cassettes as

Devotional Performance." *Ethnomusicology* 43(3): 459–89.

Grossberg, Lawrence. 1990. "Is There Rock after Punk?" In *On Rock: Rock, Pop, and the Written Word*, eds. Simon Frith and Andrew Goodwin. New York: Pantheon Books, 111–23.

Guilbault, Jocelyne, with Gage Averill, Edouard Benoit, and Gregory Rabess. 1993. *Zouk: World Music in the West Indies*. Chicago: University of Chicago Press.

Guyer, Jane I. 1996. "Traditions of Invention in Equatorial Africa." *African Studies Review* 39(3): 1–28.

———. and Samuel M. Eno Belinga. 1995. "Wealth in People as Wealth in Knowledge: Accumulation and Composition in Equatorial Africa. *The Journal of African History* 36(1):91–120.

Hall, Stuart, David Held, and Tony McGrew, eds. 1992. *Modernity and Its Futures*. Cambridge: Polity Press.

Harwood, Dane L. 1976. "Universals in Music: A Perspective from Cognitive Psychology." *Ethnomusicology* 20(3): 521–33.

Haskell, Robert E., ed. 1987. *Cognitive and Symbolic Structures: The Psychology of Metaphoric Transformation*. Norwood, N.J.: Ablex.

Helmholtz, Hermann L. F. 1863. *Die Lehre von den Tonempfindungen als Physiologische Grundlage für die Theorie der Musik*. Braunschweig: F. Viweg und Sohn. 1954. *On the Sensations of Tone as a Physiological Basis for the Theory of Music*. Edited and translated by A. J. Ellis. New York: Dover.

Herndon, Marcia. 1971. "The Cherokee Ballgame Cycle: An Ethnomusicologist's View." *Ethnomusicology* 15(3): 339–352.

Herzfeld, Michael. 1987. *Anthropology through the Looking Glass: Critical Ethnography in the Margins of Europe*. Cambridge: Cambridge University Press.

Herzog, George. 1934. "Speech Melody and Primitive Music." *Musical Quarterly* 20: 452–66.

———. 1945. "Drum Signalling in a West African Tribe." *Word* 1: 217–38.

"History." 2005. *Encyclopaedia Britannica Online*. http://search.eb.com/article-9040600 (accessed October 17, 2005).

Hobsbawm, Eric, and Terence Ranger. 1983. *The Invention of Tradition*. New York: Cambridge University Press.

Hofstadter, Douglas R. 1979. *Gödel, Escher, Bach: An Eternal Golden Braid*. New York: Basic Books.

Holst-Warhaft, Gail. 1975. *Road to Rembetika: Music of a Greek Subculture: Music of Love, Sorrow and Hashish*. Athens: D. Harvey.

Hood, Mantle. 1971. *The Ethnomusicologist*. New York: McGraw-Hill.

Hopkins, Pandora. 1977. "The Homology of Music and Myth." *Ethnomusicology* 21: 247–62.

Hornbostel, Erich M. von. 1909. "Wanyamwezi-Gesänge," *Anthropos* 4: 781–800, 1033–52.

———. 1911. "Über ein akustiches Kriterium für Kulturzusammenhänge." *Zeitschrift für Ethnologie* 43: 601–15.

———. 1928. "African Negro Music." *African Journal of the International African Institute* 1(1): 30–62.

———. 1933. "The Ethnology of African Sound-Instruments," *Africa* 6: 277–311.

Hoyningen-Huene, Paul. 1993. *Reconstructing Scientific Revolutions: Thomas S. Kuhn's Philosophy of Science*. Translated by Alexander J. Levine. Foreword by Thomas S. Kuhn. Chicago: University of Chicago Press.

Hughes, David W. 1988. "Deep Structure and Surface Structure in Javanese Music." *Ethnomusicology* 32(1): 23–74.

Hymes, Dell. 1975. "Breakthrough into Performance." In *Folklore, Performance and Communication*, eds. Dan Ben-Amos and Kenneth Goldstein. The Hague: Mouton.

Irvine, Judith T., and J. David Sapir. 1976. "Musical Style and Social Change among the Kujamaat Diola." *Ethnomusicology* 20: 67–86.

Iser, Wolfgang. 1978. *The Act of Reading: A Theory of Aesthetic Response*. Baltimore: Johns Hopkins University Press.

Jackson, Michael. 1989. *Paths toward a Clearing: Radical Empiricism and Ethnographic Enquiry*. Bloomington: Indiana University Press.

———. 1996. *Things as They Are: New Directions in Phenomenological Anthropology*. Bloomington: Indiana University Press.

James, William. 1976. *Essays in Radical Empiricism*. Cambridge: Harvard University Press.

Jameson, Fredric. 1971. *Marxism and Form: Twentieth-Century Dialectical Theories of Literature*. Princeton, N.J.: Princeton University Press.

———. 1990. *Late Marxism: Adorno or the Persistence of the Dialectic*. London and New York: Verso.

Jeffreys, M. D. W. 1961. "Negro Influences on Indonesia." *African Music* 2: 16.

Jones, Arthur Morris. 1960. "Indonesia and Africa: The Xylophone as a Culture Indicator." *African Music* 2: 36–47.

Jones, L. JaFran. 1989. "A Sociohistorical Perspective on Tunisian Women as Professional Musicians." In *Women and Music in Cross-Cultural Perspective*, ed. Ellen Koskoff. Urbana: University of Illinois Press, 69–84.

Kaeppler, Adrienne L. 1972. "Method and Theory in Analyzing Dance Structure with an Analysis of Tongan Dance." *Ethnomusicology* 16(2): 173–21.

Kant, Immanuel. 1955 [1952]. *The Critique of Pure Reason.* Translated by J. M. D. Meiklejohn, Thomas K. Abbott, and James C. Meredith. Chicago: Encyclopaedia Britannica.

Kapchan, Deborah A. 1995. "Performance." *Journal of American Folklore* 108(430): 479–508.

Kaplan, Abraham. 1964. *The Conduct of Inquiry: Methodology for Behavioral Science.* San Francisco: Chandler.

Kaplan, David, and Robert A. Manners. 1972. *Culture Theory.* Englewood Cliffs, N.J.: Prentice-Hall.

Keil, Charles. 1979. *Tiv Song.* Chicago: University of Chicago Press.

Kirby, Percival R. 1934. *The Musical Instruments of the Native Races of South Africa.* Oxford: Oxford University Press.

Kirschenblatt-Gimblett, Barbara. 1999. "Performance Studies." *Culture and Creativity.* New York: Rockefeller Foundation. www.nyu/classes/bkg/ issues/rock2.htm (accessed October 7, 2005).

Klumpenhouwer, Henry. 1998. "Commentary: Poststructuralism and Issues of Music Theory." In *Music/Ideology: Resisting the Aesthetic*, ed. Adam Krims. Amsterdam: G and B Arts International, 289–310.

Kolinski, Mieczslaw. 1967. "Recent Trends in Ethnomusicology." *Ethnomusicology* 11: 1–24.

Koskoff, Ellen, ed. 1989. *Women and Music in Cross-Cultural Perspective.* Urbana: University of Illinois Press.

———. 1992. "Ethnomusicology and Music Cognition." *The World of Music* 34(3). Includes bibliographical references.

Krims, Adam. Forthcoming. "Popular Music Studies, Flexible Accumulation, and the Future of Marxism." In *Popular Music and Social Analysis,* ed. Allan Moore. Cambridge: Cambridge University Press.

Krober, A. L. 1959. "Preface to the *Anthropology of Franz Boas.*" Edited by Walter Goldschmidt. *American Anthropologist* 61(5) part 2 (Memoir no. 89).

Krumhansl, Carol L. 1979. "The Psychological Representation of a Musical Pitch in a Tonal Context." *Cognitive Psychology* 11: 346–74.

———. 1995. "Music Psychology and Music Theory: Problems and Prospects." *Music Theory Spectrum* 17(1): 53–80.

———, and Roger N. Shepard. 1979. "Quantification of the Hierarchy of Tonal Functions within a Diatonic Context." *Journal of Experimental Psychology: Human Perception and Performance* 5: 579–94.

Kubik, Gerhard. 1965. "Transcription of Mangwilo Xylophone Music from Film Strips." *African Music* 3(4): 35–41.

Kuhn, Thomas S. 1962. *The Structure of Scientific Revolutions.* 2nd ed. Chicago: University of Chicago Press.

Kunst, Jaap. 1948. "Around von Hornbostel's Theory of the Cycle of Blown Fifths." *Medeling* 76: 3–35. Amsterdam: Publication of the Royal Institute for the Indies.

Lakoff, George, and Mark Johnson. 1980. *Metaphors We Live By.* Chicago: University of Chicago Press.

Lash, Scott. 1994. "Reflexivity and Its Doubles: Structure, Aesthetics, Community." In *Reflexive Modernization: Politics, Tradition, and Aesthetics in the Modern Social Order,* eds. Ulrich Beck, Anthony Giddens, and Scott Lash. Stanford: Stanford University Press, 110–73.

Laske, Otto E. 1977. *Music, Memory and Thought: Explorations in Cognitive Musicology.* Ann Arbor: University Microfilms.

Leach, Edmund R. 1965. *Political Systems of Burma: A Study of Kadin Social Structure.* Boston: Beacon Press.

Lerdahl, Fred. 1983. *A Generative Theory of Tonal Music.* Cambridge, MA: MIT Press.

Lévi-Strauss, Claude. 1955. *Tristes Tropiques.* Paris: Plon.

———. 1963. *Totemism.* Boston: Beacon Press.

———. 1966. *The Savage Mind.* Chicago: University of Chicago Press.

———. 1969a. *The Elementary Structures of Kinship.* Boston: Beacon Press.

———. 1969b. *The Raw and the Cooked.* New York: Harper & Row.

———. 1971. "Boléro du Maurice Ravel." *L'Homme* 11(2): 5–14.

Lomax, Alan. 1968. *Folksong Style and Culture.* Washington, D.C.: American Association for the Advancement of Science.

Lyons, John. 1970. *Chomsky.* London: Fontana.

Macarthur, Sally. 2002. *Feminist Aesthetics in Music.* Westport, Conn.: Greenwood Press.

Magrini, Tullia. 2003. *Music and Gender: Perspectives from the Mediterranean.* Chicago: University of Chicago Press.

Malinowski, Bronislaw. 1922. *Argonauts of the Western Pacific; An Account of Native Enterprise and Adventure in the Archipelagoes of Melanesian New Guinea.* London: G. Routledge.

———. 1944. *A Scientific Theory of Culture.* Chapel Hill: University of North Carolina Press.

———. 1965 [1935]. *Coral Gardens and Their Magic.* Bloomington: Indiana University Press.

Mallott, Curry, and Milagros Peña. 2003. *Punk Rocker's Revolution: A Pedagogy of*

Gender, Race, and Class. New York: P. Lang.

Manuel, Peter. 1987. "Marxism, Nationalism and Popular Music in Revolutionary Cuba." *Popular Music* 6(2): 161–78.

———. "Andalusian, Gypsy and Class Identity in the Contemporary Flamenco Complex." *Ethnomusicology* 33(2): 47–65.

Marcus, George E., and Michael M. J. Fischer. 1986. *Anthropology as Cultural Critique: An Experimental Moment in the Human Sciences.* Chicago: University of Chicago Press.

Marx, Karl. 1967 [1867]. *Capital: A Critique of Political Economy.* New York: International Publishers.

———. 1973. *Grundrisse: Foundations of the Critique of Political Economy.* New York: Vintage Books.

Maultsby, Portia K. 1975. "Music of Northern Independent Black Churches during the Ante-Bellum Period." *Ethnomusicology* 19(3): 401–20.

Mazo, Margarita. 1994. "Lament Made Visible: A Study of Paramusical Elements in Russian Lament." In *Theme and Variations*, eds. Bell Yung and Joseph S. C. Lam. Cambridge: Department of Music, Harvard University and Hong Kong: The Institute of Chinese Studies, The Chinese University of Hong Kong, 1164–1210.

McClary, Susan. 1989. "The Blasphemy of Talking Politics during Bach Year." In *Music and Society: The Politics of Composition, Performance and Reception,* eds. Richard Leppert and Susan McClary. Cambridge: Cambridge University Press, 13–62.

McDaniel, Lorna. 1994. "Memory Spirituals of the Ex-Slave American Soldiers in Trinidad's 'Company Villages.'" *Black Music Journal* 14(2): 119–43.

McLeod, Norma. 1966. "Some Techniques of Analysis for Non-Western Music." Ph.D. diss. Northwestern University.

———, and Marcia Herndon. 1980. *Ethnography of Musical Performance.* Norwood, Pa.: Norwood Editions.

Merriam, Alan P. 1964. *The Anthropology of Music.* Evanston: Northwestern University Press.

———. 1967a. *Ethnomusicology of the Flathead Indians.* Chicago: Aldine.

———. 1967b. "The Use of Music as a Technique of Reconstructing Culture History in Africa." In *Reconstructing African Culture History,* eds. Creighton Gavel and Norman R. Bennett. Boston: Boston University Press, 85–114.

———. 1977. "Definitions of 'Comparative Musicology' and 'Ethnomusicology': An Historical-Theoretical Perspective." *Ethnomusicology* 21(2): 189–204.

Merton, Robert K. 1996. Ed. Piotr Sztompka. *On Social Structure and Science.* Chicago: University of Chicago Press.

Meyer, Leonard B. 1956. *Emotion and Meaning in Music.* Chicago: University of Chicago Press.

Middleton, Richard. 2003. "Music Studies and the Idea of Culture." In *The Cultural Study of Music,* eds. Martin Clayton, Trevor Herbert, and Richard Middleton, 1–15. New York and London: Routledge.

Miller, G. A., Galanter, E., and Pribram, K. H. 1960. *Plans and the Structure of Behavior.* New York: Holt, Rinehart & Winston.

Moisala, Pirkko, and Beverley Diamond, eds. 2000. *Music and Gender.* Urbana: University of Illinois Press.

Monelle, Raymond. 2000. *The Sense of Music: Semiotic Essays.* Princeton, N.J.: Princeton University Press.

Monson, Ingrid. 1996. *Saying Something: Jazz Improvisation and Interaction.* Chicago: University of Chicago Press.

———. 1999. "Riffs, Repetition, and Theories of Globalization." *Ethnomusicology* 43(1): 31–65.

Moore, Jerry D. 1997. *Visions of Culture: An Introduction to Anthropological Theories and Theorists.* Walnut Creek, Calif.: Altamira.

Morris, Charles W. 1972. *Writings on the General Theory of Signs.* The Hague: Mouton.

Nattiez, Jean-Jacques. 1977. "The Contribution of Musical Semiotics to the Semiotic Discussion in General." In *A Perfusion of Signs,* ed. Thomas A. Sebeok. Bloomington: Indiana University Press, 121–42.

———. 1990. *Toward a Semiology of Music.* Princeton: Princeton University Press.

———. 1991. *Music and Discourse: Toward a Semiology of Music.* Trans. Carolyn Abbate. Princeton: Princeton University Press.

Nauta, Doede. 1972. *The Meaning of Information.* The Hague: Mouton.

Negus, Keith. 1996. *Popular Music in Theory: An Introduction.* Hanover and London: Wesleyan University Press.

Neisser, Ulric. 1976. *Cognition and Reality.* San Francisco: W. H. Freeman.

Nettl, Bruno. 1958. "Some Linguistic Approaches to Musical Analysis." *Journal of the International Folk Music Council* 10: 37–41.

Nicholson, Linda, and Steven Seidman. 1995. "Introduction." In *Social Postmodernism: Beyond Identity Politics.* Cambridge: Cambridge University Press, 1–35.

Nketia, J. H. Kwabena. 1958. "Yoruba Musicians in Accra." *Odu* 6: 35–44.

Norris, Christopher. 2001. "Marxism." *The New Grove Dictionary of Music and Musicians.* 2nd ed. London: Macmillan Press.

Ortony, Andrew, ed. 1979. *Metaphor and Thought*. Cambridge: Cambridge University Press.

Oxford English Dictionary, The Compact Edition. 1986. 2 vols. Oxford: Oxford University Press.

Palmer, Gary B., and William R. Jankowiak. 1996. "Performance and Imagination: Toward an Anthropology of the Spectacular and the Mundane." *Cultural Anthropology* 11(2): 225–258.

Paprotté, Wolf, and René Dirven, eds. 1985. *The Ubiquity of Metaphor*. Amsterdam and Philadelphia: John Benjamins.

Park, Robert E. 1952. *Human Communities*. New York: Free Press.

Peirce, Charles S., Max Harold Fisch, and Christian J. W. Kloesel. 1982. *Writings of Charles S. Peirce: A Chronological Edition*. Bloomington: Indiana University Press.

Phillipson, Michael. 1972. "Theory, Methodology and Conceptualization." In *New Directions in Sociological Theory*, ed. Paul Filmer et. al., 77–118. Cambridge: MA: MIT Press.

Porcello, Thomas. 1998. "'Tails out': Social Phenomenology and the Ethnographic Representation of Technology in Music-Making." *Ethnomusicology* 42(3): 485–510.

Post, Jennifer. 1989. "Professional Women in Indian Music: The Death of the Courtesan Tradition." In *Women and Music in Cross-Cultural Perspective*, ed. Ellen Koskoff. Urbana: University of Illinois Press, 97–110.

Pratt, Mary Louise. 1992. *Through Imperial Eyes: Travel Writing and Transculturation*. New York: Routledge.

Propp, Vladimir Akovlevich. 1958. *Morphology of the Folktale*. Edited with an introduction by Svatava Pirkova-Jakobson; Translated by Laurence Scott. Bloomington: Research Center, Indiana University.

———. 1984. *Theory and History of Folklore*. Translated by Ariadna Y. Martin and Richard P. Martin. Minneapolis: University of Minnesota Press.

Qureshi, Regula Burkhart. 1995 [1986]. *Sufi Music of India and Pakistan: Sound, Context and Meaning in Qawwali*. Chicago: University of Chicago Press.

———. 2002. *Music and Marx: Ideas, Practice, Politics*. New York: Routledge.

Radcliffe-Brown, Alfred Reginald. 1933. *The Andaman Islanders*. Cambridge: Cambridge University Press.

Ramsey, Guthrie P. 2003. *Race Music: Migration, Modernism, and Gender*. Berkeley: University of California Press.

Ranke, Leopold, and Robert Wines. 1981. *The Secret of World History: Selected Writings on the Art and Science of History*. New York: Fordham University Press.

Reed, Daniel. 2003. *Dan Ge Performance: Masks and Music in Contemporary Côte d'Ivoire*. Bloomington: Indiana University Press.

Reiner, Thomas. 2000. *Semiotics of Musical Time*. New York: Peter Lang.

Rice, Timothy. 1987. "Toward the Remodeling of Ethnomusicology." *Ethnomusicology* 31(3): 469–88.

———. 1994. *May It Fill Your Soul: Experiencing Bulgarian Music*. Chicago: University of Chicago Press.

Robertson, Carol E. 1979. "'Pulling the Ancestors': Performance, Practice, and Praxis in Mapuche Ordering." *Ethnomusicology* 23(3): 395–416.

———. 1989. "Power and Gender in the Musical Experiences of Women." In *Women and Music in Cross-Cultural Perspective*, ed. Ellen Koskoff. Urbana: University of Illinois Press, 225–44.

Roseman, Marina. 1989. "Inversion and Conjunction: Male and Female Performance among the Temniar of Peninsular Malaysia." In *Women and Music in Cross-Cultural Perspective*, ed. Ellen Koskoff. Urbana: University of Illinois Press, 131–50.

———. 2000. "Shifting Landscapes: Musical Mediations of Modernity in the Malaysian Rainforest." *Yearbook for Traditional Music* 32: 31–65.

Rosenblatt, Louise. 1978. *The Reader, the Text, the Poem: The Transactional Theory of Literary Work*. Carbondale: Southern Illinois University Press.

Rouch, Jean, director. 1954. *Les Maitres Fous* ("Mad Masters"). Color; VHS; 35 minutes. Watertown, Mass.: Documentary Educational Resources.

Sachs, Curt. 1929. *Geist und Werden der Musikinstrumente*. Berlin: D. Reimer.

———. 1940. *History of Musical Instruments: The Rise of Music in the Ancient World East and West*. New York: Norton.

Sachs, Nahoma. 1975. "Music and Meaning: Musical Symbolism in a Macedonian Village." PhD diss., Indiana University.

Sacks, Sheldon, ed. 1979. *On Metaphor*. Chicago: University of Chicago Press.

Said, Edward. 1978. *Orientalism*. New York: Pantheon Books.

Sakata, Hiromi Lorraine. 1989. "Hazara Women in Afghanistan: Innovators and Preservers of Musical Tradition." In *Women and Music in Cross-Cultural Perspective*, ed. Ellen Koskoff. Urbana: University of Illinois Press, 85–96.

Sanderson, Stephen K. 2002. *Social Evolutionism: A Critical History*. Oxford: Blackwell.

Sapir, J. David. 1969. "Diola-Fogny Funeral Songs and the Native Critic." *African Language Review* 8: 176–91.

Saussure, Ferdinand de. 1966 [1916]. *Course in General Linguistics.* Translated by Wade Baskin. New York: McGraw-Hill.

Sawa, George. 1981. "The Survival of Some Aspects of Medieval Arabic Performance Practice." *Ethnomusicology* 25(1): 73–86.

Schaeffner, André. 1956. "Ethnologie musicale ou musicologie comparée." In *Les Colloques de Wégimont,* ed. Paul Collaer. Brussels: Elsevier, 29–30.

Schafer, Robert J., and David H. Bennett. 1980. *A Guide to Historical Method.* 3rd ed. Homewood, Ill.: Dorsey Press.

Schechner, Richard. 1985. *Between Theater and Anthropology.* Philadelphia: University of Pennsylvania Press.

———. 1988. *Performance Theory.* New York: Routledge.

Schenker, Heinrich. 1945. *Challenge to Musical Tradition: A New Concept of Tonality.* Edited by Adele T. Katz. New York: Knopf.

———. 1977. *Readings in Schenker Analysis and Other Approaches.* Edited by Maury Yeston. New Haven: Yale University Press.

Scheub, Harold. 1970. "The Technique of the Expansible Image in Xhosa *Ntsomi* Performances." *Research in African Literatures* 1(2): 119–46.

Schieffelin, Edward L. 1985. "Performance and the Cultural Construction of Reality." *American Ethnologist* 12: 707–24.

Schippers, Mimi. 2002. *Rockin' out of the Box: Gender Maneuvering in Alternative Hard Rock.* New Brunswick, N.J.: Rutgers University Press.

Schmidt, Cynthia. 1998. "Kru Mariners and Migrants of the West African Coast." In *Garland Encyclopedia of World Music: Africa,* ed. Ruth M. Stone. New York: Garland, 2–6.

Schneider, Albrecht. 1991. "Psychological Theory and Comparative Musicology." In *Comparative Musicology and Anthropology of Music,* eds. Bruno Nettl and Philip V. Bohlman. Chicago: University of Chicago Press, 293–317.

Schutz, Alfred. 1932. *Der sinnhafte Aufbau der sozialen Welt; Eine Einleitung die Verstehende Soziologie.* Vienna: J. Springer, 1932.

———. 1971a. "Making Music Together: A Study in Social Relationship." In *Collected Papers II: Studies in Social Theory.* The Hague: Martinus Nijhoff, 159–78.

———. 1971b. "Mozart and the Philosophers." In *Collected Papers II: Studies in Social Theory,* edited and introduction by Arvid Broderson. The Hague: Martinus Nijhoff, 179–200.

———. 1976. "Fragments on the Phenomenology of Music." In *In Search of Musical Method,* ed. F. Kersten. London: Gordon and Breach.

———, and Thomas Luckmann. 1973. *The Structures of the Life-World.* Chicago: Northwestern University Press.

Scott, Derek B., ed. 2000. *Music, Culture, and Society: A Reader.* New York: Oxford University Press.

Seeger, Anthony. 1987a. "Do We Need to Remodel Ethnomusicology?" *Ethnomusicology* 31(3): 491–95.

———. 1987b. *Why Suyá Sing: A Musical Anthropology of an Amazonian People.* Cambridge and New York: Cambridge University Press.

———. 1993. "When Music Makes History." In *Ethnomusicology and Modern Music History,* eds. Stephen Blum, Philip V. Bohlman, and Daniel Neuman. Urbana: University of Illinois Press, 23–34.

Seeger, Charles. 1962. "Music as a Tradition of Communication, Discipline, and Play." *Ethnomusicology* 6(3): 156–63.

———. 1977. *Studies in Musicology 1935–1975.* Berkeley and Los Angeles: University of California Press.

Shelemay, Kay Kaufman. 1980. "'Historical Ethnomusicology': Reconstructing Falasha Liturgical History." *Ethnomusicology* 24(2): 233–58.

———. 1998. *Let Jasmine Rain Down: Song and Remembrance among Syrian Jews.* Chicago: University of Chicago Press.

Shen, Yeshayahu. 1992. "Cognitive Aspects of Metaphor Comprehension: An Introduction." *Poetics Today* 13(4): 567–74.

Shepherd, John. 1989. "Music and Male Hegemony." In *Music and Society: The Politics of Composition, Performance and Reception,"* eds. Richard Leppert and Susan McClary. Cambridge: Cambridge University Press, 151–72.

Shepherd, John, Phil Verder, Graham Vulliamy, and Trevor Wishart. 1977. *Whose Music? A Sociology of Musical Languages.* London: Latimer New Dimensions.

Shepherd, John, and Peter Wicke. 1997. *Music and Cultural Theory.* Cambridge: Polity Press.

Shiloah, Amnon, and Erik Cohen. 1983. *The Dynamics of Change in Jewish Oriental Ethnic Music in Israel.* Middletown, Conn.: Society for Ethnomusicology.

Singer, Milton. 1955. "The Cultural Pattern of India." *The Far Eastern Quarterly* 15: 23–26.

Skarda, Christine A. 1989. "Alfred Schutz's Phenomenology of Music." In *Understanding the Musical Experience,* ed. Joseph Smith. New York: Gordon and Breach, 43–100.

Slobin, Mark. 1992. "Micromusics of the West: A Comparative Approach." *Ethnomusicology* 36(1): 1–87.

Soedarsono. 1969. "Classical Javanese Dance: History and Characterization." *Ethnomusicology* 13(3): 498–506.

Solomon, Maynard. 1974. *Marxism and Art: Essays Classic and Contemporary*. New York: Knopf.

Spivak, Gayatri C. 1988. *In Other Words: Essays in Cultural Politics*. New York and London: Routledge.

Stevenson, Robert. 1973. "Written Sources for Indian Music until 1882." *Ethnomusicology* 17(1): 1–40.

Stokes, Martin. 1992. *The Arabesk Debate: Music and Musicians in Modern Turkey*. Oxford: Oxford University Press.

———, ed. 1994. *Ethnicity, Identity and Music: The Musical Construction of Place*. Oxford: Berg.

Stone, Ruth M. 1982. *Let the Inside Be Sweet: The Interpretation of Music Event among the Kpelle of Liberia*. Bloomington: Indiana University Press.

———. 1988. *Dried Millet Breaking: Time, Words, and Song in the Woi Epic of the Kpelle*. Bloomington: Indiana University Press.

———, and Verlon L. Stone. 1981. "Event, Feedback, and Analysis: Research Media in the Study of Music Events." *Ethnomusicology* 25(2): 215–25.

Strauss, Anselm L., and Juliet M. Corbin. 1990. *Basics of Qualitative Research: Grounded Theory Procedures and Techniques*. Newbury Park, Calif.: Sage.

Stumpf, Carl. 1886a. "Lieder der Bellakula-Indianer." *Vierteljahrsschrift für Musikwissenschaft* 2: 405–26.

———. 1886b. "Review of Alexander J. Ellis, 'On the Scales of Various Nations.'" *Vierteljahrsschrift für Musikwissenschaft* 2: 511–24.

———. 1911. *Die Anfänge der Musik*. Leipzig: J. A. Barth.

Sturtevant, William C. 1968. "Studies in Ethnoscience." In *Theory in Anthropology: A Sourcebook*, eds. Robert A. Manners and David Kaplan. New York: Aldine, 475–500.

Suchoff, Benjamin, ed. 1997. *Béla Bartók Studies in Ethnomusicology*. Lincoln and London: University of Nebraska Press.

Sugarman, Jane C. 1997. *Engendering Song: Singing and Subjectivity at Prespa Albanian Weddings*. Chicago: University of Chicago Press.

Sutton, R. Anderson. 1989. "Identity and Individuality in an Ensemble Tradition. The Female Vocalist in Java." In *Women and Music in Cross-Cultural Perspective*, ed. Ellen Koskoff. Urbana: University of Illinois Press, 111–30.

Tarasti, Eero. 2002. *Signs of Music: A Guide to Musical Semiotics*. Hawthorne, N.Y.: Mouton de Gruyter.

Tunstall, Patricia. 1979. "Structuralism and Musicology: An Overview." *Current Musicology* 27: 51–64.

Turino, Thomas. 1999. "Signs of Imagination, Identity, and Experience: A Peircian Semiotic Theory for Music." *Ethnomusicology* 43(2): 221–255.

Turner, Jonathan H., and Alexandra Maryanski. 1979. *Functionalism*. Menlo Park, Calif.: Benjamin Cummings.

Turner, Victor. 1967. *The Forest of Symbols: Aspects of Ndembu Ritual*. Ithaca, N.Y.: Cornell University Press.

———. 1986. *The Anthropology of Performance*. New York: PAJ Publications.

———. 1990. "Are There Universals of Performance in Myth, Ritual, and Drama?" In *By Means of Performance: Intercultural Studies of Theatre and Ritual*, eds. Richard Schechner and Willa Appel. Cambridge: Cambridge University Press, 8–18.

Tyson, Lois. 1999. *Critical Theory Today*. New York: Garland.

Vansina, Jan. 1985. *Oral Tradition as History*. Madison: University of Wisconsin Press.

———. 1990. *Paths in the Rainforest: Toward a History of Political Tradition in Equatorial Africa*. Madison: University of Wisconsin Press.

Wachsmann, Klaus P., ed. 1971. *Essays on Music and History in Africa*. Evanston, Ill.: Northwestern University Press.

Wade, Bonnie. 1998. *Imaging Sound: An Ethnomusicological Study of Music, Art, and Culture in Mughal India*. Chicago: University of Chicago Press.

Waterman, Christopher. 1990. *Jùjú: A Social History and Ethnography of an African Popular Music*. Chicago: University of Chicago Press.

Williams, Linda Faye. 1995. "The Impct of African-American Music on Jazz in Zimbabwe: An Exploration in Radical Empiricism." Ph.D. Dissertation, Indiana University.

Wong, Deborah. 2001. *Sounding the Center: History and Aesthetics in Thai Buddhist Performance*. Chicago: University of Chicago Press.

———. 2004. *Speak It Louder: Asian Americans Making Music*. New York: Routledge.

Worth, Sol. "The Development of a Semiotic of Film." *Semiotica* 1: 282–321.

Zemp, Hugo. 1978–1979. "'Aré 'aré Classification of Musical Types and Instruments." *Ethnomusicology* 22(1): 37–67; 23(1): 5–48.

Zuckerkandl, Victor. 1956. *Sound and Symbol: Music and the External World*. London: Routledge and Kegan Paul.

Index

Bib.# 512593

780.89
STO

Ollscoil na hÉireann, Gaillimh

3 1111 40235 6958